Poets, Philosophers, Lovers

Latinx and Latin American Profiles

Frederick Luis Aldama, Editor

Poets, Philosophers, Lovers

On the Writings of Giannina Braschi

Edited by

Frederick Luis Aldama

and Tess O'Dwyer

with a foreword by Ilan Stavans

University of Pittsburgh Press

Published by the University of Pittsburgh Press, Pittsburgh, Pa., 15260

Manufactured in the United States of America
Printed on acid-free paper
10 9 8 7 6 5 4 3 2 1

Library of Congress Cataloging-in-Publication Data

Names: Aldama, Frederick Luis, 1969- editor. | O'Dwyer, Tess, editor.
Title: Poets, philosophers, lovers : on the writings of Giannina Braschi / edited by Frederick Luis Aldama and Tess O'Dwyer.
Description: Pittsburgh, Pa. : University of Pittsburgh Press, [2020] | Series: Latinx and Latin American profiles | Includes index.
Identifiers: LCCN 2020034657 | ISBN 9780822946182 (hardcover ; acid-free paper) | ISBN 9780822987598 (ebook)
Subjects: LCSH: Braschi, Giannina--Criticism and interpretation.
Classification: LCC PQ7440.B67 Z84 2020 | DDC 863/.64--dc23
LC record available at https://lccn.loc.gov/2020034657

Jacket art and design by Melissa Dias-Mandoly

Contents

Acknowledgments

Thank you to Ronald Mendoza-de Jesús for co-conceptualizing this volume with the editors. Our appreciation is also extended to David Auerbach for his translations from the Spanish: Dorian Lugo Bertrán's "Leaping Off the Page: Giannina Braschi's Intermedialities"; Cristina Garrigós's "Giannina and Braschi: A Polyphony of Voices"; Laura R. Loustau's "The Poetry of Giannina Braschi: Art and Magic in *Assault on Time*"; Francisco Moreno-Fernández's "*Yo-Yo Boing!* Or Literature as a Translingual Practice"; and Francisco José Ramos's "The Holy Trinity: Money, Power, and Success in *United States of Banana*." Thanks as well to Rowman and Littlefield for granting permission to include a new version of Elizabeth Lowry's essay "The Human Barnyard: Rhetoric, Identification, and Symbolic Representation in *United States of Banana*"; an earlier version appeared in *Representing 9/11: Trauma, Ideology, and Nationalism in Literature, Film, and Television*, edited by Paul Petrovic. Finally, we would like to acknowledge all the readers, scholars, and all others who relish in the aesthetics of *making new*!

Foreword

The past is always tense, the future perfect.

—*Zadie Smith*

Boing!

I have always visto a Giannina Braschi como mi heroína. And I'm an adicto . . . There is something mágico in her juego de palabras, her exploration of tenses, her anxious, uncompromising bilingüismo que ni es de aquí ni es de aquí ni es de allá, ni tiene age ni porvenir, y ser feliz es su color, su identity. Braschi crea una lexicography that is and isn't atrapada en el presente.

¿Could she be anything but Latinéxica?

My favorite among her work is her ode—¿una oda, really?—a la ambigüedad:

> El bilingüismo es una estética bound to double business. O, 'tis most sweet when in one line two crafts directly meet. To be and not to be. Habla con la boca llena and from both sides of its mouth. Está con Dios y con el diablo. Con el punto y con la coma. Es un purgatorio, un signo gramatical intermedio, entre heaven and earth, un semicolon entre la independencia y la estadidad, un estado libre asociado, un mamarracho multicultural. No tiene cláusulas ni subterfugios, no anda con gríngolas ni con muletas, no es artrítico, no se queja—aúlla como un perro al infinito y pide maná del cielo que caiga como lluvia—no se ahoga en un vaso de agua, no deja que le doren la píldora—no anda con yeso, saltando como un güimo con muletas de aquí pá allá—no es el canario que se balancea en el columpio dentro de la jaula comiendo los pistachos—se ha ido y se sigue yendo de todas las jaulas como Pedro por su casa y no ha vuelto a mirar hacia atrás. No tiene 10 mandamientos porque no tiene pelos en la lengua, pero tiene huevos—yo los he venido poniendo desde toda mi obra que es una sola—y la llamo el manifiesto de los huevos poéticos—se hace mostrando los huevos, metiendo la pata, pisseando aquí y pisseando allá. Nace del fuego popular, del pan, de la tierra, y de la libertad. Es un perro realengo atravesando un puente entre el norte y el sur, entre el siglo XX y el siglo XXI, entre Segismundo y Hamlet,

> entre Neruda y Whitman, entre Dickinson y Sor Juana, entre Darío y Stein, entre Sarmiento y Melville—entre los dos yo's en choque está el Yo-Yo Boing!

I love the strategic diéresis. Braschi canta como la lluvia. I love her expresiones "Pedro por su casa," "no tener huevos," and also hacer una obra with "huevos poéticos." She talks the talk like Sor Juana and Emily and Rubén and Gertrude and Domingo and Herman. The map que Braschi construye is ideal for me: tiene el tamaño de mi self.

Mostly, Braschi habla de tener "pelos en la lengua." Now, how on earth can you traducir semejante alocución? It means to speak frankly but she does más que eso. She bounces de ida y de regreso, without hindrance, sin remordimiento. Como le da la gana.

She destruye la lengua only to reconstruirla en un juego de echoes y re-echoes. Nada is what it sounds. She laughs at la Real Academia Española. Se orina en el casticismo.

Hats off, Giannina. You are a semicolon—¿o un semi-Colón?—entre la independencia y la estatidad. You're el pan y la tierra y la libertad. Particularly la libertad. Language is freedom. You make el pasado un relajo and the future un regalo.

Ambiguity is also mi nombre. (Or else, my nömbre.) I'm bound to double talk. Spanish and English = Spanglish. El yo-yo que sube y baja. I love to know y not to know. I love to ser y no ser. To estar and no estar.

Gracias a ti, nuyorriqueña admirada, mi lengua también está llena de pelos y pelotas.

Boing! Boing!

Poets, Philosophers, Lovers

Introduction

Frederick Luis Aldama

Scholar, playwright, spoken-word performer, award-winning poet, and avant-garde fiction author, since the 1980s Giannina Braschi has been creating up a storm in and around a panoply of Latinx hemispheric spaces. Her creative corpus reaches across different genres, regions, and historical epochs. Her critical works cover a wide range of subjects and authors, including Miguel de Cervantes, Garcilaso de la Vega, Juan Ramón Jiménez, Gustavo Adolfo Bécquer, Antonio Machado, César Vallejo, and García Lorca. Her dramatic poetry titles in Spanish include *Asalto al tiempo* (1981) and *La comedia profana* (1985). Her radically experimental genre-bending titles include *El imperio de los sueños* (1988), the bilingual *Yo-Yo Boing!* (1998), and the English-penned *United States of Banana* (2011). With national and international awards and works appearing in Swedish, Slovenian, Russian, and Italian, she is recognized as one of today's foremost experimental Latinx authors.

Her vibrant bilingually shaped creative expressions and innovation spring from her Latinidad, her Puerto Rican-ness that weaves in and through a planetary aesthetic sensibility. We discover as much in her work about US/Puerto Rico sociopolitical histories as we encounter the metaphysical and existential explorations of a Cervantes, Rabelais, Diderot, Artaud, Joyce, Beckett, Stein, Borges, Cortázar, and Rosario Castellanos, for instance. With every flourish of her pen Braschi reminds us that in the distillation and reconstruction of the building blocks of the universe there are no limits to what fiction can do. And, here too, the black scratches that form words and carefully composed blank spaces shape an absent world; her strict selection *out* of words and syntax is as important as the precise insertion of words and syntax to put us into the shoes of the "complicit reader" (Julio Cortázar's term) to most productively interface, invest, and fill in the gaps of her storyworlds. Braschi reminds us of the power of *lexis*—asking us to deep-dive into the metaphorical, subtextual, and allegorical layers of meaning. No subject remains untouched in her fiction making. She draws from Latinx realities as well as metaphysics—even historical archive, sociopolitical, and judicial discourses. Indeed, Braschi invents new forms to express polyvalent Latinx sensibilities that shape-shift across time, place, and identity categories.

In many ways, as a contemporary Latinx author Braschi stands apart. Her radically experimental works continue to grow a genealogy of Latinx letters, but they do so from the avant-garde margins. Taken as a whole her work extends and complicates a trajectory of Latinx experimental fiction that has not received the same critical attention as, perhaps, the work of a more straightforward realist writer such as an Esmeralda Santiago or a Piri Thomas. Lisa Sánchez González sums up the realism of, say, Santiago's *When I Was Puerto Rican* as "non-confrontational" (140)—as a mainstream-consumable story that focuses on the individual triumphs at the exclusion of the "collective predicament that entails growing problems within racism, poverty, reproductive rights, education, and Colonial maldevelopment" (140). Sidestepping the easily consumable, Braschi's creative work puts pressure on and radically bends a Latinx literary canon, and with this she calls attention to the self-within-the-collective of nation and diasporic community. She converses with Isabel Rios (*Victuum*, 1976), Cecile Pineda (*Face*, 1985), Guillermo Gomez-Peña (*Codex Espangliensis*, 1998), Alejandro Morales (*Waiting to Happen*, 2001), Salvador Plascencia (*The People of Paper*, 2005), or Sesshu Foster (*Atomik Aztex*, 2005). And today we see Braschi joined by a growing number of Latinx canon-benders such as Carmen María Machado, Elizabeth Acevedo, Monica de la Torre, and Naomi Ayala. More globally, Braschi's works extend and complicate a genealogy of avant-garde women of color authors such as Theresa Hak Kyung Cha, Claudia Rankine, and Audre Lorde, and she joins with other planetary cutting-edge contemporaries such as Azareen Van der Vliet Oloomi, Pamela Lu, Zinzi Clemmons, and Sumana Roy.

Although standing apart, Braschi as creator clearly doesn't exist ex nihilo. Indeed, we see her build on and redeploy the work of feminist and queer fore-figures, including Cristina Peri Rossi, Alejandra Pizarnik, Clarice Lispector, Luce Irigaray, Helene Cixous, Marguerite Duras, and Gertrude Stein. She does so less from an identity perspective and more from a theoretical practice perspective. We see a similar dynamic with her Puerto Rican family friends and mentors playwright René Marqués and public intellectual Nilita Vientós-Gastón, and with her fiction-writing friends on the island, Rosario Ferré, Manuel Ramos Otero, Luis Rafael Sánchez, and Ana Lydia Vega. I think also of her Nuyorican poet friends who are cofounders of the Nuyorican Poets Café, Pedro Pietri and Miguel Algarín, and their precursor Julia de Burgos. From Pizarnik and Duras to Marqués and Pietri, these voices, each with their own aesthetic (some more experimentational than others) and each with their uniquely expressed antiestablishment worldviews, are forerunners to Braschi.

In response to the tremendous cultural output of Latinx (Puerto Rican/Nuyorican) culture, a rich body of scholarship has grown. This scholarship puts front and center the complex ways in which Puerto Rico and its diaspora have been caught within the imperialist web of the United States since its annexation in 1898. For instance, in *Boricua Pop* (2004) Frances Negrón-Muntaner identifies how histories of colonization and US imperialism have led to a deep shaming that informs much cultural production; conversely, she identifies a performativity that resists such shaming. In *Dream Nation* María Acosta Cruz explores how an impulse for independence as "symbolic aspiration" grows a culture that "imagines the nation" through "its heroes, its allegories, its significant stories" (1). Acosta Cruz considers how this culture springs from an influx island identity: as nation, state, commonwealth, colony. Puerto Rican/Nuyorican culture grows from a mixed yearning for sovereignty along what is caught between "dashed aspirations, and hoped-for dreams" (1). In *Defending Their Own in the Cold* Marc Zimmerman turns his attention to how Puerto Rican/Boricua cultural phenomena grow out of this fraught relationship between island and mainland identities. In what he conceptualizes as a "dis-erasure," Zimmerman identifies a nomadic, spontaneous, and resistant Latinx subjectivity to the colonial power that wraps itself around everyday life of Puerto Rican peoples. In their introduction to a 2014 special issue of *American Quarterly* titled "Las Américas Quarterly," editors Macarena Gómez-Barris and Licia Fiol-Matta characterize Puerto Rican cultural studies as a field in which scholars work to "refine the conversation on earlier colonial ruptures and Américas exchanges [and to] present the transversality of the flow of knowledge, archives, and geographic spaces . . . as critical inquiry into Las Américas" (494).

In addition to scholarly attention to issues of coloniality and sovereignty, there is a rich and necessary body of scholarship that focuses on translanguaging acts—the interfacing of English, Spanish, and code-switching linguistic registers both as unique cultural markers and as aesthetic shaping devices. (For more on translanguaging, see Francisco Moreno-Fernández's chapter in this volume.) The use of translanguaging (English/Spanish, code-switching, caló, pochismos, for instance) resists uniform monolingual expressions and also reminds readers that Latinx identities and experiences are neither island-only nor mainland-aspiring but, rather, are shaped across a linguistically nonbinary hemispheric Américas. (See Martha E. Sánchez's *A Translational Turn*.) For

Lawrence La Fountain-Stokes, an author like Braschi gives power to Latinx women subjects who actively deform and transform language in ways that invite Latinx female readers to fill in gaps and to enact transformations in the world beyond the narrative. (See Lawrence La Fountain-Stokes's *Queer Ricans.*) Likewise, in *Redreaming America* Debra Castillo considers Braschi's translanguaging as clearing a space for resistance and revolt against coercive, binary monolingual Spanish or English dominance. On one occasion, Castillo identifies how Braschi's use of an "aggressive Spanglish" in *Yo-Yo Boing!* becomes the narrative vehicle to convey a mashup of concepts and knowledge from Europe (Michelangelo Antonioni) and the Américas (Julio Cortázar)—that is, Braschi's "linguistic dissonance" gives shape to an ironic metafictional "staged performance" narrative that troubles the concept of "authenticity" itself (174).

Taken as a whole, Giannini Braschi's mixed genre, translanguaging, experimental storyworlds present "conceptions of power and resistance to empire today that is not based on the class struggle within the nation-state class but located within the rhizomatic, deterritorialized multitude" (*Latinx Studies: Key Concepts* 53). In *Yo-Yo Boing!* we see Braschi's disruptive storyworld building at play: urban Latinxs in New York City on a nomadic journey in and through different cultural zones including, of course, those zones where borders between languages do not exist. In this sense, she disrupts the assimilatory pressure and mainstream constraint: that Spanish is private and English is public; otherwise stated of this typical way that language is polarized—if Spanish-speaking, then remain Puerto Rican, and if English, then you can be US. This linguistic elasticity liberates form, where subjects engage in discussions/explorations of cultural phenomena (Nabokov, Fellini, Monique Wittig, Woody Allen, and the Nuyorican arts generally). As Kristian van Haesendonck points out, the novel's translanguaging "goes further than a postmodern linguistic game" (179). It "enjoin(s) the reader to accept the language of the other, without falling into a new marketability of 'cross-over' writing" (179). In their introduction to *Yo-Yo Boing!* Doris Sommer and Alexandra Vega-Merino identify how the novel "transmutes poetry into novel, into screenplay, dialogue, and by extension to more and sometimes unidentified variants" ("Either And" 11).

And yet, Braschi turns the table on this, too. Her translingual characters and imaginings are not anchored in named characters. All we have are speaking voices identified by a dash. Here we do encounter a variety of "characters." The novel opens with a woman performing an extended monologue in Spanish ("Close-Up") on her physical, emotional, and intellectual features. A multiplicity of translanguaging "characters" follow in the "Blow-Up" section; and in the final section, "Black-Out," we hear the voice in Spanish of the "character" Giannina. Van Haesendonck articulates this as a postmodern move whereby the "doubling and the absenting" undermines "the authority of the traditional narrator" (179). For Van Haesendonck, Braschi creates traces of formless characters who are "simultaneously antagonists of their own selves." He concludes how, "in a Beckettian way, we find nothing more than some reminders of a narrative instance: the narrator has been reduced to a disembodied, amorphous voice" (179).

Braschi stages in ways that go beyond Beckett. She stages a Latinidad. This is driven home by Debra Castillo when she analyzes how "Braschi mixes opera, salsa, rock, and Mexican folk songs with Barbra Streisand, Frank Sinatra, and *The Sound of Music*, working to capture not only the promiscuously defined cultural referent, but the very sound and rhythm of these different musical genres" (179). Castillo enriches our understanding of how Braschi stages identity and experience.

Others have also remarked on how the characterless narrative functions. For Mila Popovich, this re-creates a sense of how "migrancy, and its consequent existential form of metalives, necessitates a multiple positionality that, in turn, produces multiple reflexive modalities. Sharing an understanding that mimesis itself is a form of displacement, these authors create alternative aesthetic states inhabited by characters who experience synchronously multiple placedness in the world" (117). And for Sommer and Vega-Merino, this move creates a "roller-coaster ride of shifting subject positions" (11) that ultimately resists our locating of Latinx subjectivities either in a culture-geographic location of Puerto Rico or in that of a Nuyorican Bronx; its constant shape-shifting also calls attention to the restless sociopolitical realities of the island as nation, state, postcolonial outpost. Sommer and Vega-Merino illustrate how the novel performs "the juggling of selves: a poet who doubles as an academic; a Puerto Rican who is also an American; a woman who is a match for any man's world" (13). Presciently, translingual tongues and imaginings are indeed the common doxa for Latinxs in Braschi's world. Sommer and Vega-Merino appraise Braschi's self-reflexive translingual play as a forceful resistance to any assimilationist moves, including that of the bildungsroman typified by the progress from "Spanish intimacies to English public life" (18). Rather, it creates a spectacle out of the Spanish to English "bilateral movement" (18).

In *Permissible Narratives*, Christopher González enriches our understanding of how Braschi creates what he calls a "challenging reading situation." He attends specifically to how her translanguaging allows her to give shape to a narrative that resists the monolingual Spanish or

English reader's attempt to contain it. He asserts: "because language is inextricably bound to identity," Braschi's translingual code-switching functions as an "unabashed assault on [the] reader" (89). The net effect is that her code-switching puts "more distance between the characters and reader" and thus at once challenges storyworld construction and opens a space for the storyworld to "complicate notions of identity within the minds of the audience" (67). Thus, for González, Giannina moves "beyond the limitations of identity-bound aesthetics—of the atavisms of Latino/a literature" (106). Finally, González identifies this as a Latinx narrative that "anticipates readers who can easily decode both languages in order to co-construct the storyworld" (106). José L. Torres-Padilla argues that Braschi's translingual storyworld at once creates a poetics that "undermines the essentialist perceptions of literature and purity in language held by the island's cultural elite" and functions "to reverse colonial authority by unmasking it and showing its ambivalence" (291). However, Torres-Padilla cautions us to be mindful of bringing too much idealism to a linguistical analysis of Braschi. He identifies how relying on language alone as a "stance of resistance against imperialism and hegemony" promotes an idealism that arguably "supports the continuing colonial status of Puerto Rico and undermines any desire for self-determination that might effect real change" (292). Torres-Padilla questions whether the aesthetics of *Yo-Yo Boing!* is "elitist and bourgeois" in ways that uphold the "the status quo" (293).

In 1988 Braschi published *El imperio de los sueños*, an epic mashup of poetry and prose, deploying a myriad of storytelling forms. In her introduction to Tess O'Dwyer's 1994 English translation, Alicia Ostriker qualifies *Empire of Dreams* as a masterpiece of poetry cross-dressing "in the garb of dramatic monologue, love letter, TV commercial, diary excerpt, movie criticism, celebrity confession, literary theory, bastinado, manifesto, etc." (ix). In this work, a parade of nomadic characters and migrant voices crowd the city streets, stores, and tourist attractions of New York (such as Macy's, the Empire State Building, St. Patrick's Cathedral, Central Park). In "New/Nueva York in Giannina Braschi's *Poetic Egg*," Diane E. Marting identifies this as a "parodic elegy" to Cervantes and a contemporary example of "historiographic metafiction" that reconstructs a "fractured, cosmopolitan cityscape" populated by globally placed and displaced Puerto Ricans who make up a "global South consisting of two islands within the same country" (167). Braschi's New/eva York exists as an "ideal creative cityscape and a dystopic urban wasteland" (181). It's a city of "glitz and glamour" and where culture is coopted for "self-promotion" (181). But because it is so complexly layered, it showcases the urban Latinx "multiplicities within the identity of persons" (181). On Braschi's pairing of frivolity with the sublime, Jerónimo Arellano situates *Empire of Dreams* within the context of the McOndo movement in Latin America, alongside edgy urban novelists Alberto Fuguet and Sergio Gómez who take a stand against commercialism and magic realism. In *Magical Realism and the History of Emotions in Latin America*, Arellano identifies "a central tension" in *The Intimate Diary of Solitude* (the final section of *Empire of Dreams*) as "a conflict between the controlling narrator and a rebellious protagonist," Mariquita Samper, a Puerto Rican writer who works as a makeup artiste at Macy's, "The Greatest Store in the World" (165). Spoiler alert: Mariquita murders the ever-looming, omniscient narrator of the Latin American Boom because he keeps rewriting her diary against her will, erasing her adventures and replacing them with a suffocating solitude. Refusing to die of solitude, Mariquita shoots the narrator: "Boom! Boom! He's dead. He's dead. Mariquita has killed the narrator. Revolution in *The Intimate Diary of Solitude* (203)." This declaration of revolution—not unlike later manifestos by the Mexican "Crack Generation" writers and the McOndo novelists of the 1990s—signals "the epochal death of magical realism" in Latin America (167).

Like *Empire of Dreams* and *Yo-Yo Boing! United States of Banana* is also revolutionary in style and subject matter. In *United States of Banana* we meet an unlikely cast of disparate characters: Fidel, Artaud, Cockroach, Rubén Darío, Wishy-Washy, Puerto Rico, Hamlet, Giannina, Zarathustra, and Segismundo (a Latinxified Sigmund Freud?). As we travel from a dungeon beneath the Statue of Liberty (where Segismundo's been held for one hundred years) across the Hispanophone archipelago, Braschi asks us to seesaw between individual and collective acts as shapers of history—including the 9/11 terrorist attacks and US imperialism. María Acosta Cruz identifies the work as a "good, old-fashioned independentista tirade" (162) that "uses an everything-but-the-kitchen-sink" approach to denunciate US global imperialism: from "Puerto Rico to Iran, Iraq, and the fall of the Twin Towers" (162). But, Arnaldo Cruz-Malavé sums up *United States of Banana* as a "political-poetic, anti-imperial book [that] does not seek to attain a new space of sovereignty from which to exert an alternative, progressive hegemony; instead, it attempts to imagine and foster . . . new forms of interaction, communication, and cooperation 'from below,' literally from below" (815). Indeed, Braschi's decolonial experimental narratives clear space for readers to experience new positive and progressive forms of human relationality. Cruz-Malavé concludes that Braschi's storyworlds forge networks of "camaraderie, compañerismo, and yes, love" (816). In *Precarious Crossings*, Alexandra Perisic contextualizes a "Declaration of Love" in *United States of Banana* as a "reinvention of the language of love" through a political lens of "universal mourning" not of a "specific life but of the precariousness of life in general.(173)" Braschi dramatizes how "the immigrant condition, the dispossession of one's roots, country, and family create the conditions of possibility for an ethics of mourning"(173). Imprisoned immigrants, second class citizens, and suspected terrorists from around the globe are imprisoned under Lady Liberty's skirt, where they "share their breath and space, as they mourn together.(173)" In *Novelization in Decolonization, or Postcolonialism Reconsidered,* Peter Hitchcock observes how *United States of Banana* is "forthright in disabusing readers about how so called 'Banana Republics' come about and wonders aloud, from its title on, about the location and order of knowledge said to grow them (189)". Hitchcock affirms Braschi's clarity about the power of "cultural force" (189). Her namesake character Giannina demands that the republic open its doors to poets, philosophers, and lovers: "the powers of the world are shifting. Culture is becoming more relevant than politics. Cities more relevant than nations. Continents more relevant than nations. But continents less relevant than cities. Languages more relevant than nations. Languages are alive. Nations are dead (229)."

Without doubt, Braschi's books challenge the constructs of society and the expectations of readers. They ask us to work for our pleasures—and displeasures. As with others who have come before and those creating today, there is a kind of gatekeeping when it comes to the teaching, studying, and dissemination of Braschi and other vanguardistas of color. With radically experimental artistry, the analytical optic has traditionally been focused on men: Joyce, Barth, Danielewski, Pynchon, among many others. And yet, assuredly, readers and scholars of today's generation hunger for the kind of mind-, body-, and genre-bending work of a Braschi. And this happens in spite of the hunger for such writing. Torsa Ghosal (a former student of mine and now a professor) calls attention to this academic imbalance that skews to male authors who "feature women characters who are stalked, groped, and abused." She identifies another arguably more destructive element to this trend, calling attention to how "white, male authors often perform their dissent by sustaining illusions of possessing or plundering language imagined as the female body." Literary canons, classrooms, scholarly and mainstream writings at best don't know what to do with vanguard authors such as Braschi who trouble the reading experience—at worst they deliberately shun such authors. (See Ghosal's "How I Learned to Love Experimental Fiction as a Brown Girl by Seeking Out Books by Women of Color.")

This isn't to say that scholars, teachers, and even some mainstream reviewers haven't turned their analytical optic to Braschi. They have.

Within months of *Asalto al tiempo*'s debut in 1981, major news outlets in Barcelona, Mallorca, San Juan, and Mexico City praised the young poet's originality and sensitivity. Juan Martínez Capó was among the first newspaper critics to review *Asalto al tiempo* and proclaimed it "one of the most illuminating documents in recent Puerto Rican poetry" (15). However, much of the academic exploration is only just burgeoning in our contemporary moment. For instance, in the 2013 published *¡Muy Pop!* (coauthored with Ilan Stavans), I identify Braschi as a Latinx creator propelled by this aspiration to establish a new aesthetic relationship with her readers; how she ceaselessly searches for the new; how she radically awakens readers to new ways of perceiving, feeling, and thinking about the world; how she creates new aesthetic objects that trigger new perceptual, emotional, and cognitive relations between the narrative and the reader, constantly fighting against our habituation (paraphrase 58–59). She has been doing this since the 1980s when many of, say, her ideal readers like myself were still to become professors—and those like Torsa Ghosal were still to be born. In this sense, I consider the long game of Braschi's work as itself creating its ideal readers. I consider her work in the 1980s and 1990s as anticipating a future ideal reader, who apprehends, understands, and emotes as a Ghosal or an Aldama. And we see more of these ideal readers in the flesh and blood today; they are the ones like Ghosal, like me, and like many others who relish an aesthetics of discomfort; in narrative fictions that challenge our gap-filling and puzzle-solving capacities in and across multiple languages, identities, and experiences. (See Aldama's "Chicana/o Literature's Multi-spatiotemporal Projections & Impacts"; or "Back to the Future.") Braschi creates works that project forward to a future where they will encounter readers like myself and others whose scholarly optic didn't exist at the time of her writing, say, *Yo-Yo Boing!* These are scholars who will not only get it but—in the words of the coeditor of this volume Tess O'Dwyer—are "savvy bilingual [readers] who can enjoy the novel hot off the shelf 'as is'" (35). For instance, today a critic like Kristian van Haesendonck doesn't stop at the doorstep of *Yo-Yo Boing!* declaring it unreadable. Rather, he considers it an extension and troubling of a theater of the absurd and postmodern fiction writ large in its quest to destabilize fixed notions of the self and world. (See van Haesendonck's "Enchantment or Fright?")

The first section in this volume, "Vanguard Forms and Latinx Sensibilities" brings together chapters that focus on Braschi's narratives, identities, and worldviews. This section opens with Madelena Gonzalez's essay "The Uncommon Wealth of Art: Poetic Progress as Resistance to the Commodification of Culture in *United States of Banana*," which springboards off Jean Baudrillard's theory of the viral stage of capitalism in relation to Deleuze's theory on the societies of control. Gonzalez makes the case that Braschi's novel suggests "the utopian potential of the aesthetic as an ethical alternative to . . . the fabricated consensus of capitalism" and how art may be used as "a weapon of delegitimation of these ubiquitous structures of control and their universalizing tendencies." Next is John "Rio" Riofrio's chapter, "*Rompiendo esquemas*: Catastrophic Bravery in *United States of Banana*." Rio formulates an analytical framework based on the concept of *romper esquemas* that enriches our understanding of not only how Braschi breaks with schemas in terms of aesthetics but how *United States of Banana* powerfully wakes us from our habituated states and repetitive cognitive and emotive patterns of acting in the world. Then comes Anne Ashbaugh's chapter, "Exile and Burial of Ontological Sameness: A Dialogue between Zarathustra and Giannina." Ashbaugh's analysis of the dialogue between author, character, and ancient prophet Zarathustra sheds new light on Braschi's articulation of autonomy and freedom in *United States of Banana* and reveals otherwise occluded aspects of Nietzsche's philosophy as formulated in *Thus Spoke Zarathustra*. Next is Francisco Moreno-Fernández's chapter, "*Yo-Yo Boing!* Or Literature as a Translingual Practice." Here Moreno-Fernández uses the concept and practice of translanguaging as a way to enrich understanding of *Yo-Yo Boing!* The term "translanguaging" identifies how multilingual speakers fluidly exist at the nexus of the integration of different linguistic systems. Moreno-Fernández prefers this to identifiers such as "Spanglish" or "code-switching," which conceive of multilingual speakers' use of languages as still distinctively different. Rather, by identifying Braschi's use of translanguaging to shape *Yo-Yo Boing!* he explains how it ultimately creates the "liquid and translingual reality" experienced by Latinxs. We end the first section with Maritza Stanchich's chapter, "Bilingual Big Bang: Giannina Braschi's Trilogy Levels the Spanish-English Playing Field." Stanchich's comprehensive analysis of Braschi's unofficial trilogy—*El imperio de los sueños*, *Yo-Yo Boing!*, and *United States of Banana*—demonstrates how language informs genre and how Braschi deforms both to give shape to multilingual hemispheric Américan Latinx experiences. Stanchich finds inspiration in María Mercedes Carrión's brilliant analysis of the role of translation in *El imperio de los sueños* in "Geographies, (M) Other Tongues" (172). Although Braschi's aesthetics at once allude to European avant-gardes, her translingual linguistic deployments wrestle and forge parity with the "staggering legacies" that Spanish and English as colonial languages have left in their wake. For Stanchich, Braschi's interlingualism and translingualism clear a new borderland space for trans-canonical locutions that counter Enlightenment grammars and canons along with their consequent exclusionary politics. Finally, Stanchich situates Braschi within the work of other Puerto Rican/Nuyorican writers such as Urayoán Noel, Edwin Torres, and Edgardo Vega who clear new space for hemispheric Latinx literary traditions as a "global poetics of dissent."

The volume's second section, "Persuasive Art of Dramatic Voices," brings together chapters that focus on the different forms and locutions Braschi uses to move her audiences both emotively and cognitively. We open with the chapter "Giannina and Braschi: A Polyphony of Voices," by Cristina Garrigós. Launching from a discussion of Jorge Luis Borges (specifically, "Borges and I"), Garrigós argues that Braschi's self-reflexive and self-inscribed poetics necessitates that readers conflate author with narrative voice in all of her works. For Garrigós, Braschi writes and Giannina performs. Garrigós analyzes this in *Empire of Dreams*, where she determines the significance of the character Giannina's playing the roles of Mariquita Samper, Berta Singerman, and Uriberto Eisensweig; in *Yo-Yo Boing!* she unpacks how the voices form an anonymous authorial chorus; and in *United States of Banana*, she determines how the dialogic interplay of the authorial with the narrative opens a space that gives voice to the "subalternity, invisibility, and silence of Puerto Rico—and of Latinos, in general." In her chapter, "The Poetry of Giannina Braschi: Art and Magic in *Assault on Time*," Laura R. Loustau analyzes the transformative power of Braschi's first book of poetry *Asalto al tiempo* (1981). Loustau uses Merleau-Ponty to formulate a Braschian poetics that shows how Braschi creates a poet-artist/poet-reader dyad that at once pays homage to César Vallejo (specifically, *The Black Heralds* and *Trilce*) and radically innovates poetic forms to open us to new ways of physically sensing and acting in the world. In "The Human Barnyard: Rhetoric, Identification, and Symbolic Representation in *United States of Banana*," Elizabeth Lowry explores how Braschi creates a complex life tableau to reconstruct the politically charged event of 9/11. Lowry uses a rhetorical studies analytic to demonstrate how Braschi's cross-genre aesthetic persuades readers to step close to the discomforting and ontologically different. For Lowry, Braschi "communicates the problematics of singular representation by resisting formal genre conventions, thus refusing to fix the very shape of her text." This allows Braschi to deploy a tactic of "rhetorical listening" whereby multiple worldviews are presented and understanding is achieved across cultural and national differences. Then, in "Gamifying World Literature: Giannina Braschi's *United States of Banana*," Daniela Daniele analyzes how Braschi's alchemical and vernacular *United States of Banana* gives shape to playful picaresque drama formed in and between a Caribbean and mainland US Latinx experience. As "alien poet who carries the weight of a bookish tradition while walking with a light foot in the ruins of Ground Zero," Braschi pushes the envelope on a European/United States–rooted avant-garde art-making tradition to breathe new life into representations of a post-traumatic 9/11 global scene. Daniele identifies how Braschi revamps video-game poetics and cartoonish, programmatic consistency to make for a critical gamification of the literary tradition that wakes us to the brutalities of US imperialism.

The final section of the volume, "Intermedial Poetics and Radical Thinking" brings together chapters that analyze how Braschi's aesthetics reflect on and refract questions of existence. We open with "Leaping Off the Page: Giannina Braschi's Intermedialities," in which Dorian Lugo Bertrán analyzes the strategies Braschi deploys across hybridized genres (novel, short story, chronicle, essay, diary, theater, prose poetry), inter- and intra-textual referencing, and intermediality to move readers beyond the notion of in-betweenness. Bertrán points to adaptations by other artists of Braschi's writings—into paintings, lithographs, video, theater, photography, sculpture, drawings (such as Joakim Lindengren's graphic novel adaptation of *United States of Banana* published in Swedish in 2017). Bertrán points to instances of "sound in writing" that lead readers to a place akin to Nuyorican spoken word and slam poetry performances where image/word and the visual/performative create new ways of articulating a poet's "inter-life." In Ronald Mendoza-de Jesús's chapter, "Free-dom: *United States of Banana* and the Limits of Sovereignty," we see how Braschi shares common ground and worldviews with the French-Algerian philosopher Jacques Derrida. For Mendoza-de Jesús, the fact that Braschi and Derrida are exiles who live in and around the legacies of colonization leads to common expressions of unfixity and the concept of unconditionality; Mendoza-de Jesús defines the latter as "the absence of any internal or external constraints" that is often invoked "implicitly as a synonym of freedom, if not as its very essence." Braschi and Derrida seek to have us "rethink unconditionality, and therefore freedom as such, . . . [so as] to dismantle the hegemonic political and juridical configurations that transform the force of unconditionality into the power of sovereignty, beginning with that political machine known as the sovereign self, who understands itself as a political entity by making its existence coincide with its ability to *possess itself*." Finally, Mendoza-de Jesús identifies how both Braschi and Derrida leave readers at the displaced center of paradox, where "the liberation of freedom from freedom is the entrance into a space of doubt without end." It is from this "unstable place" that Braschi and Derrida, he states, "invite us to rethink what we mean by freedom, what we regard as a right, and what we understand by sovereign power." We end this final section with "The Holy Trinity: Money, Power, and Success in *United States of Banana*." Here Francisco José Ramos uses Herbert Marcuse, Guy Debord, and Gottfried Wilhelm Leibniz to scaffold a higher appreciation of the "specular game" that Braschi constructs in *United States of Banana*. In the society of the spectacle where we no longer have direct access to the experiential and authentic, Braschi creates "an open work of art" whereby theater morphs into philosophical essay into prose poem and operetta to dismantle capitalism and its neoliberalist tenets. Indeed, Braschi's specular game—created out of the intermixture of the author, the character Giannina, and her theatrical voices—destabilizes fixed notions of subjectivity and a reality constructed out of spectacle. Braschi's specular game also, he writes, functions "as political satire, a trenchant dramatization of Puerto Rico's pathological dependence on the nation that invaded the island in 1898 and imposed US citizenship in 1917, which was consecrated in 1952 as a colonial experiment that has since served as a launching pad for America's imperial proclivities." Braschi's dramatic texts resist categorization as either "Spanglish" or "postmodern literature." For Ramos, Braschi takes literature to the "limit of its possibilities," a writing practice "that is fully installed out in the open air, and its flight rises skyward, like the birds, those prodigious and free messengers of the void." The volume concludes with Rolando Pérez's interview with Giannina Braschi, conducted specifically for this endeavor. Here Pérez and Braschi take us on a journey through deep time that explores aesthetics, metaphysics, language, politics, and her buoyancy in life and poetry.

Braschi smuggles into a US imagination a sensibility created in and across a hemispheric Américan history, aesthetic, and culture. And she does so to create hard-hitting, no-holds-barred, mind-expanding storyworlds. She wakes us to the world in and across languages, ontologies, metafictional epistemologies. In closing, I would like to say how excited I am to be publishing Joakim Lindengren's graphic novel adaptation of Giannina Braschi's *United States of Banana* in English, with scholarly commentary by Amanda M. Smith and Amy Sheeran. This along with Braschi's magisterial corpus will at once build on a planetary literary past and anticipate a reader today and tomorrow. I look forward to seeing, too, how new generations of multi- and translanguaging Latinx authors and comic book creators will be inspired to shape radically experimental fictions. I look forward to seeing what materializes from Braschi's invitation for us to look into and beyond dreams of the self and to open to the limitless possibilities for transforming tomorrow's selves in the world.

Works Cited

Acosta Cruz, María. *Dream Nation: Puerto Rican Culture and the Fictions of Independence*. Rutgers UP, 2014.

Aldama, Frederick Luis. "Chicana/o Literature's Multi-spatiotemporal Projections & Impacts; or Back to the Future." *The Routledge Handbook on Chicana/o Studies*, edited by Denise Segura, Francisco Lomelí, and Elyette Benjamin-Labarthe,: Routledge, 2019, pp. 193–203.

Aldama, Frederick Luis, and Christopher González. *Latinx Studies: The Key Concepts*. Routledge, 2018.

Aldama, Frederick Luis, and Ilan Stavans. *¡Muy Pop! Conversations on Latino Popular Culture*. U of Michigan P, 2013.

Arellano, Jerónimo. *Magical Realism and the History of Emotions in Latin America*. Bucknell UP, 2015.

Capó, Juan Martínez. "Giannina Braschi, *Asalto al tiempo*." *El Mundo*, 1981.

Carrión, María Mercedes. "Geographies, (M)Other Tongues and the Role of Translation in Giannina Braschi's *El imperio de los sueños*." *Studies in Twentieth-Century Literature* vol. 20, no. 1, Winter 1996, pp. 167–91.

Castillo, Debra. *Redreaming America: Toward a Bilingual American Culture*. State U of New York P, 2005.

Cruz-Malavé, Arnaldo. "Under the Skirt of Liberty: Giannina Braschi Rewrites Empire." *American Quarterly*, vol. 66, no. 3, 2014, pp. 801–18.

Foster, Sesshu. *Atomik Aztex*. City Lights, 2005.

Ghosal, Torsa. "How I Learned to Love Experimental Fiction as a Brown Girl by Seeking Out Books by Women of Color." *Bustle*, January 25, 2019, www.bustle.com/p/how-i-learned-to-love-experimental-fiction-as-a-brown-girl-by-seeking-out-books-by-women-of-color-15863937.

Gómez-Barris, Macarena, and Licia Fiol-Matta. "Introduction." *American Quarterly*, vol. 66, no. 3, special issue "Las Américas Quarterly," September 2014, pp. 493–504.

Gomez-Peña, Guillermo. *Codex Espangliensis*. Moving Parts Press, 1998.

González, Christopher. *Permissible Narratives: The Promise of Latino/a Literature*. The Ohio State UP, 2017.

Hitchock, Peter. "Novelization in Decolonization, or Postcolonialism Reconsidered." *Other Globes, Past and Peripheral Imaginations of Globalization*, edited by Simon Ferdinand, Irene Villaescusa-Illán, and Esther Peeren, Palgrave Macmillan, 2020, pp. 177–94.

La Fountain-Stokes, Lawrence. *Queer Ricans: Cultures and Sexualities in the Diaspora*. U of Minnesota P, 2009.

Lindengren, Joakim. *United States of Banana*. Cobolt, 2017.

Marting, Diane E. "New/Nueva York in Giannina Braschi's 'Poetic Egg': Fragile Identity, Postmodernism, and Globalization." *Global South*, vol. 4, no. 1, 2010, pp. 167–82.

Morales, Alejandro. *Waiting to Happen*. Chusma House, 2001.

O'Dwyer, Tess. "Grunting and Grooming in a Room of One's Own: On Translating Giannina Braschi's *Yo-Yo Boing!*" *Artful Dodge* 34–35, 1999, pp. 70–79.

Ostriker, Alicia. "Introduction." *Empire of Dreams*, by Giannina Braschi, translated by Tess O'Dwyer, Yale UP, 1994, p. ix.

Perisic, Alexandra. *Precarious Crossings: Immigration, Neoliberalism, and the Atlantic*. The Ohio State UP, 2019.

Pineda, Cecile. *Face*. Viking, 1985.

Plascencia, Salvador. *The People of Paper*. McSweeney's Books, 2005.

Popovich, Mila. "Metafictions, Migrations, Metalives: Narrative Innovations and Migrant Women's Aesthetics in Giannina Braschi and Etel Adnan." *International Journal of the Humanities*, vol. 9, no. 10, 2012, pp. 117–27.

Rios, Isabel. *Victuum*. Diana-Etna, 1976.

Sánchez González, Lisa. *Boricua Literature: A Literary History of the Puerto Rican Diaspora*. New York UP, 2001.

Sheeran, Amy, and Amanda M. Smith. *United States of Banana: A Graphic Revolution*. The Ohio State UP, 2021.

Sommer, Doris, and Alexandra Vega-Merino. "Either/And." *Yo-Yo Boing!* Latin American Literary Review Press, 1998, pp. 11–18.

Stanchich, Martiza. "'Borinkee' in Hawai'i." *Writing Off the Hyphen: New Critical Perspectives on the Literature of the Puerto Rican Diaspora*, edited by Jose L. Torres-Padilla and Carmen Haydée Rivera, U of Washington P, 2008, pp. 201–20.

Torres-Padilla, José L. "When Hybridity Doesn't Resist: Giannina Braschi's *Yo-Yo Boing!*" *Complicating Constructions: Race, Ethnicity, and Hybridity in American Texts*, edited by David S. Goldstein and Audrey B. Thacker, U of Washington P, 2007, pp. 290–307.

Van Haesendonck, Kristian. "Enchantment or Fright? Identity and Postmodern Writing in Contemporary Puerto Rico." *Cultural Identity and Postmodern Writing*, edited by Theo D'haen and Pieter Vermeulen, Editions Rodopi B.V., 2006, pp. 169–84.

Zimmerman, Marc. *Defending Their Own in the Cold: The Cultural Turns of U.S. Puerto Ricans*. U of Illinois P, 2011.

Suggested Further Reading

Aldama, Frederick Luis. *The Routledge Concise History of Latino/a Literature*. Routledge, 2012.

Allatson, Paul. "From 'Latinidad' to 'Latinid@des': Imagining the Twenty-First Century." *The Cambridge Companion to Latina/o American Literature*, edited by John Morán González, Cambridge UP, 2016, pp. 128–46.

Barnstone, Willis, and Tony Barnstone, eds. "Giannina Braschi, Puerto Rico–New York." *Literatures of Asia, Africa, and Latin America: From Antiquity to the Present*, Prentice Hall, 1999, pp. 1954–55.

Beck, Evelyn. Review of *United States of Banana*, by Giannina Braschi. *Library Journal*, October 1, 2011.

Bergmann, Emilie L., and Edward H. Friedman. "Imitation and Adaptation: A Meeting of Minds." *Bulletin of Spanish Studies*, vol. 93, no. 7–8, 2016, pp. 1445–67.

Beroiz, Luciana. "Las heterotopías posmodernas de Marlene Nourbese Philip, Giannina Braschi y Howardena Pindell." *Cuadernos del Sur/Letras*, vol. 42, 2012, pp.11–30.

Beroiz, Luciana. "Urban Postmodern Chronicles: Translation Issues in the Collections of Giannina Braschi and David Trinidad." *Estudios de Teoria Literaria Revista Digital Artes/Letras/ Humanidades*, vol. 6, no. 12, 2017, pp. 111–23.

Carroll, Julia. "Spanish Affect and Its Effects: Bilingual Process in Giannina Braschi's *Yo-Yo Boing!*" *Leading Ladies: mujeres en la literatura hispana y en las artes*, edited by Yvonne Fuentes and Margaret R. Parker. Louisiana State UP, 2006, pp. 93–106.

Clarkson, Shaun. "Torching the Symbols of Liberty in *United States of Banana*." *Creative Sanctions: Imaginative Limits and the Post-9/11 Novel*. PhD dissertation, Purdue University, West Lafayette, Indiana, 2017.

D'Amore, Anna Maria. *Translating Contemporary Mexican Texts: Fidelity to Alterity*. Peter Lang, 2009.

De Mojica, Sarah González. "Literaturas heterogéneas e hibridaciones créoles: sujetos andinos y caribes." *Cuadernos de Literatura*, vol. 6., no. 11, 2000, pp. 67–85.

De Mojica, Sarah González. "Sujetos híbridos en la literatura puertorriqueña: *Daniel Santos* y *Yo-Yo Boing!*" *Revista de crítica literaria latinoamericana*, 2002, pp. 187–203.

Dessús, Virginia. "Identidades postmodernas: *Yo-Yo Boing!* de Giannina Braschi." *La Torre: Revista General de la Universidad de Puerto Rico*, vol. 6, 2001, pp. 413–26.

Diaz, Nancy Gray. "Performing Soledad: The Demythification of Identity in Giannina Braschi's *El Imperio de los sueños*." *Romance Notes*, vol. 37, no. 3, 1997, pp. 331–37.

Enghels, Renata, and Margot Vanhaverbeke. "La expresión de valores diminutivos en contextos escritos de cambio de código. Un análisis comparativo de novelas latinas." *Academia Norteamericana de le lengua Española*, no. 38, 2020.

Estill, Adriana. Review of *Yo-Yo Boing!*, by Giannina Braschi. *Letras Femeninas*, vol. 25 no. 1, 1999, p. 224.

Flores, Juan, and George Yúdice. "Living Borders/Buscando América: Languages of Latino Self-Formation." *Latinos in Education: A Critical Reader*, edited by Antonia Darder, Rodolfo D. Torres, and Henry Gutiérrez. Routledge, 1997, pp. 174–200.

Foster, David William. Review of *Yo-Yo Boing!*, by Giannina Braschi. *Review of Contemporary Fiction*, 1999, pp. 202–3.

Garrigós, Cristina. "Bilingües, biculturales y posmodernas: Rosario Ferré y Giannina Braschi." *Insula*, no. 667–68, 2002, pp. 16–18.

Gonzalez, Madelena. "*United States of Banana* (2011), *Elizabeth Costello* (2003) and *Fury* (2001): Portrait of the Writer as the 'Bad Subject' of Globalisation." *Études britanniques contemporaines. Revue de la Société d'études anglaises contemporaines*, no. 46, 2014.

Kuebler, Carolyn. "Empire of Dreams." *Review of Contemporary Fiction*, vol. 15, no. 1, Spring 1995, pp. 168–70.

Lonsdale, Laura. *Multilingualism and Modernity: Barbarisms in Spanish and American Literature*. Palgrave Macmillan, 2020.

Loustau, Laura. *Cuerpos errantes: Literatura latina y latinoamericana en Estados Unidos*. Beatriz Viterbo Editora, 2002.

Loustau, Laura R. "Nomadismos lingüísticos y culturales en *Yo-Yo Boing!* de Giannina Braschi." *Revista Iberoamericana*, vol. 71, no. 211, 2005, pp. 437–48.

Osborne, Elizabeth. "El espacio del entremedio como espacio de negociación y provocación en *Yo-Yo Boing!* de Giannina Braschi." PhD dissertation, University of Chile, 2010.

Pérez, Rolando. "The Bilingualisms of Latino/a Literatures." *The Oxford Handbook of Latino Studies*, edited by Ilan Stavans. Oxford UP, 2020, pp. 282–306.

Ramos, Francisco José. "Asalto al tiempo de Giannina Braschi." *Plural*, vol. 1, no. 2, 1982, pp. 197–99.

Ramos, Francisco José. "Postfacio." *El imperio de los sueños*. Barcelona: Anthropos, 1988.

Riofrio, John. "Falling for Debt: Giannina Braschi, the Latinx Avant-Garde, and Financial Terrorism in the *United States of Banana*." *Latino Studies*, vol. 18, no. 1, 2020, pp. 66–81.

Rivera, Carmen Haydée. "Embracing Alternate Discourses on Migration: Giannina Braschi's and Luisita López Torregrosa's Multi-dimensional Literary Schemes." *Revista Umbral*, vol. 8, 2017, pp. 6–20.

Rivera, Carmen Haydée. "El poder de la palabra y la experiencia transnacional: una entrevista con Giannina Braschi." *Op. Cit. Revista del Centro de Investigaciones Históricas*, vol. 20, 2011–2012, pp. 181–201.

Sheeran, Amy, and Amanda M. Smith. "A Graphic Revolution: Talking Poetry and Politics with Giannina Braschi." *Chiricú Journal: Latina/o Literature, Arts, and Culture*, vol. 2, no. 2, 2018, pp. 130–42.

Waldron, John V. "Killing Colonialism's Ghosts in McOndo: Mayra Santos-Febres and Giannina Braschi." *CIEHL: Cuaderno Internacional de Estudios Humanisticos y Literatura*, 2010.

Waldron, John V. Review of *Estados Unidos de Banana*, by Giannina Braschi. *Feministas Unidas, Inc.*, vol. 38, no. 1, Spring 2018, p. 16, people.wku.edu/inma.pertusa/encuentros/FemUn/newsletters/news/FemU_Spring2018.pdf.

I

Vanguard Forms and Latinx Sensibilities

1

The Uncommon Wealth of Art

Poetic Progress as Resistance to the Commodification of Culture in *United States of Banana*

Madelena Gonzalez

Staged in a surreal post-9/11 New York and Puerto Rico, *United States of Banana* is a politically charged metaphor for the fall of the US empire and the collapse of the World Trade Center as well as a plea for subject minorities to free themselves from the yoke of domination by the majority, whether such domination be economic, linguistic, cultural, or ideological. Braschi's sophisticated aesthetic challenges the banality of the contemporary clichés of global McCulture and allows her to rewrite radical politics as high art. Thanks to what she terms her "Hierarchy of Inspiration," "the demon, the duende, the angel and the muses" (63), Braschi's narrator affirms the unique status of the artist whose function is to reconnect with truth and authenticity through the aesthetic, emphasizing the artist's role as seer and visionary whose poetry can be the source of a powerful transformation of reality. She proposes a new commonwealth or "United Nations without nations" (*USB* 118), which eliminates the elements of power and authority that are sources of oppression in the hands of the majority. Ultimately, what is suggested by Braschi's novel is the utopian potential of the aesthetic as an ethical alternative to the dominant ideology of the neoliberal imperative and the fabricated consensus of capitalism.

With the rise of globalization studies in academia, notably in the social sciences and economics, postcolonialism and its reliance on alterity and hybridity is starting to seem out of sync with the generalized cultural homogenization that results from the global expansion of capital. For some, the current state of affairs is merely a continuation of colonialism by other means, allowing for the continuation of the postcolonial paradigm; for others the necessity for a "new cartography" is palpable and urgent (Hardt and Negri 92). Postcolonialism, as its name suggests, was constructed in relation to colonization, on the back of the disillusionment with the failure of nationalism, hence the fear of essentialism and the Enlightenment project that it evinces. However, the globalized era has ushered in new, more insidious and more ambivalent forms of economic imperialism as well as a new epoch of post-nationalism, which may be couched in the form of the reinvigorated internationalism of a traditional Marxist cast or be closer to Hardt and Negri's utopian vision of "global citizenship" (92). Even if both phenomena are situated historically, neither can be glibly assimilated to the postcolonial as we know it to date.

In the field of literary criticism and the study of fiction, there is a time lag in relation to this new state of affairs. The postcolonial label is still persistently and systematically applied to certain writers who are seen as representative of its main tropes, for both ethnic and aesthetic reasons, although a clear definition of the postcolonial aesthetic has yet to arise. The work of Braschi, a Puerto Rican living in New York, would seem to fulfil the necessary criteria of biculturalism, bilingualism, migrancy, hybridity that are required for gaining entry into the postcolonial canon. Indeed, the panel session dedicated to *United States of Banana* at the convention of the Modern Language Association in January 2013 had recourse to this familiar paradigm. Braschi, it would seem, inhabits a space that is hotly contested by both high postcolonial studies and the world book industry, which exists within the new paradigm of global culture or what Wallerstein and other analysts have classed as the world capitalist system. Indeed, it is worth noting that *United States of Banana* is published by AmazonCrossing, the Internet giant's publishing arm. This double interpellation affects her performance as a writer but also that of readers of her work. Her novel is seemingly ideally poised for analysis within existing critical parameters but obstinately refuses to conform to the protocols laid out for it.

Three different aspects of the novel seem particularly relevant to my hypothesis of a poetics of resistance. First, the return to form and style is a way of reasserting control over the novel as artefact. Second, the artist figure is seen as a "bad subject," declining to occupy the role assigned her within globalization. Third, the emphasis is on the creative imagination as a source of agency and transformative power, both locked in battle with the hyperreal simulacrum of the technoverse and obliged to seek out a compromise with mimesis and rationality in order to reaffirm real emotion via the expression of an ethical universal.

The Return to Form and the Potency of Style

Braschi's text certainly both encourages and resists a certain type of referential illusionist reading in familiar postmodern fashion and deals in some measure with postcolonial themes such as migration and identity but seeks to situate itself above and beyond such totalities in an unidentifiable elsewhere, which makes it difficult to pin it down to any one location on the literary-critical map. The author chooses to set most of her novel in contemporary New York, the very epicenter of globalization, but she "outsources" the second part to a recognizably postcolonial location, Puerto Rico. The theme addressed, however, is not so much the oppressive legacy of colonialism as the challenge to independence and self-determination that is constituted by the hegemony of world capitalism—on which the narrator, a writer/poet/artist, tries to persuade her fellow travelers to declare war. Resistance is seen from within the prism of this invasive model and ironically expressed in the rephrasing of a celebrated refrain from an old Andrews Sisters' song, "drinking rum and Coca-Cola / and working for the Yankee dollar" into "drinking rum and Coca-Cola / and working for your own nasty dollar" (*USB* 244–48), which punctuates her conversation with the other characters.

A few specific examples will show how the return to formalist concerns and the potency of style can be used as tools to question accepted values and interpretative strategies, as encapsulated in the shocking reaction of Braschi's eponymous writer figure, Giannina, one of the multiple narrators of the novel, to the events of 9/11. The startling pronouncement "Inspiration made an installation that day" (*USB* 86) occurs in part 2 of the novel, itself entitled "United States of Banana." The statement comes near the beginning of a chapter named "Burial of the Sardine," which charts the progress of Giannina, a sort of duenna, and her unlikely companions, Hamlet and Zarathustra, through a surreal post-9/11 New York on their way to bury the aforementioned "rigorous but retarded sardine" at the foot of the Statue of Liberty (72). It is part of a seemingly absurdist philosophical dialogue she holds with her comrades and the recently deceased "salaried sardine" that mocks the enslavement of contemporary Americans to capitalism: "Every two weeks—it brought me a salary—the stinky sardine—and I brought home all I could with that salary—confinement, imprisonment. Depending on a salary made me salivate" (72). Braschi's wordplay, linguistic patterning, and literalization of metaphor give her poetic licence for her critical intent in relation to the enslavement to materialism that she depicts at the heart of the American empire. The triumph of commodification is portrayed as total in the novel and the difficulty consists in finding a position outside the market from which to combat its mechanisms. What is being lamented is the fact that art has long ago lost its aura to a logic of mechanical, and now virtual, reproduction. The narrator's anxiety concerns her status as individual and artist within the accelerated flows of an information society drained of real human emotion, in short, the loss of individuality that is attendant on the fragmentation of the human, as modernization extends into globalization via information highways and the omnipresent digiverse, described by Deleuze in his "Postscript on the Societies of Control" (1992).

The Puerto Rican Giannina could be construed ethnically as postcolonial outsider, but her exile is self-enforced and eminently desired. Her interest is in dismantling the global empire from within by making its workings visible to the naked eye or by baring the device, thanks to a self-conscious and defamiliarizing poetics based on wordplay. Rather than assume the mantle of the exoticized postcolonial Other, she affirms the superiority of the elite cosmopolitan radical, exploring the new empire from a position of intellectual and economic privilege that allows her the luxury of informed dissent. It is from this vantage point that she proceeds to demolish the American dream and its myths with the undiplomatic immunity of her poetry:

> I used to hear the voices of the people in taxi drivers—but now their voices are hooked up to cell phones, iPods, or Blackberries. If you talk to them—they disconnect only for a second—and return to their gadgets. Human beings can't bear very much reality. . . . And now they use electronics to formalize the fact that they're busy with the dread of daily living that produces nothing creative but the monotony that they call pragmatism . . . they're fire-breathing dragons at the office of their mouths. What would happen if we snipped the wires of their busyness. Progress would happen—as it did to us on September 11. Inspiration made an installation that day. (*USB* 86)

The stylistic flourishes, syllepsis, alliteration, the internal rhyme of the last sentence, the reference to literary modernism via the application to our contemporary networked existence of a line from part 1 of Eliot's "Burnt Norton," "human kind / Cannot bear very much reality" (178), are the marks of a sophisticated and elitist aesthetic that challenges the banality of contemporary cultural clichés and allows the author to rewrite radical politics as high art. Poetic mastery creates a defamiliarized alternative to the symbolic poverty of consumer society. Artistic inspiration is reinstated as resistance to the oppression of the North American business ethos and enables the writer, empowered by her craft, to create an oppositional model of poetic progress, condensed in the epiphany of 9/11, seen as a work of art.

Such manifestations of stylistic potency underline the importance of art as ideological intervention, thanks to the artist-figure's special status as antagonist as well as protagonist. According to Deleuze, the pervasive structures of our current "societies of control" are more dangerous than those of more traditional models because they are less immediately visible, an analysis which is reminiscent of Baudrillard's theory of the viral stage of capitalism, instituting a fourth order of simulacra (see Baudrillard 13–18). However, unlike Baudrillard, and like Deleuze who encourages us to look for new forms of resistance, Braschi's novel suggests that art may be used as a weapon of delegitimation of these ubiquitous structures of control and their universalizing tendencies. It moves beyond the postmodern and the postcolonial to envisage the reinstatement of a different (ethical?) type of universal—based on love, feeling, the human heart—that can only be mediated through the romantic imagination of the artist, thus reasserting her uniqueness and importance as an exceptional individual.

The Artist as "Bad Subject"

Within the new totality of globalization, one possible role available to the artist is that of the "idiot savant," who, as Giannina puts it, "is taught but doesn't learn" (*USB* 173), the "bad subject" in the Althusserian sense who refuses to submit to the dictates of authority and uses poetic licence to reinvent the world. The incipit of Braschi's novel, for example, presents the poet-narrator creatively stimulated by the tragedy of 9/11: "It's the end of the world. I was excited by the whole situation. Well, if everybody is going to die, die hard" (3). This is presented as a solution to her fellows' subjugation to the capitalist model: "No more fear of being fired—for typos or tardiness—digressions, or recessions—and what a way of being fired—bursting into flames—without two weeks notice—and without six months of unemployment—and without sick leave, vacation, or comp time" (3). Not only does 9/11 become the vehicle for a bizarre romantic transcendence, it is also rewritten as a shockingly unpolitically correct corrective to the prevailing narrative of sentimentality about the disaster. Instead of recognizing the immensity of the event as unprecedented personal and collective tragedy, as has been the case in the majority of post-9/11 novels, Braschi's narrator restages the catastrophe around a single grotesque synecdochic snapshot, "Death of the Businessman," where the exploded body parts of the victim signify the ultimate comic reification of humanity consonant with the logic of materialism:

> I saw a torso falling—no legs—no head—just a torso—tumbling in the air—dressed in a bright white shirt—the shirt of a businessman—tucked

> in—neatly—under the belt—snuggly fastened—holding up his pants that had no legs . . . he was dead—dead for a ducat, dead—on the floor of Krispy Kreme—with powdered donuts for a head . . . and this businessman on the ground was clutching a briefcase in his hand—and on his finger, the wedding band. I suppose he thought his briefcase was his life—or his wife. (3)

The narrator's point of view is that of the elite inside-outsider or outside-insider, the superior and rebellious aesthete, the artist as exceptional being, situated above the common run, who cannot be assimilated into the oppressed Other of postcolonialism but forces the reader to confront issues of class rather than race and of ideology rather than identity. As Giannina journeys south with her troupe of philosophers and exceptional individuals loudly proclaiming that "the powers of the world are shifting" (*USB* 220), these figures seem to flirt with what Soo Yeon Kim has called "radical cosmopolitanism," that is to say, "a type of non-allegiance that deconstructs a utopian rendition of cosmopolitanism and refuses to commit to either cosmopolitanism or nationalism" (65). Giannina is a beleaguered, quixotic, perverse, elitist aesthete, an unattractive but inspired antiheroine who pits imaginative self-creation against social construction and rewrites society's expectations of the artist in bizarrely challenging if not to say shocking ways by refusing the consensual narrative options on offer. If, as Emerson stated, "the true romance, which the world exists to realize, will be the transformation of genius into practical power" (247), how can this be realized in a world where art is subsumed into global popular culture and the human spirit is enslaved to commodity production? The theme park of contemporary McCulture seems to reflect the death of artistic creativity within globalization where transcendence is collapsed into an inescapable immanent totality. Can the Romantic intuition of an artist like Giannina redeem and renew the affectless real and provide the consolation of authentic experience within a spiritually empty cosmos?

Disconsolate Utopias and Rational Delirium

United States of Banana resembles an embattled Künstlerroman, offering us a portrait of the artist in a permanent state of disquietude, the natural condition of the inspired creator, striving to reconnect with real emotion, to reinstate the language of the heart through recourse to the myth of the Romantic imagination, negative capability, and the creative energy or special madness of poetry. This echoes Ernst Bloch's vision of the novel of the artist, taken up by Fredric Jameson to illustrate the concept of the utopian sublime: "Bloch's conception of the novel of the artist, which carries the unknown unrealized work of art inside itself like a black hole, a future indeterminacy suddenly shimmering in the present, the absent Utopian sublime suddenly opening up like a wormhole within the empty everyday" (Jameson 110). Thanks to what she terms her "Hierarchy of Inspiration," "the demon, the duende, the angel and the muses" (*USB* 63), Braschi's narrator affirms the unique status of the artist whose function is to reconnect with truth and authenticity through the aesthetic: "But the nature of the poet is to see through the mud. To throw dirt in people's faces without distinguishing a king from a beggar. . . . All of them should feel the mud—and smell it—and find a sapphire in a pig's shit" (64). The potent poetic image of Eliot's "garlic and sapphires in the mud" is plucked from part 2 of "Burnt Norton (178) and rewritten with a certain alliterative crudity to emphasize the artist's special role as seer and visionary whose poetry can be the source of a powerful transformation that turns the base into the beautiful, in short, the alchemical art, conjured up by the term "duende," which in Spanish signifies both master and demon and represents the primitive power, the fire and soul of the artist.

However, the spirituality of any ideal self, accomplished through revelation is subject to a double dissolution, first in the abyssal sublime of Giannina's creative frenzy and, second, in the alienating aphasia of the global totality that has no use for the artist within its economy of representation and thus effects the death of the author and of character: "all the world's a stage—And all those characters that appear on those stages—merely players—are all dead—even the poet as a character that represents me—there is nobody representing me on that stage" (*USB* 235). In order to be attained, the ineffable must be harnessed to representation, the ideal must be made material. This is the challenge faced by the artist if s/he wishes to clear a significant space for the truth of an ethical universal to combat the ersatz of globalization. It is up to the writer to reinvent a form of creative mimesis that will make this ethical universal a tangible reality. S/he must rediscover the link between art and life, between the poet and the multitude, find a compromise between her aspiration to the sublime and the constraints of representation, in short, reinstate authentic experience within the simulated or coded structures that have superseded direct experience. In order to achieve this, Giannina offers her audience a rogue aesthetic that reconnects them to the real and contests the dominant ideology enshrined in the state, thanks to a "Declaration of Independence," the title of chapter 4 of the novel's second part:

> Not even the poet represents the me that I have inside—so you—character/poet who through the centuries has tried to represent the role I supposedly

> have inside—you—poet—cannot understand the feelings that are swimming in the river of my mind. . . . It is this rebellious being that has come to the surface of all of us in the audience who have been misrepresented by those of you who don't understand the transformations that have happened in our *derrumabaciones*—in those states where chance and expectation have been the measurement of the mathematics of affliction—and the relation has been broken between creation and representation, love and fiction—and the reality of packing meat in the meatpacking district. (*USB* 234–35)

Linking the material and the transcendent, thanks to the aesthetic, enables the poet to make room for an alternative ideology. Thus, the first part of the book, entitled "Ground Zero" with its images of apocalypse and destruction, prepares the terrain for the reversal of the balance of power that occurs in the second part and that is reflected in the name of the novel itself. By ascribing the status of banana republic to the United States and redefining its former satellites as the new seat of power, an enlightened universalism, what the narrator terms "a United Nations—without nations" (*USB* 118), can come to the fore.

Giannina's rational delirium suggests a possible mode of existence for the artist within globalization, a mode that rests on the paradoxical coupling of the Romantic sublime with Enlightenment rationality. In the novel's final chapter, which takes the form of a Socratic dialogue between the narrator and an immigrant taxi driver in Central Park, philosophical reasoning interweaves with a Molly Bloomish rhapsody on artistic intuition and love. Giannina suggests the utopian potential of the aesthetic as an ethical alternative to the dominant ideology and the neoliberal imperative, thanks to the ability of that same aesthetic to create a new value: "Can't there be a work of art that is a great event and that at the same time creates a new value?" (*USB* 140).

Although rational delirium may confer on the artist the superior energy of rebellion, it also means that the promise of ultimate recognition, growth, and artistic fulfilment is withheld. In his study of "The Politics of Postcolonial Modernism," Neil Lazarus proposes the term "disconsolation" (431) to describe a certain type of literature: "writing which resists the accommodationism of what has been canonized as modernism and that does at least what some modernist work has done from the outset: namely, says 'no'; refuses integration, resolution, consolation, comfort; protests and criticizes" (431). Although Giannina, the poet trying to woo her way into Plato's Republic, may seem consigned to such a disconsolate utopia, the formal, linguistic, and thematic originality of the novel helps its readers to travel to another dimension, a hyperspace that is constructed out of the real transcended by art. By situating herself outside frontiers, whether real or figurative, Braschi offers with humor and conviction a philosophico-poetical alternative to the paradigm of the commodification of culture within globalization, the unacknowledged ideological universalism of official culture and its intangible strategies of control. Her writing says no to fear and self-censorship in the age of terror and resists the consolation and the comfort offered by the certainties of the fabricated consensus of capitalism. It dares to interpellate the world order instead of succumbing to interpellation, protests against the status quo, and criticizes the received wisdom of a society in thrall to empty materialism. In her rational delirium, the narrator not only produces the great event that she so ardently desires in order to combat the recuperation by the media of history and affect but also reveals the utopian potential of a dissident aesthetics which uses art to create a new value that may constitute an ethical response to our globalized condition.

Works Cited

Althussser, Louis. "Ideology and Ideological State Apparatuses. Notes Towards an Investigation." *Lenin, Philosophy and Other Essays.* Monthly Review Press, 1972. Translated by Ben Brewster, www.marxists.org/reference/archive/althusser/1970/ideology.htm/.

Baudrillard, Jean. *La Transparence du mal.* Galilée, 1990.

Braschi, Giannina. *United States of Banana.* AmazonCrossing, 2011.

Deleuze, Gilles. "Postscript on the Societies of Control." *October*, vol. 59, Winter 1992, pp. 3–7, www.spunk.org/texts/misc/sp000962.txt/.

Eliot, T. S. *Collected Poems, 1909–1962.* Faber and Faber, 2002.

Emerson, Ralph Waldo. "Experience." *The Annotated Emerson*, edited by David Mikics, The Belknap Press of Harvard University Press, 2012, pp. 223–47.

Hardt, Michael, and Antonio Negri. "The Multitude against Empire." *Literature and Globalisation: A Reader*, edited by Liam Connell and Nicky Marsh, Routledge, 2011, pp. 87–92.

Jameson, Fredric. "Fear and Loathing in Globalization." *New Left Review*, vol. 23, September–October 2003, pp. 105–14.

Kim, Soo Yeon. "Ethical Treason: Radical Cosmopolitanism in Salman Rushdie's Fury." *Ariel*, vol. 42, no. 1, January 2011, pp. 63–84.

Lazarus, Neil. "The Politics of Postcolonial Modernism." *Postcolonial Studies and Beyond*, edited by Ania Loomba, Survir Kaul, Matti Bunzi, Antoinette Burton, and Jed Esty, Duke UP, 2005, pp. 423–38.

Wallerstein, Immanuel. *The Modern World System.* Academic Press, 1974.

2

Rompiendo esquemas

Catastrophic Bravery in *United States of Banana*

John "Rio" Riofrio

There is a phrase in Spanish, *romper los esquemas*, that loosely translated means "to break with established norms." This phrase is used in any number of contexts. It might refer to a performer who resists expectations of gender or social mores; it might refer to a new partner who shows one an entirely distinct way of perceiving the world; it might be used to describe a newly elected politician who resists the siren call of big donor funding and, as such, "breaks with established norms." In contemplating the heft, insight, and sheer philosophical ambition of Giannina Braschi's remarkable novel *United States of Banana*, I can think of no better way to describe both this work and Braschi's career than to say that, at every step, she has sought to *romper esquemas*. As this singular volume proves, she has broken with a seemingly endless list of established norms. It is my contention, however, that *United States of Banana* is Braschi's masterpiece, a volume as much a masterclass on how to *romper esquemas* as it is a manifesto on the increasing urgency to do so.

At its core *United States of Banana* is a paradoxical work. At times visceral, grotesque, disorienting, and deeply pessimistic, it evinces a lingering social malaise that feels like probing at a festering wound. Yet, somehow, simultaneously, the novel is also light, humorous, thought provoking, and inspiringly hopeful. How, we might be inclined to ask, does Braschi do this? And more important, why? At every turn she purposefully frustrates our expectations. The novel's book jacket offers a summary of the plot that, although outlandish and fantastic, preps the reader with some form of generic expectations, suggesting that the novel "takes place at the Statue of Liberty in post-9/11 New York, where Hamlet, Zarathustra, and Giannina are on a quest to free the Puerto Rican prisoner Segismundo."

From the outset, and despite the confident assertions in the jacket copy, it soon becomes clear that Braschi does not intend to offer her readers anything as recognizable as a standard novel. Instead, as Madelena Gonzalez argues in this volume, the notion of an identifiable story is quickly subsumed in order to make way for a deeper proposition. Gonzalez writes: "Staged in a surreal post-9/11 New York and Puerto Rico, *United States of Banana* is a politically charged metaphor for the fall of the US empire and the collapse of the World Trade Center as well as a plea for subject minorities to free themselves from the yoke of domination by the majority, whether such domination be economic, linguistic, cultural, or ideological" (23). Gonzalez's insightful reading of the novel and her prescient use of the word "plea" capture perfectly the sense that Braschi's novel, more than just a brilliant, playful intertextual romp, also has something urgent to say about issues of power, inequality, and the ways in which comfortable habituated lives obscure our recognition of these issues.

Braschi's novel is divided into two sections, and the first part reads more like an essay, but one that takes enormous creative liberties. Braschi uses the chaos and destruction of 9/11—the teeming sense that the world was literally and figuratively coming apart—to draw thought-provoking comparisons between the terror of terrorism, the daily terror of financial insecurity in a world marked by rampant, seductive consumerism, and the terrifying oppression of a market-driven society persistently opposed to critical thought. By contrast, the second half of Braschi's work is a play in which, among others, characters such as Hamlet, Zarathustra, Giannina, Segismundo, and Antonin Artaud tell the story of Puerto Rico's century-long imprisonment under the skirt of "Lady Liberty" and of the overturning of the world order wrought by Segismundo's eventual liberation. *United States of Banana*, more than a novel, is an archaeological layering of intertextual references culled from the canons of literature and philosophy. A dizzying work, it leaps from one philosophical discussion to another, interspersing moments of plot with language play as well as weighty assertions about empire, postcolonialism, inequality, revolution, and social (dis)order. Stated clearly, my assertion is that Braschi's novel is a manifesto, a call to arms about the US betrayal of its own "American" ideologies of freedom, liberty, and democracy.

How is Braschi's manifesto—with its attendant call for a reconfiguration and a reconceptualizing of our social values—inextricably bound to her willingness to break established norms? In this context, attentive consideration of the Spanish word *esquemas* lays the groundwork for a discussion of its English-language cognate *schema*. Both words have their etymological roots in the Greek word *σχῆμα*, meaning "form or figure." Although originally associated with the notion of a physical shape, over the centuries the words *schema* and *esquemas* have accrued a series of meanings related less to the idea of form and more to the "shape" of a "structure." Perceived in this way, we could argue that schema are the forms that give shape to our lives. It is precisely this definition that is the focus of the book *The Social Imperative* (2015) by literary scholar Paula Moya.

Moya engages with the field of social psychology to offer a cogent, urgent argument about the privileged position that literature holds in our coming to a more complete, more thoughtful understanding of our social world. She notes: "When it comes to understanding how significant social categories like race, ethnicity, gender, and sexuality structure individual experience and identity as well as why it is necessary to appreciate and engage 'worlds of sense' that are anchored in experiences and identities other than one's own, there may be no more efficient and effective approach than the close reading of individual works of literature" (6). Moya's insight is twofold. On the one hand, she foregrounds the way in which literature—through the craft of storytelling and a latent investment in the lives of the protagonists—offers readers an opportunity to empathize with others. Though not guaranteed, this possible empathic connection bears enormous pedagogical potential. For Moya, in a historical moment that has seen the resurgence of social segregation, empathy encourages segregated communities to come to a better understanding of the subtle contours of another's lived experience. This is not merely because literature has the capacity to narrate the experiences of distinct groups. This world of possible connection stems from the fact that literature is produced by cultural ideologies, at the same time also reflecting and revealing those same ideologies.

For Moya, insightful multiethnic literature is compelling because it refuses to offer what journalist Juan González has dismissed as the "one sided safari approach" (xvii) to learning about other, often marginalized, communities. Instead, literature's capacity for social change hinges on its ability to indicate what Moya has called "the world of sense" (8). In arguing that it is "via the individual text that literature is a sensitive indicator of the ideological underpinnings of human experience" (8), Moya is making an essential point about literature's underlying ability to cut across the various sociohistorical ideologies that contribute to the fracturing of our complexly heterogeneous society. For Moya, the ideologies of, for example, racism, patriarchy, or homophobia often function at a low frequency that barely registers amid the "noise" of daily life. Literature, she proposes, cuts through the noise and offers a coherent way for us to pick out these subtle frequencies in order to make sense of them and, as such, our own lives and the lives of others.

I argue that this reading of what literature can do would likely resonate with Braschi's own sense of the power and purpose of writing. Where Braschi might differ—or more accurately, want to push further—would be in considering this very idea of "coherency." In *United States of Banana*, unlike the novels examined by Moya, the belief is that the "world of sense" is composed of a fabricated coherence, which rests within an underlying (dis)ordered chaos. Seen in this light, the absolute brilliance of Braschi's work is how it demonstrates the complexities of a social world that is ordered in its inequities but confusing and chaotic in the way these various systems of inequality coalesce and combine to give our lives a semblance of order.

For Braschi the disorder of persistent contrived inequality is masked by an ordered status quo. This status quo, which hides itself in plain sight, is manifest in a strict adherence to social rules, patterns, and preexisting structures—what Moya would refer to as "schema." Because social rules and patterns function to maintain an unfair, seemingly inviolable status quo, Braschi wrestles with expectations throughout *United States of Banana* in an effort to redefine and reinvigorate the interrelated ideas of liberty and choice. More subtly, but no less importantly, Braschi theorizes the deep intact connections between presumably distinct categories of freedom and constraint. Early in the play, for example, Giannina, Zarathustra, and Hamlet sneak under the skirt of Lady Liberty seeking the imprisoned Segismundo (who is also a metaphor for the colonial relationship between the United States and Puerto Rico). There, they find a Segismundo who alternates between profound despair over his century-long imprisonment and an almost euphoric optimism, fueled in part by the tectonic sociopolitical shifts wrought by 9/11. Segismundo declares: "Down with the divisions that keep putting us down. Si, we can. Yes, se puede. Yes, we can. / —What can you? / —Yes, we can. I don't know how. But we certainly can. And we will. Yes, we will break the divisions between genres and genders and races. Fuckers. You will not divide us anymore. Yes, we will. Yes, we can—the voice of the people is breaking down the doors of the dungeon" (*USB* 123). Most notable is Braschi's careful and provocative use of Spanglish. Instead of offering the established Spanish phrase, *si se puede* alongside the English phrase "Yes we can," Braschi mixes the two phrases in order to enact the breaking down of constraints imposed by notions of discrete languages.[1] The intermixing of the languages embodies her larger project of confronting the restrictions imposed by all manner of expectation. In this way, within the complexly layered ecosystem of the novel, the inherent constraints of language or literary genre, for example, parallel the limitations enforced by categories of race and gender. For Braschi the schemas of social constraints go well beyond the categories of our social lives. These schemas impose structures that function as the architecture for the modern workplace and the ongoing neocolonialism of the United States.

The dizzying mix of languages, ideas, and poetic registers of ideas form a backdrop for Braschi's thoughtful strategic inclusion of self-doubt. The line "what can we do? / I don't know" emerges from within the optimistic revolutionary call to action in order to articulate two urgent ideas. First, the "world of sense" that is manifest in the novel suggests reason for both optimism and pessimism, hope but also despair. Second, this world of sense is visible only because of the work of the poet.

Although skeptical of the poet's ability, the character of Zarathustra gives us a clue as to the possible import and weight of the poet's social function. He says: "Poets don't mean what they say. They take no responsibility—no accountability—they have light feet—they run like rabbits after carrots—intuitions—and leave the tortoise behind—with jetlag—and myopia and eyeglasses—studying studiously the flight of the rabbit" (*USB* 80). Fleet of foot but, more important, fleet of thought, the poet chases down intuitions, glimmers of half-formed thought that do not necessarily conform to fully formed ideas. Point of fact, it is only the poet, brave enough to exist outside the norms and constraints of society, who has the ability to feel the disorder under the surface and to put that disorder into words. Zarathustra's categorization of non-poets as myopic sufferers of "jetlag" indicates the complicating issue; the poet is neither accountable to nor necessarily responsible for putting those intuitions into words that will be comprehensible to all. In fact, for Braschi, it is quite possible that reconfiguring inchoate feelings into a form that makes sense—feelings that fit neatly into the schema from which they were lifted—would change them and, as such, make them victim to the constraint of expectation.

To make better sense of this, I propose we return to Moya's work with "schemas." Drawing on the field of social psychology, Moya defines "schemas" as the "active organization of past experiences (physical and emotional) and past reactions (sensory-motor and cognitive-affective) through which a person apprehends and interacts with incoming stimuli" (15). In particular, what makes schemas such a powerful device for understanding our social identities is the fact that, because they are constructed out of our experiences and behaviors, schemas build up over time so that they become identifiable patterns of behavior both present and future. They are reactive in that they form a framework for our emotional response to events that are socially constructed, but they are also extrapolative in their ability to "go beyond the information given" (15). More thought provoking still, Moya suggests that schemas "have a temporal dimension characterized by evolution across time—they are *anticipatory* as well as retrospective, even as they orient a person's behavior in the present" (15; my emphasis).

The beauty of schemas is that they order our social world and thus provide a stable framework upon which to make sense of complex social and historically situated interactions. The problem, however, is that schemas, as both a product and a reflection of our own limited social locations, can themselves be limited and limiting in the view of the world they provide us. As Moya further explains: "Schemas, then, are more than just mental states that people use to perceive the world around them. They *are* mental states . . . [that] also involve us completely as Beings" (23). Seen in this way, we *are* our schemas. The coherence they provide can thus either reveal new meanings or further entrench extant misleading social norms. There is nothing inherently liberating about schemas in the same way that the revelations of the poet have no inherent power to reshape our understanding of our world.

Braschi—in her role as novelist, poet, essayist, and most important, philosophical thinker—is acutely aware of the way in which our social world frequently refuses to speak to us in coherent phrases, offering instead only glimmers, carrots, of intuition. As is patently clear throughout her oeuvre, it is often the case that we move through our daily existence with little appreciation for the entrenched, often contradictory, ideological forces at play in the architecture of our daily reality. In her novel Braschi acknowledges the fact that our lives often do not feel like our own, by calling attention to the *feeling* that our lives are constrained and curated not simply via the choices we make but, rather, via the deeply subsumed reality of a *lack of choice*. For Braschi, this social (dis)order masks the lack of meaningful choice with a paradoxically overwhelming array of consumerist choices that simply do not matter. Inherent, then, in the easy acceptance of the status quo is a refusal to think beyond established norms and ways of doing things as they have always been done.

In distinct but resonant ways, the literary scholar Ralph Rodriguez is similarly concerned with the status quo of the field of Latinx literature. More specifically, he questions the utility of the very category of "Latinx" literature: "As critics, we can do better than yoke writers beneath a label that they themselves resist because of its limiting qualities. If labels and taxonomies fail to advance our critical understanding, then they should be abandoned" (14). Although polemical, Rodriguez's effort to interrogate whether the label of "Latinx" does more good than bad is compelling. The question at the heart of his book—whether longstanding categories such as "Latinx Literature" do, in fact, advance our critical understanding—stirs the pot in ways that I suspect will advance our critical understanding. This said, there is an intriguing irony in considering Rodriguez's question in light of Braschi's work. On the one hand, *United States of Banana* articulates Braschi's desire to resist categorization. On the other hand, the novel is both "Puerto Rican" and "Latinx" in meaningful ways. By that (a propos Rodriguez's argument), it goes well beyond the exploration of "traditional" Puerto Rican themes.

From Rodriguez and Braschi's shared perspective, categories are arbitrary, constructed after the fact and in such a way as to reshape what has been written without categorization into neat preestablished categories that conform to schemas already in place. Whereas the genre expectations of Puerto Rican literature demand a focus on topics such as migration, urban violence, and ethnic identity within a context of white Eurocentrism, Braschi's novel is in dialogue with those expected issues but also with a profoundly philosophical, canonical genealogy not typically accorded to ethnic literatures. Braschi's novel is as much a critique of the systems that have sought to exclude ethnic literatures from that canon while also an effort to undermine the very construction of those same intellectual canons. More specifically, *United States of Banana* foregrounds the case of Puerto Rican colonialism in order to launch a scathing critique of the US usurpation and subsequent betrayal of the universal philosophical idea of Liberty.

Braschi's focus on Puerto Rico, as both the subject of her novel and as a metaphor for a much larger confluence of historical and social practices, is timely and prophetic. She anticipates, to a degree, the suffering wrought by both the landfall of Hurricane Maria in 2017 and the debt crisis of 2018. Both events temporarily brought Puerto Rico to the foreground of national and international attention. Although news coverage of the hurricane—its aftermath and the debt crisis—was both noticeable and significant, media outlets soon tired of the topic and Puerto Rican was, again, summarily forgotten. We turn, therefore, to the ethnic-studies scholar and filmmaker Frances Negrón-Muntaner's exceptional essay "The Emptying Island" to get a sustained analysis of Puerto Rico's larger significance.

Negrón-Muntaner uses literary studies to frame Puerto Rico's long history as an objectified territorial possession that both reveals but is also a product of colonialist desires. Focusing on the narrative of Puerto Rico as "la isla que se vacia," Negrón-Muntaner places the recent exodus of Puerto Ricans within an ongoing history marked by a centuries-long "colonial-capitalist practice of expulsion." Negrón-Muntaner labels this desire—to empty the island of its people in ways that are both material and symbolic—as "foundational" and "recurrent" and identifies it as "coterminous with the island's three distinct forms of colonial-capitalist modernity (plantation, industrial, and neoliberal) from the fifteenth century to the present."

Negrón-Muntaner thoughtfully situates the recent upheaval caused by both Hurricane Maria and the debt crisis within a much longer history of colonialist aggression. She makes abundantly clear that the fantasy of an empty Puerto Rico—one simply available for consumption and repopulation by wealthy white populations—is a centuries-old desire with profound consequences for the Puerto Rican people past, present, and future:

> [If] Operation Bootstrap emptied the island in order to impose the rhythms of industrial capitalism, expand the island's consumer market for US goods, and efficiently expel "surplus" labor, then PROMESA marks a transition to a new iteration of colonial-capitalism.[2] In this scenario, what is desired is all that finance capital can devour, namely housing, public spaces, and indebted subjects consuming privatized services. Although population expulsion is not a stated objective of the governing board, the Junta's policies knowingly fuel migration by imposing drastic cuts in essential human services such as education, health, and pensions.

What is particularly striking about Negrón-Muntaner's assessment of Puerto Rico's current debt crisis is the central role the US government has played both historically and contemporaneously. In particular the creation of a junta tasked with enacting the policies of the sardonically named PROMESA clearly articulates a set of values that places securing financial interests well above the safety and security of US citizens who just happen to be Puerto Rican. Negrón-Muntaner's insight into the voracity of neoliberal capital's appetite for acquisition enabled, in part, by its astonishing (albeit familiar) disregard for human suffering offers strong evidence for the distinct possibility that Puerto Rico's riches will be summarily devoured by neoliberal, neocolonial interests.

Similar to Braschi's perceptive intuition into the larger neoliberal terror lurking beneath the smoldering remains of 9/11, Negrón-Muntaner contends that the astonishing destruction wreaked by Hurricane Maria pales in comparison to the astonishing, willful destruction wrought by a neoliberal greed marked by austerity (for others) and willful neglect (of others). Built upon a sturdy foundation of (neo)colonial racist ideology, the "marketplace" sees in Puerto Rico's suffering a strategic opening for the fulfillment of the long-held colonial desire to possess Puerto Rico without having to worry about the existence of the less desirable Puerto Ricans. Staring, unblinkingly, at the destruction during and after the hurricane, one of the first lines in *United States of Banana* seems particularly a propos. Describing the narrator's reaction to seeing a human torso falling from the burning World Trade Tower, Braschi writes: "I am redundant because I can't believe what I saw" (*USB* 3).

Given their shared ability to describe in stark unflinching terms the aftershocks of these enormous signal events, it is worth noting that both Negrón-Muntaner and Braschi, in the midst of describing earth-shattering ruin, have found something redemptive. Negrón-Muntaner posits that the devastation of Hurricane María unearthed a long history of political and colonial suffering while simultaneously signaling a moment of subtle opportunity:

> I propose to build on literary scholar Alexandra Perisic's (2017) observation that catastrophes—a term derived from the "Greek katastrephein, meaning to 'overturn'"—can be understood not as a "disaster" but as a moment of "overturning" in which collective reflection and action are still possible (118). A catastrophic reading of the "emptying island" then, does not assume that debt or hurricane-induced mobility will lead to a fatal end. Rather, it suggests that in the current context of rapid neoliberal restructuring and refusal to this process, the so-called "emptying island" may offer one way to imagine and enact alternatives to colonial-capitalist modernity.

Fueled, perhaps, by the clear sense that Puerto Rico's history has always been one of resilience in the face of legitimate suffering, both Negrón-Muntaner and Braschi foreground tragedy as comprised of a potent paradoxical mix of pain and hope. Negrón-Muntaner's description of catastrophe as an overturning that "may offer . . . alternatives to colonial-capitalist modernity" bears a striking resemblance to the way in which Braschi in *United States of Banana* narrates a similar paradox embedded within the catastrophe of 9/11.

Having successfully snuck their way into the prison under the Statue of Liberty's skirt, Giannina, Hamlet, and Zarathustra find Segismundo, who treats them to a long soliloquy about his life as the prisoner of Lady Liberty. The scene is beautiful and disturbing, an extended metaphor of the way in which Puerto Rico's ongoing status as a colony reveals the truth about the US ongoing desire to be a global empire. Segismundo describes the camaraderie he enjoys with the many other, mostly Middle Eastern, prisoners who were similarly imprisoned following the events of 9/11: "If the twin towers hadn't fallen, I would have never met a Pakistani, Iraqi, or Iranian friend, or a Chinorican, or an Egyptian. I am thrilled to be able to talk to prisoners of war from around the world. It's becoming a gathering of tribes—a United Nations—without nations—not the whore of the U.S. of Banana—but a think tank where new ideas are brewing in the cauldron of races and genders and religion" (*USB* 118). It should, perhaps, come as no surprise that Segismundo, the stand-in for Puerto Rico, is the one to voice these words, for what Braschi makes clear is that Puerto Rico, like the poets of the world, is a meaningless nothing. In a world that has given itself over to rampant capitalism, a small island such as Puerto Rico has no significance on the world stage. Analogously, in a social order framed by consumption and the voracious acquisition of wealth, the poet is a nobody. Given this cruel reality, the inclination, in the case of the poets, is to follow the rules in the hopes of getting some recognition, any recognition. Braschi, however, in an effort to slough off the easy gains of conformity, comes to an urgent realization regarding the price, and reward, of liberation:

> There was always a problem with my creativity—and the crane always came to demolish the problem—but when it demolished the problem—it demolished my way of thinking—because it was not the American way of thinking—the American way of life—the correct way of doing things . . . the crane of the smart and clever—and it demolishes my thought structures—and it says—*this is wrong and this is wrong and this is wrong and what is right is because it is wrong*—it is always like that—that what is wrong is wrong because it is right. Once came a stupid man to tell me—you are wrong. I believed him because he spoke with authority. (*USB* 174–75)

With an emblematic mix of chaotic clarity, Braschi articulates one of her central ideas: the schemas of a society built around conformity are premised upon an unquestioning faith in authority, present and past. Braschi's struggle to reclaim her own authorial voice, to believe in her creative mind despite its unwillingness to conform, mirrors our collective investment in a historically embedded status quo marked by structures of searing, persistent inequity.

Ultimately, *United States of Banana* is a sustained meditation on contentment and freedom. Both values, on the surface of things, seem positive, and the United States, with its "peaceful" state of freedom and contentment, has always been eager to promote itself as the manifestation of both. Braschi, however, rejects the voice of authority. Arguing assertively that the choice to conform is no choice at all, Braschi pulls apart the lie(s) at the heart of the persistently invoked representation of the United States as the land of liberty. Braschi attacks this notion of contentment as a self-sustaining lie—a lie with a profound, expansive, almost empire-like reach. For fulfilment and even happiness are not about contentment but, rather, the bravery to embrace both critical thought and discomfort.

Notes

1. The phrase *si se puede* has become ubiquitous. Latin American in origin, it has historically been used as a chant during protests and manifestations in Latin America. Translated as "it can be done" or "yes, we can," the phrase has migrated to the United States and can now regularly be heard at demonstrations and political rallies that feature Latinx political figures and/or audience members.

2. Negrón-Muntaner's explanation of the passing of legislation and the formation of the board, or junta, intended to oversee Puerto Rico's debt obligations is far better than anything I might compose. So I will defer to her precise wording: "On June 30, 2016—one day before the island failed to make a bond payment—Congress passed the Puerto Rico Oversight, Management, and Economic Stability Act (PROMESA). This federal law appointed a seven-member fiscal control board composed of individuals with deep ties to the banking and investment world—including some involved in producing the debt crisis—and granted them broad powers over Puerto Rico's elected government to assure that creditors will be paid."

Works Cited

Braschi, Giannina. *United States of Banana*. AmazonCrossing, 2011.

González, Juan. *Harvest of Empire: The History of Latinos in America*. Viking, 2000.

Moya, Paula. *The Social Imperative: Race, Close Reading, and Contemporary Literary Criticism*. Stanford UP, 2015.

Negrón-Muntaner, Frances. "The Emptying Island: Puerto Rican Expulsion in Post-Maria Time." *Hemispheric Institute*, vol. 14, no. 1, 2018, www.hemisphericinstitute.org/en/emisferica-14-1-expulsion/14-1-essays/the-emptying-island-puerto-rican-expulsion-in-post-maria-time.html/.

Rodriguez, Ralph. *Latinx Literature Unbound: Undoing Ethnic Expectation*. Fordham UP, 2018.

3

Exile and Burial of Ontological Sameness

A Dialogue between Zarathustra and Giannina

Anne Ashbaugh

We are burying sameness.

—***United States of Banana***

Identities are not tangible anymore. If you look for an identity you find inequality. . . . The self has been refracting.

—***United States of Banana***

Whatever is always in motion is immortal.

—***Phaedrus, 245c***

It is difficult to analyze Giannina Braschi's writings because her texts sustain a constant motion, introducing perspective after perspective through which characters, actions, and language itself all transform. The Socrates of Plato's *Phaedrus* would have had to characterize her works as immortal precisely for this incessant flow. The very feature that immortalizes the works, though, prevents analysis, making it impracticable to resort to traditional hermeneutical strategies. It is as futile, for instance, to seek to define one of Braschi's texts according to some distinguishing mark as it is to search for a comparable work, even among Braschi's corpus. *United States of Banana*, in particular, thrives in this elusiveness. In respect to the meaning and importance of the sardine in Giannina's conversation, for example, we find that she defends the sardine against its trivialization by Zarathustra, yet she confesses that her relationship with the sardine is horrifying because "it had fangs and it bit me like a rabid squirrel" (*USB* 72). Appealing as questions concerning the symbolism of the sardine may seem, the task becomes nightmarish when we discover that Braschi subverts this critical convention as well by endowing the sardine with a multitude of symbolic meanings, none of them primary or specially related to the fish. Instead, the symbolic meanings attach themselves more closely to the ways in which sardines are jam-packed in a can for mass distribution and to a related popular saying used to describe crowded conditions as one of being "packed like sardines." Reading the work we experience a charming and humorously delightful pleasure in not dwelling on elements of the work by refusing to burrow into the work in search for some profound meaning rather than allowing the text to move according to Braschi's circuitous grace.

Regarding the relationship of *United States of Banana* to other works, we discover early in our reading the futility of comparing Braschi even to authors who radically transformed the act of writing, like Borges, Cortázar, Perec, and more recently, Anne Carson. Braschi is autonomous, self-propelled, and as such unique. Labels only throw mud at her text. In this essay, for that reason, I approach *United States of Banana* indirectly, using a literary shield analogous to Perseus's so as to reflect possible connections between two characters, Giannina and Zarathustra, characters that Braschi reincarnates and radically transforms. Giannina is and is not Braschi herself. Zarathustra is the character that Nietzsche created out of a dwindling Zoroastrian monotheism to teach the "overman," but Braschi embodies him into her text, assigning to him a dialogue that at times sounds noble yet is mostly voluble and occasionally frivolous. To this end I examine the abundance of perspectives unfurled by both Zarathustra and Giannina in their struggle for autonomy. I say "self-liberation" or "autonomy," and not simply "freedom," because all liberation from outside the self ends up colonizing. Liberators tend to impose measures that are foreign to the apparently liberated entity and to foster conditions that prevent self-overcoming: consider, for example, Segismundo gnawing at the womb of the Statue of Liberty.

> What the eye doesn't see, the heart doesn't grieve over.
> There is *only* a perspectival seeing, *only* a perspectival "knowing."
> (Nietzsche, *GM* III.12)

The Zarathustra in *United States of Banana* is Polish, entangled with the historical Nietzsche but resembling neither Nietzsche nor the

Persian prophet. This interplay between author, character, and ancient prophet enriches the dialogue between Zarathustra and Giannina and reveals important elements of Nietzsche's philosophy that otherwise are hidden.[1] We see for example, in "Burial of the Sardine," that Giannina identifies the sardine with the corpse that Zarathustra, too, carries. She refers to the sardine as "the dead body I carry on my back" (*USB* 71). Her description foreshadows and appropriates the image of the prophet carrying the corpse of a tightrope walker who fell at his feet when a jester disturbed his equilibrium. In *Thus Spoke Zarathustra*, Zarathustra's care of the corpse creates an intensely dramatic and concrete experience of the debt a liberated spirit owes to the vanquished ideal without which he may have perished under the weight of pessimism before reaching liberation.[2] Zarathustra must bury the dead ascetic ideal but not in the earth—ascetic ideals bear no fruit and devalue the earth. Embodied in the tightrope walker, furthermore, this ascetic ideal expresses the end of the "last man," who is paralyzed by his own uselessness and able only to blink. As such, the ideal cannot handle opposition or randomness or meet the creative perspectival challenge represented by the impatient buffoon who jumps onto the tightrope and disrupts the tightrope walker's routine. When the acrobat fell at his feet, Zarathustra received his last breath and recognized in the corpse his last burden.[3] Zarathustra carried the acrobat's corpse during a whole sleepless night and left him once and for all in the hollow space of a tree, where the body could do no harm and no harm would come to it.

Turning the acrobat into a sardine, Giannina exposes the monumental frivolity that underlies the seriousness of the ascetic ideal.[4] The transformation adds an ironic aspect that helps Zarathustra bear his burden and overcome it. Braschi's Zarathustra complains about having to walk miles just to bury a mere sardine, and Giannina reprimands him, saying: "It worked its whole life in the sludge of oil and vinegar. I'll sprinkle incense, myrrh, and a pound of gold to be buried with it under the sand" (*USB* 71). The admonition serves simultaneously as a humoristic revaluation that weaves together seriousness, triviality, puerility, and the basic needs of life. Thus, in Giannina's experience, the sardine is also a war and the monstrous dominion of an absurd capitalism that has mechanized life itself. For example, she explains, she doesn't eat sardines because she finds their helplessness repugnant (72). This disgust invites into the text Nietzsche's philosophy and its warnings against pitying the weak, since pity is the weapon of mass destruction that attacks the human will at its core. Burying the sardine, Giannina conquers two epidemics that Nietzsche identifies as "*the great nausea at man*" and "*the deep compassion for man*" (*GM* III.14).

In a still greater blow against the two epidemics, near the end of the book Giannina remorselessly and without pity claims to have eaten Zarathustra so that she can converse with Diotima. Another humorously rendered blow strikes Zarathustra himself this time, when Segismundo declares he is not the overman because he "is not over," adding that over him a bridge will be built between "two nationalities that become one and one nation that becomes many" (*USB* 135). The overman in Segismundo's conversation breaks through geographical boundaries and colonial stereotypes as it self-overcomes. With a single pun Segismundo points toward the self-overcoming that the overman requires, but he does so adding a sociopolitical dimension and a mockery of the seriousness with which most philosophers who study Nietzsche have hidden the ludic elements of his Zarathustra. Through this Calderonian character Braschi grasps and communicates a vision of Zarathustra that is more exact and faithful to Nietzsche than we find in many treatises dedicated to explaining Nietzsche's difficult text.

Self-overcoming requires a shift of perspective, a transformation of eyes adapted to see humanity and the earth as worthless when compared to the perfection of a god. The devaluation of the earth by the Christian moral ideal closely resembles the disparagement experienced by colonized populations when they view themselves in comparison with the supposed superiority of style exhibited by the dominant culture. Subverting the devaluating perspective involves individuation and the development of one's own style, but neither process can take place in the context of exile. The predicament supported by the Christian moral ideal, therefore, cannot be altered without ending the exile by affirming the value of the earth and declaring ourselves citizens of the earth.

Expressed in mythological terms, the first exile (in Spanish, *destierro*, or leaving someone without earth or land) was simultaneously a burial (in Spanish, *entierro*, or placing into the earth). Separated from the Tree of Life and with a knowledge of good and evil, Adam and Eve were displaced and thrown into a foreign world where they would die estranged. The theology accompanying this myth adds that human beings inhabit the earth but are not of it. Symbolically speaking, then, Cain and Abel were born into an exile similar to that of any expatriate forced to leave the motherland. (Their speech and their accent must have sounded jarring to the god who banished their parents from Paradise.) It is precisely this experience of being alien to the earth that Nietzsche overcomes with his Zarathustra and that Braschi challenges with her Statue of Liberty. Nietzsche frees the will that has been colonized by religious paradigms. Braschi frees Latinx creativity that has been colonized by empires. By situating the dialogue between Giannina and Zarathustra in this context of oppression and liberation, we uncover a special relationship between Nietzsche and Braschi taking shape in the dialogue. We should also keep in mind the perspective added to this dialogue by the presence of Segismundo imprisoned in the Statue of Liberty.[5]

Nietzsche's subversion of the first exile—in which humans are thrown onto land that will never be their home—shows, through the person of Zarathustra, that traditional metaphysics and the ontological sameness on which its model of perfection is based are simply a fiction as fake as Hollywood and more enslaving to the human spirit. It is a fiction designed to fetter and weaken the will. Believing that "this" life is not the real life and that this earth is "a vale of tears" imprisons humans in a tower of beliefs analogous to Segismundo's prison and for the same reasons: terror of what human instincts can do to absolutists. The freedom denied to Segismundo is as natural to his will as are scales to a fish's body. The degradation of individuality effected by the ideal of ontological sameness similarly breaks with the vital flux of experience, of the specificity with which we feel joy or pain, and ends up alienating us from our own humanity. Alienated, we cannot join the majority group in power without compromising who we are. Giannina recognizes the predicament when she admits, "familiarity doesn't bring nearness—it breeds stagnation—ease. . . . What I do to control myself is shout and scream—the opposite of what is required of me to enter the grammatical system of my foreign language. . . . I have to be who I am on both sides of the speeding highway—unable to cross—until I shout and scream my head off" (*USB* 41).

Breaking the fetters imposed by colonizing ideals requires an affirmation of the value and importance of particular circumstances and emotions experienced individually. Presumably with this and other ends in mind, Braschi imbues *United States of Banana* with countless perspectives intertwined with each other to form a dialogical net of authors and literary characters who are diverse in their language and their historical time. Their language and their time, however, do not persist through the Braschian metamorphoses. For example, Theaetetus emerges as a "tit" boy and Laches as milk, both puns born in the English translation of the Greek names but available only through Spanish (referring to *teta* and *leche* respectively). Artaud, Hamlet, and Rubén Darío, to mention a few, converse eloquently and quite naturally as their dialogue opens new horizons from which one can understand why Segismundo's freedom is as problematic as his imprisonment—and thus why the colonization of a people is as complicated as their liberation. Although in reading the text we do not hear the multiple accents of characters for whom English is a foreign tongue, the dialogue does not allow readers to forget this crucial perspectival element. Zarathustra, for example, reminds Giannina that she doesn't count because her English is "macaronic" (*USB* 85).

In the same manner, Nietzsche introduces perspectives that reveal self-denial as the origin of the preference for objectivity. The new perspectives, in turn, end the exile of the human will. Caught in the search for objectivity, the will had become insatiable. Each indulged fancy left the will empty—exactly as Giannina feels at the end of a shopping spree. How can the human will free itself from this consumeristic moral slavery imposed by modern culture and supported by the ascetic ideal? Nietzsche and Braschi share this concern for strengthening the human will, and they resort to creative experiences in order to instill self-worth in an otherwise ineffectual will.

In Nietzsche's epistemology, for example, perspectives supplant dichotomies, in particular the dichotomy between subject and object that is so useful to traditional approaches. Nietzsche affirms reality sensuously, as he would affirm any outcome of perceptual experience. In this respect his approach is aligned with scientific naturalism. He insists, however, that knowledge be rooted in perception both structurally (accessing its subject matter from a perspective or perspectives) and in content (measured by what the observations yield).

Not every perspective is effective to the same degree for the process of self-overcoming. Some perspectives, in fact, hide experience and enslave us. The priestly ascetic perspective leads to the devaluation of the body, of human emotions, and of life as we experience it on earth. That perspective, furthermore, cancels out all others and, from no human perspective whatsoever, declares the reality of heaven and of another, still better life worthy of our desire. Such a view from nowhere speaks about everywhere as a source of objective truth. Other perspectives, like the aesthetic perspective, clarify and affirm the value of human life leading to a revaluation of our life on earth and manifesting the centrality of sensuousness, bodily pleasures, and human creativity. The more any perspective supports life, the more valuable it is for knowledge, too.

There, in short, lies the value of Nietzschean perspectivism. What does perspectivism mean? "The ascetic treats life as a wrong path he has to walk along backwards . . . like a mistake . . . an ascetic life is a self-contradiction . . . satisfaction is looked for and found in failure, decay, pain, misfortune, ugliness, . . . and self-sacrifice" (*GM* III.11).

When we ask "What does perspectivism mean?" we shift perspectives and expectations. No longer do we seek an answer that is indifferent to the subject or an intrinsic quality that marks its essence. The new question points to a meaning or meanings, not essences. The question treats its subject matter as something that preoccupies inquirers and recognizes that it matters who asks the question—so much so that the questioner at every turn permeates the outcome of the study. The illusion of pure knowledge is pushed to the margins of our concern. When we ask what something means, we have to add a second question, "for whom?"—and this second question introduces perspectives or points of view that cannot be ignored. We can say, for example, that for the ascetic philosopher, perspectivism is a threat, a dangerous subjectivism; for the priest, it means the death of god; for the artist, it means the possibility of experiencing the world by creating. For the overman, perspectivism means the subversion of epistemological dichotomies that prevent a thinker from proceeding with mind and will in unison. By thinking and willing non-dichotomously, perspectivism empowers the will and the mind simultaneously.

Nietzsche favors aesthetic perspectives over ascetic values, and his philosophy gives primacy to experience over abstraction and to vital activity over ideals. Creativity nourishes the will because, in the act of creation, the artist does not obey some exterior force but, rather, responds to a "thus I will it" from within herself. Perspectivism, therefore, goes hand in hand with self-overcoming and with the affirmation of life. Perspectivists do not deny that there are external entities. They challenge the belief that humans grasp external entities objectively without affecting them in any way by perceptual habits, thinking, culture, language, and the like.

Zarathustra's first speech, "On the Three Metamorphoses," adds three perspectives for the will to value and desire. First, the human spirit turned camel becomes lion and the lion, child (*TSZ* I). The camel carries the burden of unquestioned traditional values imposed upon it by the culture to establish systems of values that are universally acceptable and chosen by those in power. It is the camel that accepts and carries with it the enslaving asceticism mentioned above, and that perceives all else from the horizon of this ideal. The burdened spirit takes on the heaviest loads by humbling itself, by "letting one's foolishness glow in order to mock one's wisdom" to "loving those who despise us" (*TSZ*, I.1). "But in the loneliest desert" spirit becomes lion. The obedient "Yes" of the camel cannot be heard once the roaring "No" of the lion fills the solitude. The lion rejects the orders of the last master and the last god. Its no-saying tears apart the camel, to consume from it only what nourishes spirit and strengthens the will. It is the first moment of a self-overcoming.

The lion, however, cannot create. It must become child to utter their authentic "Yes"—the "Yes" of an artist who carves out of stone willfully and not at another's command. The lion creates "freedom for oneself and also a sacred No to duty . . . [to] take the right to new values." Zarathustra asks: "Why must the preying lion still become a child?" (*TSZ*, I). Presumably, the child is needed to overcome any kind of resentment build-up during the camel metamorphosis and to initiate a new beginning. The child builds and destroys, joyfully aware that every destruction is for creating, not for revenge. The child, furthermore, works as a "wheel rolling out of itself" (*TSZ*, I) exercising her will without the burdens of history, culture, and ideals. Zarathustra calls the "Yes" of a child a sacred affirmation because the child's speech creates the world. By contrast, the "Yes" of the camel is servile, weighted down by the enormous heaviness of tradition and ideality. The camel expresses a domesticated animal's servile acquiescence. In terms of *On the Genealogy of Morals*, we could call the camel the result of the force that asceticism exerts upon the human will. Epistemologically speaking, this metamorphosis corresponds to the perspective of inquirers who habitually demand objectivity as a test for knowledge because they distrust their senses. Clearly, this perspective manifests a weak and sickly will.

The lion's perspective, on the other hand, initiates a revaluation of values. The beast of prey tears the beast of burden to pieces. From the lion's perspective, we recognize the urgent need to shed the burdens if we are to become our own person or overman. To Zarathustra's comment that the human is something that must be overcome, and his question, "what have you done to overcome him?" (*TSZ*, prologue 5), the lion responds with a resounding denial of the ascetic ideal and drowns the "Thou shalt" of the tradition. The lion's "No" subverts practices, beliefs, and ideals that devalue life. The lion attacks everything that is toxic to the human spirit, including the weakness of will that blocks self-overcoming—a weakness that deceives humans, leading them to believe everything is fine even as the tradition gradually undermines humanity and human life. Finally, the lion offers a symbolic enactment of the nobility of spirit that preceded the Christian moral ideal's demand for vengeance against the strong, an enactment of the relentless tearing of what must be consumed to survive, to reach the third metamorphosis.

In the final metamorphosis a triple creative perspective arises: creation of values, artistic creation, and self-creation. The child's innocence and ability to forget and not hold grudges results in joyful play. Juxtaposing this metamorphosis to a fragment preserved from Heraclitus's work on Nature, we can notice the elemental force entailed in this metamorphosis. The fragment reads: "Lifetime is a child at play moving pieces in a game. Kingship belongs to the child" (Heraclitus, B 52).[6] This perspective, shared by Heraclitus and Nietzsche reveals the power of play to create outside the limits of resentment and guilt. For example, children construct towers with blocks and gain as much pleasure from dismantling the towers as they did from assembling them. The parents, on the other hand, film or photograph the construction to preserve it. Likewise, children at play hit each other and instantly forget and stay friends. The parents hold grudges. This letting go of the child is what makes the child's "Yes" sacred, because it is an affirmation that follows the flow of life, the path of coming to be and passing away.

Three other perspectives pervade Zarathustra's speech: his own, his eagle's, and his serpent's. The eagle presents the panoramic vision from on high, and the serpent provides a perspective tightly knit with the earth, which it touches with its whole body. Zarathustra, in turn, ascends to the mountain and descends to the marketplace, shifting views. On high, he relates to his animals but is fundamentally alone with his thoughts and desires. Below, he speaks to his audience aware of their predicament and experiences. Readers, however, pierce the solitude of the prophet and glimpse reality from many vantage points simultaneously. For example, when the animals first affirm to Zarathustra the eternal return, they do so from their shared perspective: "To those who think as we do, all things themselves approach dancing; they come and reach out their hands and laugh and retreat—and come back" (*TSZ* III). Thus, the eternal return is not a theory, nor a metaphysical claim for camels to transport through deserts. It is an affirmation made from multiple perspectives by Zarathustra's animals, understood by the prophet as a harbinger of joy emanating from the liberation of being and of time from stasis. The eternal return affirms the meaning of becoming for those who can fly over and slide on the earth simultaneously. The animals add: "Everything goes, everything comes back; the wheel of being rolls eternally" (*TSZ* III). The image of the wheel brings to mind the child metamorphosis announced earlier and the rhythm of life. As such, the eternal return liberates and creates a space for our own becoming by affirming joyfully a sensuous, elemental aspect of being. The affirmation, like perspectivism, joins eyes and mind guaranteeing not objective truth but embodied experiences.

Much more could be said about *Thus Spoke Zarathustra* and Nietzsche's perspectivism, but the scope of our essay limits us. Suffice it to say that perspectivism in Nietzsche's epistemology becomes the antidote to heal the human knower from having consumed too many indigestible truths. With perspectivism we do not seek to justify beliefs; we overcome the ascetic need to insist on traditional truths rendered plausible by familiarity. With perspectivism, we seek to calibrate our desire for truth so that it, too, strengthens the human will. Thus Nietzsche redefines "objectivity" in the third essay of *On the Genealogy of Morals* (section 12) stating that the preparation of the mind to receive or even desire "objectivity" took place over a long period of time when the mind turned against itself and sought to see otherwise than it saw. The rest, as we read in *The Gay Science*, section 110, was a matter of having some errors prevail until the force of a belief depends not on its truth but on its age. In *United States of Banana* Giannina and Zarathustra expand these realizations and affirmations in a dialogue framed by the brute fact of the death and destruction of the 9/11 attacks on the United States, a dialogue that carries the horror of those attacks into the sinews of colonialism and the slow death by deprivation of self-esteem. A deprivation to which colonized populations succumb without recourse to revolutions, be they political, economic, or literary, like that of Giannina, Zarathustra, and Segismundo.

Indeed, what I find most authentic about the relationship between Giannina and Zarathustra is the fact that they engage in a dialogue intensely committed to subverting colonialisms, disembodied truths, and the death of experience by mechanized consumerism—taking the latter to involve the intellectualization of experience to cancel out individuality. We can observe this transformation and this shared passion for unmediated experience in the following passages from *United States of Banana* and *Thus Spoke Zarathustra*:

> *Giannina*: We are burying sameness . . . the three [Giannina, Zarathustra, and Hamlet] together—at the same time—holding hands—burying bodies in the same hollow tree—and running free from freedom. Free. (*USB* 74)
>
> *Zarathustra*: All men are created equal. . . . But I am looking for inequality. My thirst is unequal. (*USB* 75)
>
> *Zarathustra (invoking the will to truth immaculate perceiver)*: And to me the *immaculate* perception of all things would be that I desire nothing from things, except that I may lie there before them like a mirror with a hundred eyes. (*TSZ* II.96).

Immediately before and after characterizing those who desire pure perceptions, Zarathustra calls them *lechers* and *sentimental hypocrites*, adding: "You do not love the earth as creators, begetters, and enjoyers of becoming!" (*TSZ* II.96).

In this essay, being neither literary criticism nor a search for absolute truth, I remain forever grateful for having experienced Giannina and Zarathustra without the need of a mirror with a hundred eyes—in the flesh, as it were.

Notes

The epigraphs are from *United States of Banana*, 74, 55; Plato, *Phaedrus*, 245c.

1. I owe this realization about the play between authors and characters to Dr. Kael C. Ashbaugh.

2. Nietzsche explains that, under the direction of the ascetic priests, the ascetic ideal is used to fight depression without resorting to courage. This consists in a mechanical activity: "It is beyond doubt that with this an existence of suffering is alleviated to a not inconsiderable extent: today people call this fact, rather dishonestly, 'the blessing of work.' The alleviation consists in completely diverting the interest of the sufferer from the pain" (*GM* III.18). A series of distractions saturates consciousness, lessening the pain but unfortunately decreasing also a human's range of experience. Suffering dissipates in the intellectualized explanation of the reasons for suffering to which the priests give a lofty purpose: collaboration in the redemption of humanity. The process leads also to self-forgetfulness and self-depreciation, and although worse off and alienated from actual living, ascetics believe they are leading a meaningful life.

3. In the three metamorphoses of the spirit, Zarathustra becomes a lion to carry the burden of the ascetic ideal.

4. We can observe the coincidence between the sardine and the ascetic ideal embodied in the tightrope walker when Giannina explains why she doesn't eat sardines: "Because I detest their helplessness. . . . They never lived. They're dead even when they're alive. . . . It's their deadliness that lingers over me every day of my life—the dead inertia of the sardine that obeys and begs for water, gallons of water, and does what it's asked to do in spite of no water and denies itself so much—that it doesn't realize it doesn't have a being anymore—and it lets itself be canned" (*USB* 73–74).

5. Hamlet's presence, in turn, densely marks the colonization that the English language enabled in North America and in the colonies of the United States. Spanish is virtually absent from the text but, nonetheless, palpitates in each soliloquy of Segismundo that is memorized by Puerto Rican children from the seventh grade onward.

6. See Kahn, *Art and Thought of Heraclitus*.

Works Cited

Braschi, Giannina. *United States of Banana*. AmazonCrossing, 2011.

Kahn, C. H. *The Art and Thought of Heraclitus*. Cambridge UP, 1979.

Nietzsche, Friedrich. *The Gay Science*. Translated by Josefine Nauckhoff. Cambridge UP, 2016.

Nietzsche, Friedrich. *On the Genealogy of Morality*. Translated by Carol Diethe. Cambridge UP, 1997.

Nietzsche, Friedrich. *Thus Spoke Zarathustra*. Translated by Adrian Del Caro. Cambridge UP, 2006.

Plato. *Phaedrus*. Translated by A. Nehamas and P. Woodruff. Hackett, 1995.

4

Yo-Yo Boing!

Or Literature as a Translingual Practice

Francisco Moreno-Fernández

In her review of *Yo-Yo Boing!* Jean Franco praises Giannina Braschi's virtuosity at switching between English and Spanish. In the prologue to the novel, Doris Sommer and Alexandra Vega-Merino distinguish between the use of English, Spanish, and Spanglish, noting that these are the alternating linguistic realities of the narrative. Yet, what if these in fact are not alternations? Spaces of contact may lead to translingual practices where languages constitute a continuous reality, where bilingualism translates into translingualism and languages into translanguage. This is an analytical strategy based on the text itself.

From this standpoint, I propose a thesis that is basically twofold. On the one hand, the work under consideration is a translingual narrative, in its formal essence. On the other, it might be characterized as "liquid" in its content. For the first proposal, I build on the contributions made over the past ten years regarding the notion of "translanguaging," a concept emerging from the field of learning and language acquisition, but which has expanded to encompass a far greater scope and a far more powerful explanatory capacity. For the interpretation of *Yo-Yo Boing!* as "liquid" literature, I rely on the hypothesis of the Polish philosopher Zygmunt Bauman, although I have my own approach to the "liquid" in this particular application. According to Bauman, interpersonal relationships in the contemporary world are no longer rigid, stereotyped, or structured but, rather, flexible, adaptable, multiform, and unpredictable—in other words, liquid.

What Is Translanguaging?

Why don't bilingual children react when they are instructed to "translate"? Or why, when we move about in bilingual environments, do we lose consciousness of the language we are reading, or the one we are hearing, or even the one we are speaking (about)?

To understand why processes of this kind occur, resorting to the concept of "bilingualism" does not seem sufficient. This is why since the 1990s, there have been discussions concerning translanguaging, a term that was coined by Cen Williams (applied in Welsh as *trawsieithu*) in his unpublished thesis titled "An Evaluation of Teaching and Learning Methods in the Context of Bilingual Secondary Education." However, the actual dissemination and consolidation of the term, and of the related concept, have only gained traction over the past five years, thanks mostly to Ofelia García (García and Wei).

Translanguaging is the process by which multilingual speakers use their languages as an integrated communication system. It is a dynamic process in which multilingual users perform complex social and cognitive activities through the strategic use of multiple semiotic resources in order to act, know, and be. Translanguaging presupposes that, beyond mere linguistic production, the use of the language also involves effective communication, the functions of the language, and the processes of thought. Translanguaging is characterized by the unintentional integration of linguistic systems, becoming an interpretive alternative to the concept of bilingualism, which would be seen more as a "double monolingualism" or as an alternation between languages. From this perspective, the mono/multi and uni/pluri binaries would lead to a reductionist interpretation of communication and competence.

The prefix "trans" denotes that these are fluid practices, which go beyond (i.e., transcend) the systems and structures of socially constructed language, thereby involving different meaning-generating systems. Translingual practices have a transforming capacity that affects not only linguistic systems but also the cognition and social structures of the individual. This conception has transdisciplinary consequences, which lead to a reconceptualization of language, language learning, and the use of languages in the fields of linguistics, psychology, sociology, and education (García and Wei). Translanguaging is manifested in writing, the writing acts of the bilingual individual (Horner, Lu, Royster, and Trimbur), in literacy studies (cross-cultural literacy, multi-literacy, heterography), in sociolinguistics (multilingualism, fragmented multilingualism), and in applied linguistics (dynamic bilingualism). I propose that these transdisciplinary consequences and this reconceptualization of the use of language also affect literary creation.

The use of the prefix "trans," on the other hand, situates us on a plane where it is possible to understand or interpret globalization, superdiversity (Vertovec), and globalized contexts, such as those experienced in large cities or among groups of speakers in open connection with multiple international referents. Hence, theories of translanguaging can be readily linked to Alastair Pennycook's theories of globalization in his work titled *Global Englishes and Transcultural Flows*. Pennycook interprets globalization as a multivocal and diverse phenomenon, in which any analysis cannot be approached from static positions but only through transversal standpoints. This is why he resorts to terms such as "transdisciplinary," "transcultural," "transtextual," "translocal," or "transidiomatic"; and it is also why he pays special attention to hip-hop as a worldwide phenomenon, as a reference for a transmodal semiotics incorporating music, writing, dress, dance. Pennycook focuses on the local manifestations arising within and as a result of globalization, as a counterpoint that both explains and complements it.

All of this fits perfectly into a translingual paradigm, the characteristics of which have been outlined by Suresh Canagarajah:

> Languages are always in contact and influence each other.
> Speakers treat all available languages as codes of a single repertoire in their daily communication, not as codes separated by labels.
> Speakers do not have separate competences, but an integrated skill.
> Languages are not necessarily at war with one another but complement each other in communication.
> Texts and speech form a whole mediated by different codes.
> In context, negotiations are common practices.
> Languages are always open to negotiation and reconstruction.
> Communicative norms are relocalized.
> Languages are mobile resources that adapt to each purpose.
> Semiotic resources are involved in a physical and social environment, aligned with contextual factors (participants, human body, scenario).

The Liquidity of Yo-Yo Boing!

The characterization of Braschi's work as liquid (Bauman) interests me since I see it as being perfectly complementary to its interpretation as translingual. In this characterization, I prefer to define the content of *Yo-Yo Boing!* as being liquid and its linguistic form as being translingual. When I speak of "liquid," I mean the fluidity between disparate elements that are contrary or contradictory within the work. Thus, the constant, fluid, liquid movement between the sublime and the vulgar, dream and reality, tenderness and violence, eroticism and eschatology, the spiritual and the physical, the cultured and the popular, and the autobiographical and the fictitious. Or, more important, between the universal, the general, and the local. This would explain the manipulation of all manner of universal cultural references (literature, film, art) in tandem with social issues such as the discrimination against Hispanics in the United States, as well as local manifestations—or rather, relocalized manifestations—in the form, for example, of dialectalisms, and of specific Puerto Rican cultural references (*dar pon*, *vejigantes*, *chinas*; *¡Ay, bendito!*), all of which express the indexicality of Braschi's literary language.

The liquidity of Giannina Braschi's work can be clearly seen in the importance the author gives to movement. *Yo-Yo Boing!* is a work filled with movement; movement that is internal and external, physical, and sometimes without a reference invoked to any specific type of movement:

> Y Por qué ahora—y no antes—soy yo la que ahora y no antes tiene razón en inculparse; por donde estoy ahora no recuerdo haber estado nunca y por eso vuelvo a pasar a ver si lo reconozco o si me lo aprendo de memoria o si lo olvido alucinando con la memoria a cuestas. Yo soy la que soy sin ser quien fui. (196, 197)

> Y por qué ahora—y no antes—soy yo la que ahora y no antes tiene razón en inculparse . . . por donde estoy ahora no recuerdo haber estado nunca y por eso vuelvo a pasar a ver si lo reconozco o si me lo aprendo de memoria o si lo olvido alucinando con la memoria a cuestas. Yo soy la que soy sin ser quien fui. (196, 197)

> Estar haciendo sin estar en un ser que no soy yo y que no me conoce porque ya no me habita, se ha ido de mí, me ha dicho adiós tantas veces—y con tanta premura, y con tanta desilusión en sus alas—como si lo inculpara el estar siendo sin mí. (203)

> Por eso me estoy yendo desde hace tiempo a donde el irse es lo único cierto que me llama la atención, el irse lejos de aquí, el nunca más estar aquí, donde yo nací, donde yo crecí, donde yo me reproduje. (202)

> Cuando hablo me estoy yendo de un barco. . . . Lo importante es que ninguno tenga una frontera—que no sepamos por dónde vamos pero que vayamos siempre a donde vayamos vayámonos de todos—y de nadie—a nadie consideremos tan importante para no partir en este viaje que nos

lleva—adiós—hacia fronteras insospechadas—donde la frontera es la única sospecha que sospecha—porque no hay sospechosos a bordo de la frontera que nos afronta. (202)

And why now—and not before—am I the one who, now and not before, is right to blame myself. . . . I don't remember ever having been where I am now and that's why I am returning to see if I recognize it or if I can memorize it or if I will forget, hallucinating with memory in tow. I am what I am without being who I was. (196, 197)

To be doing without being in a being that is not me and does not know me because it no longer inhabits me, because it has left me, it has bid farewell to me so many times—and with so much haste, and with so much disappointment on its wings—as if I were blaming it for being without me. (203)

That is why I have been going for a long time where leaving is the only certain thing that appeals to me, going far from here, never being here again, where I was born, where I grew up, where I reproduced myself. (202)

When I speak, I am leaving a ship. . . . The important thing is that no one has a border—that we do not know where we are going but that we always go where we go, and let's leave everyone—and no one—and we consider no one that important that we can't just leave on this journey that takes us—farewell—to unsuspected borders—where the border is the only suspicion that suspects—because there are no suspects onboard at the border confronting us. (202)[1]

In this last example, we find another key to understanding the liquidity of Braschi's work: the word "frontera" (frontier/border/boundary). This liquidity finds its ideal habitat in border situations, be they cultural, social, linguistic, environmental, or personal. The reality presented by Braschi could be better defined through the form adopted by the frontier—by her own frontier(s)—than through the features of each of the realities with which this frontier comes into contact. To better understand this idea, I suggest we refer to Walter Benjamin's reflections on color. For Benjamin, a color cannot be defined or described by its intrinsic characteristics but, rather, by the way it contrasts with adjacent colors; this contrast occurs precisely at the edge of surfaces—at the border. A blue surface is not appreciated in the same way if it borders a black surface as if it abuts a green surface. It is the border/boundary that gives us the key to understanding why things look the way they look and are the way they are.

This notion of frontier, border, or boundary, applicable to a situation of contact, is not exclusive to the realm of philosophical reflection. The notion has also been employed as a fundamental term in socio-ethnic and ethnographic studies. Parallel to the observations made by Benjamin, in 1969 Fredrik Barth, for example, stated that "the ethnic boundary . . . defines the group, not the cultural stuff that it encloses" (15). Although we speak of social boundaries, there may be actual geographical correspondences for such boundaries. Ethnic groups are not necessarily based on the occupation of exclusive territories or on an initial ascription but, rather, are based on ongoing expression and validation. The ethnic border channels social life and gives rise to a complex and conflicting organization of behaviors and social relations. This is exactly what we have observed in Braschi.

Giannina Braschi is quite aware of the existence and importance of this border; and even if she weren't, it would be of little consequence because it is evident that she somehow appreciates and lives that border. And this evidence is obtained from many elements of content and thought expressed in *Yo-Yo Boing!*—particularly in its metalinguistic awareness, or epilinguistic awareness, as French linguistics might describe it (Gombert). This awareness emerges when the author states literally that "somos bilingües" (*YYB* 167); when she speaks of "barreras lingüísticas" (12); when she resorts to pseudo phonetic writing to represent colloquialisms, in Spanish or English; when she discusses improving her pronunciation; or when she has a character say: "I know five words in Spanish: *coño, pendejo, puta, maricón, carajo*" (127). And, certainly, this epilinguistic awareness is apparent in the constant language games and in the way in which she so often plays with this translingual reality and with all the factors with which it contrasts and among which it moves so liquidly.

The Translanguaging of *Yo-Yo Boing!*

But now let us return to the matter of translanguaging. If we analyze how the already enumerated characteristics of translanguaging are manifested in *Yo-Yo Boing!* we can see that practically all of them would allow us to qualify this work not as bilingual, in a strict sense, but simply as translingual. The supposed code-switching between languages observed in the long central section of the work ("Blow-Up") indicates that the speakers in the narrative treat their languages as elements of a daily repertoire, that there is no separate competence but, rather, an integrated skill, and that the distinctions between languages do not point to an underlying conflict but to communicative complementation. Braschi's text also reveals the manipulation of various literary codes in an integrated whole (direct and indirect discourse, prose, poetry, even lyrical prose), as well as a constant negotiation of content, which is also interwoven with a semantic and pragmatic negotiation. Finally, *Yo-Yo Boing!* provides an excellent example of the deployment of localized norms, given how a reindexed Puerto Rican identity is integrated into the Americanness of the text.

Because of all of these elements, *Yo-Yo Boing!* is a perfect illustration of translingual practice, a practice that is situated within a contact space (a Bakhtinian chronotope) and that manifests itself within each speaker/character, in the aggregate of their interactions, and in the themes touched upon in many of these interactions, which, significantly, include such topics as translation. Thus, translanguaging is not seen as a reflex or a consequence—not even a symptom—but the very essence of a social and individual reality. This translanguaging is revealed in multiple forms and in countless passages, which can even lead readers to lose consciousness of the language they are reading at any given moment. And it is not as if the languages cease to be social constructs, where the boundaries are arbitrarily established by criteria that have nothing to do with a strictly linguistic nature.

This novel, like those of many other authors, has been characterized as a work in Spanglish. My interpretation is that this "Spanglish" is nothing more than an expression of translanguaging or, more appropriately, various expressions of translanguaging. This is why we find countless examples of that translingual reality in *Yo-Yo Boing!* including loan words ("goldfish" instead of *pez dorado*), grammatical and orthographic adaptations (*mumi, pissear, machinas, in-betweenes* [170, 60, 93, 118]), code-switching elements of all kinds (intra-sentential, extra-sentential, intra-syntagmatic, referential), even the use of false cognates, which is not so frequent in the literature traditionally termed "bilingual" (*granos* as "grains"; "I don't treason the people I love"; "revolting gavetas").

Despite the meaning and importance of all these phenomena, Baschi's translanguaging also employs a very special and relevant element, one that is not so frequently used in literature: onomatopoeia. In *Yo-Yo Boing!* we find them in Spanish (*kikiriki, tacata, trocotrí* [48, 83, 94]); in English (ouch!, gulp, oops [95, 113]); in Spanish inserted within English constructions (Muuu, mooo [109]); and of course, onomatopoeias that are part of the overall language game. These examples also corroborate the arbitrariness of the linguistic sign, something known to semiologists but rarely exemplified in such border spaces. These examples also open the discussion to broader issues of translingual writing.

Other Interpretations and Conclusions

A work as rich as Braschi's can certainly be open to multiple readings, all of them warranting respect. I would like to refer only to the interpretations given by two authors—Laura Loustau and Anastasia Gameza—specifically with regard to Braschi's "bilingualism" and the supposed use of "Spanglish" in her work. I concur with both authors on the relevance given to the notion of movement: Loustau speaks of "nomadism" and Gameza of "displacements." Nonetheless, Loustau affirms that *Yo-Yo Boing!* subverts linguistic conventions by incorporating a bilingualism that the author uses to avoid anchoring the work to national and cultural definitions. Loustau has opted for a political/nationalistic interpretation that, for coherence with my own analytical strategy, I do not share. It is not that politics does not surface in Braschi's work but that her writing transcends it. From my perspective, this supposed bilingualism responds to something deeper, which has to do with the essence of the language: translanguaging, understood as a natural linguistic process that Braschi transports to literature. There are other manifestations of translingual writing (among students of foreign languages, for example), however the importance of translingual literature has not been sufficiently foregrounded (Pratt), and Braschi certainly offers a magnificent example.

As for Gameza's contribution, which is enormously meritorious as an academic thesis, the author discusses the transgression of genres and subversion in *Yo-Yo Boing!* in which code-switching and Spanglish are seen as transgressive instruments and resources. To a large degree I would concur with Gameza's interpretation, but I prefer to see the work as expressing a liquid and translingual reality. In my view, we will never come to understand *Yo-Yo Boing!* by employing the labels of Spanglish and code-switching exclusively. It is not a matter of code-switching between English with Spanish as a form of rebellion; it is not about knowing more or less English or finding the exact word in either language at any given moment. It is about being liquid and translingual and living in a border reality where expression is adapted to the environment so that it is perfectly in sync with the globalized and "super-diverse" reality that surrounds us, a reality that is not fixed, which has no unique or stable referents. As Braschi notes: "Es un perro realengo atravesando un puente entre el norte y el sur, entre el siglo XX y el siglo XXI, entre Segismundo y Hamlet, entre Neruda y Whitman, entre Dickinson y Sor Juana, entre Darío y Stein, entre Sarmiento y Melville, entre los dos yo's en choque está el *Yo-Yo Boing!*" ("Pelos en la lengua," 50).[2] Giannina Braschi provides the key herself, and here she does not discuss politics or nationalism, or subversion, but literature. In the key that Braschi offers us we find the fundamental ideas I have attempted to explore: movement, borders, liquidity, and translanguaging.

Notes

1. English translation of *Yo-Yo Boing!* by David Auerbach.

2. "It's a stray dog crossing a bridge between north and south, between the twentieth century and the twenty-first century, between Segismundo and Hamlet, between Neruda and Whitman, between Dickinson and Sor Juana, between Darío and Stein, between Sarmiento and Melville, and between the two shocked 'yo's' is the *Yo-Yo Boing!*"

Works Cited

Barth, Fredrik. *Ethnic Groups and Boundaries: The Social Organization of Culture Difference.* 1969. Waveland, 1998.

Bauman, Zygmunt. *Vida líquida.* Paidós Ibérica, 2006.

Benjamin, Walter. "The Rainbow." *Early Writings (1910–1917).* 1915. Edited and translated by Howard Eiland. Harvard UP, 2011, pp. 214–27.

Braschi, Giannina. "Pelos en la lengua." *Hopscotch: A Cultural Review,* vol. 2, no. 2, 2001, p. 50.

Braschi, Giannina. *Yo-Yo Boing!.* Translated by Tess O'Dwyer. AmazonCrossing, 2011.

Gameza, Anastasia. "Desplazamientos lingüísticos y literarios en la obra de Giannina Braschi *Yo-Yo Boing!*" Graduate thesis, Universidad de La Laguna, 2015.

Canagarajah, Suresh. *Translingual Practice: Global Englishes and Cosmopolitan Relations.* Routledge, 2013.

García, Ofelia, and Li Wei. *Translanguaging: Language, Bilingualism and Education.* Pala grave Macmillan, 2014.

Gombert, Jean-Émile. *Le développement méta-linguistique.* PUF, 1990.

Horner, Bruce, Min-Zhan Lu, Jones Royster, and John Trimbur. "Opinion—Language Difference in Writing: Toward a Translingual Approach." *College English,* vol. 73, no. 3, 2010, pp. 303–21.

Loustau, Laura R. "Nomadismos lingüísticos y culturales en *Yo-Yo Boing!* de Giannina Braschi." *Revista Iberoamericana,* vol. 71, no. 211, 2005, pp. 437–88.

Pennycook, Alastair. *Global Englishes and Transcultural Flows.* Routledge, 2007.

Pratt, Mary Louise. "Linguistic Utopias." *The Linguistics of Writing: Arguments between Language and Literature,* edited by N. Fabb, D. Attridge, A. Durant, and C. MacCabe, Manchester UP, 1991, pp. 48–66.

Sommer, Doris, Alexandra Vega, and Alexandra Vega-Merino. "Either and." *Yo-Yo Boing!* Latin American Literary Review Press, 1998, pp. 11–18.

Vertovec, Steven. "Super-Diversity and Its Implications." *Ethnic and Racial Studies,* vol. 30, no. 6, 2007, pp. 1024–54.

Williams, Cen. "Arfarniad o ddulliau dysgu ac addysgu yng nghyd-destun addysg uwchradd ddwyieithog" [An evaluation of teaching and learning methods in the context of bilingual secondary education]. PhD dissertation, University of Wales, Bangor, UK, 1994.

5

Bilingual Big Bang

Giannina Braschi's Trilogy Levels the Spanish-English Playing Field

Maritza Stanchich

Giannina Braschi's *United States of Banana*, taking off from the end of her groundbreaking quasi-novel *Yo-Yo Boing!*, marks a paradigmatic shift in the millennial poetics of witness of Whitman and Martí's New York with a high/low trans-canonical and trans-American postmodern performance that levels the playing field of the charged terrain of Spanish-English bilingualism. *Banana* enacts simultaneously postmodern and protest poetics in dizzying global/local contexts, as US global hegemony declines after 9/11, as the United States has become the second-largest Spanish-speaking country in the world, and as Braschi's homeland of Puerto Rico gets mired in a colonial debt crisis now turned climate catastrophe after Hurricane Maria. Her avant-garde Spanish-English bilingualism wrestles the staggering legacies of both these colonial languages in the Americas to forge parity between them, in the process exposing discourses that sought to officialize them as languages of national literary canons and imperial powers on a global stage.

The *United States of Banana* culminates the trilogy, with each book formed of distinct parts, as a meditation on Spanish and English as bilingual lingua franca in a trans-American poetics emanating from a New York City transcending its epicenter of US empire.[1] *El imperio de los sueños* (1988) was written in Spanish, *Yo-Yo Boing!* (1998) is brashly bilingual, and *United States of Banana* (2011) is in English; all three have also been published in translation (1994, 2011, 2016).[2] Braschi's vanguard bilingual performance in *Yo-Yo Boing!* breaks with previous theorizations of the functions of interlingualism in diasporic Puerto Rican and Chicano theory (Aparicio; Bruce-Novoa; Flores and Yúdice), as well as with Puerto Rico's insular cultural nationalist linguistic discourses (Duany; Flores, *Insularismo*; Janer). Braschi challenges a transimperial history of global power relations between English and Spanish (Mignolo), with literary language that exceeds canonical traditions and literary genres and that forges parity between the two languages in global trans-American terms. How Braschi engages these literary canons also reveals their contours, with translingual—in Lydia Liu's sense of that term—and trans-canonical implications.[3]

Doris Sommer and Alexandra Vega-Merino describe the language of *Yo-Yo Boing!* as "shoring up creative energy for the challenge to develop a nuanced, original, playful and productive bilingualism" (18). Lourdes Torres characterizes Braschi's work as "radical bilingualism" (86) along the lines of the "Weird English" proposed by Evelyn Nien-Ming Ch'ien's book of that name (2005), which posits an English language pollinated by other languages at the level of syntax in the oeuvres of novelists such as Junot Díaz and Salman Rushdie. That fact that *United States of Banana* deals most directly with the question of Puerto Rico's struggle against US colonialism and that it is, of all three works, the most completely written in English also demonstrates how Braschi marshals the productive power of such bilingualism in local and global terms.

Walter Mignolo has argued that, although the idea of linking languages with territories predates the Enlightenment (initiated with Castilian by the seventeenth century), with the development of grammar directly linked to state control and global power Spanish has since become a subaltern language in relation to English, especially since the Second World War (257–59). Puerto Rico's struggle for cultural autonomy against systematic US imposition of English until 1948, during an era when English was the language of instruction in all subjects throughout the colonial school system, exemplifies the subalternity of Spanish in global imperial terms. Yet that Braschi dedicates *United States of Banana* in part to the trail-blazing legal and literary figure Nilita Vientós Gastón, who successfully defended Spanish as a language of instruction in Puerto Rico, suggests that Braschi purposefully challenges such subalternity. Mignolo posits that the explosive growth of Spanish-speaking populations within the United States is a step in the decline of global Spanish prestige, though this remains contested as US Latinos expand political power and resist discourses and policies of xenophobia (now akin to border fascism in the Trump era).

Mignolo's elucidation both of border languages as an alternative to national languages and of bilanguaging as "a fundamental condition of border thinking" (253) is crucial to Braschi's invocation of these two powerful colonial languages of the Americas and among the top four languages in the world in terms of numbers of speakers. By "bilanguaging," Mignolo does not mean bilingualism, though bilanguaging may or may not also be bilingual or plurilingual. Rather, bilanguaging goes beyond the grammatical system of language to reveal "the ideology of monolanguaging (and particularly the idea of national languages in the imaginary of nation-states), that is, of speaking, writing, thinking within a single language controlled by grammar, in a way similar to a constitution's control over the state" (252). Mignolo is concerned with the geopolitics of such grammars of language—and with how national languages are consolidated in complicity with the state and regulating institutions, with both nations and national languages persistently seeming "natural" (Hobsbawm 13). In *United States of Banana*, Braschi repeatedly refers to this dominating role of grammar, in passages that deal explicitly with the unmooring of English and Spanish in the Americas from such colonial designs and North/South binaries in relation to canonicity (*USB* 38, 39, 42, 62, 135). The wordplay on gender and genre also echoes that they are the same word in Spanish, *género* (121, 123). In *Yo-Yo Boing!* a key reference to Puerto Rico's colonial condition hinges on a grammatical joke comparing Puerto Rico's ambivalent political status to semicolons: "Los puertorriqueños son puntos y comas. No pueden decidirse o por el punto o por la coma" [Puerto Ricans are semicolons. They can't decide between the period or the comma]. (*YYB* 182). Here grammar symbolizes the country's predicament.

Mignolo defines bilanguaging as a way of life, living between languages, a celebration of the "conflictive tension" of in-betweenity, "a dialogic, ethic, aesthetic, and political process of social transformation" (265, 276), which also describes Braschi's linguistic experimentation. Bilanguaging opens up the possibility of "post-national" ideology and imaginary that is potentially post-Occidental and postcolonial (253–54, 276–77) and reveals the fissures that monolingual nationalism disavows, allowing enunciations from those fissures to disrupt or intervene in official monolingualism.[4] For a historically specific example, Kelvin Santiago-Valles's examination of the regimes of power and discipline in Puerto Rico during the first half of the twentieth century, *"Subject People" and Colonial Discourses* (1994), reveals that a Spanish lingua franca was not a given between 1788 and 1898. First, as late as the 1830s most captive laborers had been born in Africa, and second, Afro-Caribbean cane cutters from the British West Indies who migrated to and later settled the eastern and southern coasts did not commonly know Spanish (44).

Cultural nationalism in Puerto Rico—discussed in depth by Jorge Duany, among others (for example, Scarano)—promoted Spanish as the bulwark of Puerto Rican identification, marshaling intelligentsia and canonical writers of the 1930s to consolidate popular support for particular local elite interests during the 1940s and 1950s period of industrialization known as Operation Bootstrap and culminating in the formation of the country's Free Associated State status in 1952. In contesting Spanish as the only language befitting Puerto Rican letters, a critique of such monolanguaging does not reinscribe colonial US English imposition but, rather, interrogates what such prescriptions have hidden, as well as in whose interests they have been made. As Arcadio Díaz Quiñones asserts, "la afirmación de una identidad cultural monolítica y excluyente no permite reconocer los muchos espacios, tiempos, creencias y contextos locales que conforman la constitución misma de lo puertorriqueño" (76).

Harnessing such a critique against both Puerto Rico's and the United States' monolanguaging, Braschi's triumphant Spanglish in *Yo-Yo Boing!* is also crucial to the linguistic politics and experimental aesthetics of *United States of Banana*, where Braschi declares it one of Puerto Rico's three languages, with a style that also exceeds previously theorized functions of literary and performed interlingualism. Her interlingual and trans-canonical vanguardism demonstrates language invention in that it unequivocally refuses official monolingualism and strict standardization while blurring multiple registers and genres. Interlingualism intimates a more complex intermingling of languages than suggested by bilingualism and perhaps approximates what Nien-Ming Ch'ien's *Weird English* is documenting. Interlingualism constitutes the improvisational syntactical interfacing of both languages—suggested by the lived practices of Spanglish—and has been contrasted to bilingualism in seminal Chicano studies by Juan Bruce-Novoa, though he refers to the "common speech" practiced by communities, whereas Braschi's inventions are often defamiliarized from such everyday contexts, as has also been pointed out by Sommer and Vega-Merino (16).

Braschi's vanguard interlingualism exceeds the interlingual formulations expounded by Juan Flores and George Yúdice in a then seminal essay for Puerto Rican studies, "Living Borders/*Buscando America*" (1997). Exploring how "Latino usage tends necessarily toward interlingual innovation," they contend that the "interfacing of multiple codes serves to de-canonize all of them, at least in their presumed discrete authority, thus allowing ample space for spontaneous experimentation and punning" (190). Yet, as Persephone Braham contends, although Braschi's "refusal to reject one language for the other reflects the eternal dilemma of Puerto Rico's status, it is also a measure of Braschi's debt to Joyce and other Modernists (y Modernistas)" (85–87). Braschi's usage departs markedly from Nuyorican usage in that her interlingual adventurousness does not necessarily function to document the vernacular practices of the broader diasporic community, though these are also much more varied than Nuyorican literature alone attests both in terms of location and genre, as I elaborate elsewhere (Stanchich).

Although Braschi's books might not display a widely recognized Spanglish, she does deploy an irreverence that is also the hallmark of what Flores and Yúdice characterize as the "intercultural variability and transferability" of "trans-creation," theorizing the *gufeo*, from the colloquial American "goof," in the traditions of Puerto Rican *vacilón* and *relajo*. In Braschi, the *gufeo* operates at full blast, taking irony and satire to the level of lampoon, while enunciating bilingualism as a lingua franca of a new New World, exploding North/South binaries. For Braschi, the intercultural is cultural (as she posits is the case for Hamlet, Zarathustra, and Segismundo too). She exalts the bi- or multilingual as the twenty-first-century subject par excellence by simultaneously invoking the postmodern present along with the English Renaissance and the Spanish Golden Age, in a world with more Spanish than English speakers, and from an immigrant New York in which more than 150 countries are represented, with the borough of Queens as one of the most linguistically diverse places on the planet (including endangered languages). By invoking the globalized present and the worlding past, Braschi goes to the heart of power struggles between North–South language transactions, and indeed to the linguistic birth of modernity in the Americas, armed with the artistic spirit of poetic neologisms and ancient dramas in contemporary tongues.

As part of a multiple heterogeneous diaspora literature, Braschi's oeuvre simultaneously helps disrupt Puerto Rico's cultural nationalist prescriptives, such as regarding its constellation with language and race, and helps historicize an important and historically often minimized part of Puerto Rican history, the postwar mass migration of the Muñoz era, with population displacement now at a new historic peak because of the collapse of the Estado Libre Asociado. Arlene Dávila in *Sponsored Identities* (1997) registers the potential of diaspora cultural productions for making such discursive interventions: "While 'modernity' itself was encouraged, its by-products—the rise of mass culture, the transnational community of Puerto Ricans, and hybrid forms of language and culture—were considered direct challenges to the image of the nation constructed around a folklorized and utopian peasant past" (254). This heeds Juan Flores's call that the mining of "the seams and borders of national experience need to be understood not as absences or vacuums but as sites of new meaning and relations" (*Bomba*, 51) and also his point in *The Diaspora Strikes Back*

(2009) that the diaspora's cultural production needs to be taken seriously for new developments and not just for how it reflects island culture. Such analysis also expands on book-length studies engaging Puerto Rican diaspora literature, on the more discrete formation of an organically resistant diaspora canon in Lisa Sánchez González's *Boricua Literature* (2001), and the relation of select women's works to island discourses and canons in Marisel Moreno's *Family Matters* (2012) and Ramón Soto-Crespo's multidisciplinary apologia for the island's current political status *Mainland Passage* (2009).

The issues germane to Braschi—interlingual vanguardism, generic experimentation, postmodern high-brow and popular cultures, trans-American and trans-Atlantic canonicity, cosmopolitanism, poetics, drama, and philosophy—nonetheless engage insular and diasporic Puerto Rican literature. Yet Braschi's style and language dramatically depart from characteristic traits and functions of both while forging transformative linguistic and aesthetic practices that are epic in scope, abandoning North/South binaries, and exalting in-betweenity. Braschi's language experiments highlight a vein of contemporary avant-garde literature of the Puerto Rican diaspora along with the distinct projects of Lawrence La Fountain-Stokes, Urayoán Noel, Edwin Torres, and the late Edgardo Vega Yunqué—including poets who uniquely venture into broadly comparative and international terrains such as Victor Hernández Cruz, whose most recent collections explore Arabic and African linguistic influences in Spain, and Martín Espada, whose oeuvre engages pan-Latino, trans-American literary traditions as well as a global poetics of dissent. The fantastic mode of *United States of Banana* resonates with emergent stateside Puerto Rican authors who use light sci-fi, fantasy, and magical realism to challenge and innovate aesthetic, cultural, gender, and sexual dictates, including Lyn Di Iorio, Charlie Vazquez, and playwright Quiara Alegría Hudes. *Banana* notably nods to the Nuyorican poets, mentioning poet and playwright Pedro Pietri by name (*USB* 124), and invoking his play *The Masses Are Asses*, which was published in a bilingual edition by the Institute of Puerto Rican Culture in Puerto Rico (1997). Pietri's often absurdist plays were also internationally recognized, translated, and staged. In Caribbean literature, bringing Puerto Rico's plight into play with other nations, states, and semi-nation states of the region, I read the vanguard politics of *Banana* alongside experimental oeuvres such as those by Robert Antoni, Kamau Brathwaite, Erna Brodber, Wilson Harris, and Pauline Melville.

In insular terms, Braschi's trilogy breaks with previous discourses of what Zilkia Janer (2) calls "colonial nationalism," referring to the cultural nationalism of the founding of the Estado Libre Asociado, and with nary a nativist *jíbaro* or *jibarista* discourse in sight, lending Puerto Rico an epic of inventive independence.[5] References to Puerto Rico's specific Spanish vernacular and popular culture run deep, as with the title of *Yo-Yo Boing!*—the stage name of the Puerto Rican comedian and radio personality Luis Antonio Rivera, widely recognized by those on the island close to or of Braschi's generation. *Banana*'s romp is rife with playful local references, such as the colloquial phrase *Ni fú, ni fá* (neither here nor there), the pest control service Oliver Exterminators, and the burial of the sardine, which is still performed in the carnival of Puerto Rico's southern city of Ponce (as in regions of Spain). This, while making linguistic and political commentary, such as the refrain on Puerto Rico's three main political parties "wishy" (independence), "wishy-washy" (the free associated state), or "washy" (statehood), which correspond to "spanish, spanglish or english," "nation, colony or state" (*USB* 114) and the impasse between the three, here relating Segismundo's mind-set as a Puerto Rican who "grew up thinking he was not free—but that he could choose between three options—":

> Wishy: You are only Fú
> Washy: You are only Fá
> Wishy: You only wash
> Wishy: You only wish. And I am sick at heart.
> Wishy-washy: You say I'm neither Fú nor Fá. But I say I am Fú and Fá. You are only Fú. How can Fú be more Fú than Fá? (*USB* 107)

In *Antillano* fashion, this echoes *Oscar Wao*'s *fukú* (J. Díaz) in theme and tone. These are serious matters to *United States of Banana*'s story line, linked to the attempted prison break for Segismundo, while critiquing the governance by partisan obstruction that has so hampered politics in Puerto Rico: "If they vote for Wishy—Segismundo will be liberated from the dungeon. If they vote for Wishy-Washy, the status quo will prevail. If they vote for Washy, he will be sentenced to death, and nobody will have the honor of hearing his songs rise from the gutters of the dungeon of liberty. Every four years the citizens of Liberty Island vote for Wishy-Washy. They can choose between mashed potato, french fries or baked potato. But any way you serve it, it's all the same potato" (*USB* 7). The crab walking backward in *United States of Banana* (80, 87, 192, 246) echoes what in Puerto Rico is called *jaibería* (a cultural tendency toward avoidance of direct conflict named for a crab that backs away), as theorized by Ramón Grosfoguel, Frances Negrón-Muntaner, and Chloé S. Georas and Arcadio Díaz Quiñones, rather than T. S. Eliot's "pair of ragged claws" in "Prufrock."

At the same time, the summoning of Hamlet, Zarathustra, and Segismundo builds a canonical capaciousness rivaled by few, perhaps also akin to the high modernism of Eliot but for very different ends. The somewhat Socratic dialogues of *Yo-Yo Boing!* between the voices named Giannina, Zarathustra, and Hamlet strike a philosophical pose, yet as Plato's Socrates was not the real Socrates, Nietzche's Zarathustra and Shakespeare's Hamlet are here simultaneously both characters and not characters who go on to take center stage in *United States of Banana*. As *Yo-Yo Boing!* levels the playing field of power dynamics between English and Spanish, by being bookended front and back in its erudite Spanish, *United States of Banana* reverses and subverts assumptions concerning which country gets deemed a banana republic. It is almost completely in English—with lead characters from the Spanish Golden Age, such as Segismundo as a prisoner trapped by his father for one hundred years under the skirt of the Statue of Liberty, as if also to stave off a terrible prophecy à la Sophocles. *United States of Banana* invokes Pedro Calderón de la Barca's *La vida es sueño* (1635), in which the father of the imprisoned prince is king of Poland—on equal if not more central footing than Shakespeare's *Hamlet* (1603), the prince of Denmark—and so highlights the cross-cultural subtexts and crossover potential of among the most enshrined texts in the English and Spanish literary canons, as the following exchange shows, exalting the internationalism of New York while interrogating themes of belonging, displacement, language, tradition, and national literatures:

> Spain: Where is Segismundo?
> Giannina: He is the prince of Poland.
> Spain: Return him to Spain where he belongs.
> England: No I won't return the Elgin Marbles to Greece, so you can keep Hamlet.
> Giannina: In Denmark?
> England: In New York. (*USB* 254)

The fact that key Spanish Golden Age poetry was in part produced by the era's cross-cultural translation and influence with Italianate poetry indebted to Petrarch is part of the linguistic tension inherent in the canonicity that Braschi's experimentalism highlights and subverts in trans-American New Worldings.

All the more fitting that Braschi culminates this trilogy in a rhetorically supercharged romp through genres, registers, canons, popular cultures, and dramatis personae to imagine a carnivalesque end to US colonialism (suggested by the burial of the sardine, as enacted in Ponce carnivals, and culminating carnival seasons through much of Spain), forging what Madelena Gonzalez characterizes as a "rogue aesthetic" that seeks to "rewrite radical politics as high art" (10, 20). Indeed Braschi's trilogy culminates with a fantastic end to the so-called American Century and a send-up of Western literary canonicity, running the gamut of poetry, prose, drama, film, philosophy, in modes by turns classical, absurd, and kitschy. The as yet unpublished French afterword to *United States of Banana*, also by Gonzalez, uses Julia Kristeva's observation of "exaggerated sophistication" of the outsider's words relying on "naked rhetorical force" to produce extravagant baroque tendencies, characterizing Braschi's style for its "overloaded artifice, exaggerated effects and a certain grandiloquence" (paragraph 11). Cristina Garrigós reads *United States of Banana* as "'The Waste Land' of the 21st century," though there is a big difference between Eliot's lament and Braschi's irreverence; and Braschi's multiple allusions open up the many linguistic and cultural fissures in such foundational civilizational thinking, rather than conservatively shoring them up (paragraph 2). That Eliot aimed to be as much or more an English poet than an American one and is formally recognized as both fits the tensions inherent in Braschi's many allusions, in terms of their linguistic, cultural, and national crosscurrents. *Banana*'s opening epigram by Rubén Darío, Nicaragua's preeminent *modernista*, also echoes his overt indebtedness to French literature. The bilingual performance in *Yo-Yo Boing!* borders on obnoxious defamiliarization in a Gertrude Stein vein, but equally important would be Stein's extended expat Paris circles as well as, of course, her sexuality.

Yo-Yo Boing! unfolds in three sections, suggesting filmic techniques, as critic Laura R. Loustau notes, with the section titles "Close-Up," "Blow-Up" and "Black-Out." But these also refer to films that share affinities with these canonical literary tensions, linguistic patrimonies, and cross-cultural productions.[6] A close-up is a type of shot that frames the subject tightly, and indeed in this first section we get up close and personal with Giannina as a character. But *Close-Up* is also a 1990 Iranian film masterpiece, referred to as docufiction, by director Abbas Kiarostami who was also a poet, painter, graphic artist, and a part of the Iranian New Wave cinema known for its poetic dialogues and allegorical philosophical and political subjects. The film is a favorite at New York City art film houses such as Film Forum. Blow-ups enlarge photographs, and the second section famously alludes to Michelangelo Antonioni's tour de force film *Blow-Up* (1966), which is considered a "mod masterpiece," the Italian director's first English-language film inspired by Julio Cortázar's short story "Las babas del diablo" (1959) ("The Devil's Drool"), as noted by Debra A. Castillo (174) and María M. Carrión (185). "Black-Out" suggests staging in a theater, and indeed *United States of Banana* also picks up from here more in terms of genre.

Braschi's trilogy in *United States of Banana* gives way to drama and to a more radical stance on Puerto Rico's colonial condition, with *Yo-Yo Boing!* being read by some critics as being more status-quo oriented (Torres-Padilla). The experimental theatrics of Braschi's Hamlet might owe more to "Hamletmachine," by Heiner Muller of East Germany, where it was at times banned. "Hamletmachine" was denounced in the 1970s and was produced with a full-length version of Shakespeare's *Hamlet* in Berlin in 1990, in what Muller called "a national requiem." Or its shockingly violent 2000 New York City production by the Argentine theater company El Periferico de Objetos, whose Spanish-language production *Maquina Hamlet* (with English supertitles) at the Harvey Theater caused some patrons to walk out (a softer version was produced in New York by Robert Wilson in 1986). *La vida es sueño* was also adapted in 1975–1978 into a three-act opera *Life Is a Dream*, by American composer and academic Lewis Spratlan, which won the Pulitzer Prize in music in 2000 when it was partially produced. It was not performed completely until 2010 in Santa Fe. So it follows that an experimental work such as *Banana* would be adapted to the stage in New York (by Colombian director Juan Pablo Felix in 2015) and inspire a graphic novel in Sweden (by Joakim Lindengren in 2017). The implied frisson of such translations, adaptations, and performances—again temporal, linguistic, canonical, national, and global—reverberates beyond Spanish-English bilingualism.

Braschi deploys English in *United States of Banana* to interrogate how canonicity corresponds with Spanish-English officializing discourses in national, hemispheric, and global terms, in chapters such as "Foreign Speaking English," "Tongue Machine," and "Language of Mass Destruction," from her vantage point as a native Spanish speaker unhinging the imperial ideology of such correspondences. These epic tensions recall a passage from a Braschi reading/performance of *Yo-Yo Boing!* at the Seventh Annual International Caribbean Women Writers and Scholars Conference held in Mayagüez, Puerto Rico, in April 2000, and often cited, which switches back and forth from English to Spanish but invokes officializing linguistic tensions beyond these language traditions and their respective canon building. In Braschi's reading/performance, her switching to Spanish, back to English, and back again to Spanish received crescendo treatment with the line "El muro de Berlín fue derribado. Why can't I do the same." Bilingual audience, readers, and perhaps bicultural subjects roll right along, for Braschi does not italicize, much less translate the switch. This follows with the ultimate translation metaphor of the tower of Babel, invoked from New York as its maximum expression.

> —If I respected languages like you do, I wouldn't write at all. El muro de Berlín fue derribado. Why can't I do the same. Desde la torre de Babel, las lenguas han sido siempre una forma de divorciarnos del resto de la humanidad. Poetry must find ways of breaking distance. I'm not reducing my audience. On the contrary, I'm going to have a bigger audience with the common markets—in Europe—in America.
>
> And besides, all languages are dialects that are made to break new grounds. I feel like Dante, Petrarca and Boccaccio, and I even feel like Garcilaso forging a new language. Saludo al nuevo siglo, el siglo del nuevo lenguaje de América, y le digo adíos a la retórica separatista y a los atavismos. (*YYB* 142–43)

By invoking Dante, Petrarch, and Boccaccio, Braschi alludes to the official legitimizing processes of nation-states, turning to other European languages not included in Mignolo's formulation, in recalling the way architects of Italy marshaled the language of Petrarch and Dante to establish an official language excluding other regional dialects. And as the critic Carrión notes, *El imperio de los sueños* also makes explicit this theme: "The idea of an only tongue ruling over a considerable number of different nations and peoples is fundamentally questioned in one of the most exaggerated instances of textual buffoonery." Carrión cites Braschi here: "El mundo es un gran sistema gramatical. Mariquita vuelve a subrayar esta frase. 'The world is a great grammatical system. Mariquita underlines this phrase'" (172).

In resignifying the US empire and the American dream from the perspective of migrant New York City at the end of the century, starting with *El imperio de los sueños*, *Banana* picks up from where *Yo-Yo Boing!* leaves off to get the job done, as Zarathustra accusingly points out in the "Burial of the Sardine" chapter: "You think you are a visionary just for saying: I am going to bury the 20th century. In 1998 you said it—and here we are in 2006—and you are still trying to bury the body" (*USB* 76). Indeed, the drama of the fall of the Berlin Wall as "end of history" thesis is checked by 9/11. As Braschi experiences the event firsthand, 9/11 portends the end not just of the twentieth century but of the American Century, the end of the United States as global hegemon and colossus of the North. The death and destruction of 9/11 leads to the funeral procession and burial of the sardine as a carnivalesque rite, rooted in the Hispanophone Caribbean, to bring these global/local tensions home. In the ultimate trans-American gesture, Segismundo as Puerto Rican political prisoner symbolically conquers "feardom" or fear of freedom (*USB* 17), Puerto Rico is liberated and US passports are awarded to all Latin Americans, prophesizing a conceptual anti-wall for *nuestra América* in productive contemporary terms, releasing the historical tensions between the hemisphere's two most powerful colonial languages, which Gloria Anzaldüa characterized as "linguistic terrorism" (38). Rather than reconcile these tensions, Braschi's trilogy supersedes and transforms them as perhaps only daring conceptual art can start to do.

Notes

1. I use the term "trans-American" in the same sense as José David Saldívar in *Trans-Americanity*. Also see his earlier work, *Border Matters*.

2. Assessing all three works together as a trilogy produces important insights. See the arresting gender and sexuality implications of Braschi's poetic vision of New York City in Arnaldo Cruz Malavé, "Under the Skirt of Liberty."

3. In applying the term "translingual" to Braschi's trilogy, I am interested in "the ways in which ideas operate through translingual practice" (Liu 20). Liu's conceptualization of translingual mediations, however, distinguishes East–West from North–South relations because European languages are particularly incommensurable with distinct language systems and global historical relationships as represented by such languages as Arabic and Chinese. Liu posits that the linguistic transactions between East and West are fraught with "unidirectional" language influence as opposed to mutual influence, which means that one language is more affected or changed by contact and influence than the other.

4. I use the term "post-national" to interrogate particular nation-state projects, influenced mainly by Charles V. Carnegie's *Postnationalism Prefigured* and Shalini Puri's *The Caribbean Postcolonial*.

5. For example, on discourses of the *jíbaro* (or peasant) of Puerto Rico's interior, see Francisco A. Scarano's "The *Jíbaro* Mascarade."

6. By "cross-cultural" I am referring to the use of the term by the Caribbean novelist and philosopher Wilson Harris. His theories of the cross-cultural imagination eschew umbrella discourses for deeper mutual engagements that are profoundly interactive. In *Womb of Space*. Harris defines the cross-cultural imagination in cross-national and inter-regional terms and locates counter-hegemonic fissures in the writer's unconscious and intuitive cultural imagination. However, the cross-cultural imagination also intuits mutual exchanges or "gifts" that can barely be discerned on the threshold of cross-cultural contact. He also touches on this in his essay "Creoleness."

Works Cited

Anzaldúa, Gloria. *Borderlands/La Frontera*. Aunt Lute Books, 1987.

Aparicio, Frances. "On Subversive Signifiers: Tropicalizing Language in the United States." *Tropicalizations: Transcultural Representations of Latinidad*, edited by Frances Aparicio and Susana Chávez-Silverman, UP of New England, 1997, pp. 194–212.

Aparicio, Frances. "Tato Laviera y Alurista: Hacia una Poetica Bilingue." *Centro de Estudios Puertoriqueños Bulletin*, vol. 7, no. 13, 1988, pp. 86–96.

Braham, Persephone. "*Yo-Yo Boing!* Review." *Latin American Literature and Arts Review: New Writing and Arts in the Americas*, vol. 33, no. 60, 2000, pp. 83–93.

Braschi, Giannina. *Estados Unidos de Banana*. Translated by Manuel Broncano, AmazonCrossing, 2016.

Braschi, Giannina. *El imperio de los sueños*. 1999. Editorial de la Universidad de Puerto Rico, 1st ed. Editorial Anthropos, 1988.

Braschi, Giannina. *United States of Banana*. AmazonCrossing, 2011.

Braschi, Giannina. *Yo-Yo Boing!* Latin American Review Press, 1998.

Bruce-Novoa, Juan. "Spanish-Language Loyalty and Literature." *Retrospace: Collected Essays on Chicano Literature Theory and History*. Arte Publico, 1990, pp. 41–51.

Bruce-Novoa, Juan. "Surviving Our Decade." *Retrospace: Collected Essays on Chicano Literature Theory and History*. Arte Publico, 1990, pp. 125–31.

Carnegie, Charles V. *Postnationalism Prefigured: Caribbean Borderlands*. Rutgers UP, 2002.

Carrión, María M. "Geographies, (M)Other Tongues and the Role of Translation in Giannina Braschi's *El imperio de los sueños*." *Studies in Twentieth Century Literature*, vol. 20, no. 1, Winter 1996, pp. 167–91.

Castillo, Debra A. *Redreaming America: Toward a Bilingual American Culture*. State U of New York P, 2005.

Cruz Malavé, Arnaldo. "'Under the Skirt of Liberty': Giannina Braschi Rewrites Empire." *American Quarterly*, vol. 66, no. 3, 2014, pp. 801–18.

Dávila, Arlene M. *Sponsored Identities: Cultural Politics in Puerto Rico*. Temple UP, 1997.

Díaz, Junot. *The Brief Wondrous Life of Oscar Wao*. Riverhead/Penguin, 2007.

Díaz Quiñones, Arcadio. *El Arte de Bregar: Ensayos*. Ediciones Callejón, 2000.

Duany, Jorge. *The Puerto Rican Nation on the Move: Identities on the Island and in the United States*. U of North Carolina P, 2002.

Eliot, T. S. "The Love Song of J. Alfred Prufrock." 1917. *The Norton Anthology of American Literature*, 9th ed., edited by Robert S. Levine et al., Norton, 2017, vol. D, p. 355.

Flores, Juan. *The Diaspora Strikes Back*. Routledge, 2009.

Flores, Juan. *From Bomba to Hip-Hop: Puerto Rican Culture and Latino Identity*. Columbia UP, 2000.

Flores, Juan. *Insularismo e ideologia burguesa*. Ediciones Huracán, 1979.

Flores, Juan, and George Yúdice. "Living Borders/*Buscando América*: Languages of Latino Self-Formation." *Latinos in Education: A Critical Reader*, edited by Antonia Darder, Rodolfo D. Torres, and Henry Gutiérrez, Routledge, 1997, pp. 174–200.

Garrigos, Cristina. "Giannina Braschi. United States of Banana." *Evergreen*. Evergreen Book Review no. 128, June 2012.

Gonzalez, Madelena. "*United States of Banana* (2011), *Elizabeth Costello* (2003), and *Fury* (2001): Portrait of the Writer as 'Bad Subject' of Globalisation." *Études Britanniques Contemporaines, Revue de la Société d'Études Anglaises Contemporaines*, vol. 46, 2014.

Grosfoguel, Ramón, Frances Negrón-Muntaner, and Chloé S. Georas. "Beyond Nationalist and Colonialist Discourses: The Jaiba Politics of the Puerto Rican Ethno-Nation."

Puerto Rican Jam: Rethinking Colonialism and Nationalism. U of Minnesota P, 1997, pp. 1–38.

Harris, Wilson. "Creoleness: The Crossroads of a Civilization?" *Selected Essays of Wilson Harris: The Unfinished Genesis of the Imagination*, Routledge, 1999, pp. 237–47.

Harris, Wilson. *The Womb of Space: The Cross-Cultural Imagination*. Greenwood, 1983.

Hobsbawm, E. J. *Nations and Nationalism since 1780: Programme, Myth, Reality*. Cambridge UP, 1990.

Janer, Zilkia. *Puerto Rican Nation-Building Literature: Impossible Romance*. U of Florida P, 2005.

Liu, Lydia H. *Translingual Practice: Literature, National Culture, and Translated Modernity—China, 1900–1937*. Stanford UP, 1995.

Loustau, Laura R. "Conciencia Nómada y Traslados Geo-Literarios: *El Imperio de los sueños* de Giannina Braschi." *Cuerpos Errantes: Literatura Latina y Latinoamericana en Estados Unidos*. Beatriz Viterbo Editora, 2002, pp. 117–56.

Mignolo, Walter. *Local Histories/Global Designs: Coloniality, Subaltern Knowledges, and Border Thinking*. Princeton UP, 2000.

Moreno, Marisel C. *Family Matters: Puerto Rican Women Authors on the Island and the Mainland*. U of Virginia P, 2012.

Nien-Ming Ch'ien, Evelyn. *Weird English*. Harvard UP, 2005.

Pietri, Pedro. *The Masses Are Asses/Las massas son crasas*. Translated by Alfredo Matilla Rivas, Instituto de Cultura Puertorriqueña, 1997.

Puri, Shalini. *The Caribbean Postcolonial: Social Equality, Post-Nationalism, and Cultural Hybridity*. Palgrave, 2004.

Saldívar, José David. *Border Matters: Remapping American Cultural Studies*. U of California P, 1997.

Saldívar, José David. *Trans-Americanity: Subaltern Modernities, Global Coloniality, and the Cultures of Greater Mexico*. Duke UP, 2012.

Sánchez González, Lisa. *Boricua Literature: A Literary History of the Puerto Rican Diaspora*. New York UP, 2001.

Santiago-Valles, Kelvin A. *"Subject People" and Colonial Discourses: Economic Transformation and Social Disorder in Puerto Rico, 1898–1947*. State U of New York P, 1994.

Scarano, Francisco A. "The *Jíbaro* Mascarade and the Subaltern Politics of Creole Identity Formation in Puerto Rico, 1745–1823." *American Historical Review*, vol. 101, no. 5, 1996, pp. 1398–431.

Sommer, Doris, and Alexandra Vega-Merino. "Either/And." *Yo-Yo Boing!* Latin American Literary Review Press, 1998, pp. 11–18.

Soto-Crespo, Ramón. *Mainland Passage: The Cultural Anomaly of Puerto Rico*. U of Minnesota P, 2009.

Stanchich, Maritza. "'Borinkee' in Hawai'i: Rodney Morales Rides the Diaspora Wave to Trans-regional Imperial Struggle." *Writing Off the Hyphen: New Perspectives on the Literature of the Puerto Rican Diaspora*, edited by Carmen Haydée Rivera and José L. Torres-Padilla, U of Washington P, 2008, pp. 201–20.

Torres, Lourdes. "In the Contact Zone: Code-Switching Strategies by Latino/a Writers." *MELUS*, vol. 32, no. 1, 2007, pp. 75–96.

Torres-Padilla, Jose L. "When Hybridity Doesn't Resist: Giannina Braschi's *Yo-Yo Boing!*" *Complicating Constructions: Race, Ethnicity and Hybridity in American Texts*, edited by David S. Goldstein, U of Washington P, 2007, pp. 290–307.

II

Persuasive Art of Dramatic Voices

6

Giannina and Braschi

A Polyphony of Voices

Cristina Garrigós

Despite fruitless attempts by literary critics in the 1960s to detach authors from their works or to kill the author, to paraphrase Roland Barthes, to speak about Giannina Braschi's writing is to speak about the author. Even if Braschi's work is not entirely autobiographical, there are undoubtedly elements that make it difficult for us to analyze her texts without referring to the person who holds the pen. For starters, she names herself as a character who engages in conversation with numerous alter egos. Braschi's literature and life are indissolubly enmeshed, and yet there is a profound difference between the person and the literary figure(s). As Borges wrote in his famous prose-poem "Borges and I":

> I live, I let myself live, so that Borges can spin out his literature, and that literature justifies me. It is not difficult to admit that he has managed to write a few worthwhile pages, but those pages cannot save me, perhaps because what is good really belongs to no one, not even to the other one, but to language and tradition. In any event, I am destined to become lost once and for all, and only some moment of myself will survive in the other one. . . . And so, my life is a fugue, an escape, and I lose everything, and everything is left to oblivion or to the other one.
>
> I don't know which one of us is writing this page. (186)[1]

Like Borges, Braschi writes and Giannina performs, or as the author put it in an interview published in *Voces de América*: "A poet and actress, Giannina brings words to life, assumes the roles of characters, creates identities" (Garrigós, "Chicken" 148). In *Empire of Dreams*, the character Giannina plays the roles of Mariquita Samper, Berta Singerman, and Uriberto Eisensweig, and "they are all clowns, malleable like dough, indefinable and indistinguishable, multiple and fragmentary" (148). In *Yo-Yo Boing!* the voices form an anonymous chorus, "an idea I took from T. S. Eliot, taking poetry out of the context of poetry, bringing poetry back to the theater, to dramatic voices" (150). In *United States of Banana*, Giannina joins Hamlet and Zarathustra to free Segismundo, who is locked away inside the Statue of Liberty. The author explains the pairing of princes:

> Because if Segismundo thinks, Hamlet becomes restless. Hamlet and Segismundo are princes of Denmark and Poland, respectively, yet their native languages are English and Spanish. When I read them, I read them in exile, the exile of their native languages, and this distance from the native makes me love what is foreign. This is the dichotomy felt by Latinos living in the United States. Socrates preferred to die in his native land than to live in exile. I prefer to live and not feel comfortable in any land or in any language. I wonder why I was selected to integrate and disintegrate languages in exile, but I also wonder why the selected are never the most prepared. And why they were chosen when they never asked to be selected. (Garrigós, "Chicken" 153)

Giannina is impatient, restlessly active; Braschi intuitive, reflective. Thirty years have elapsed since her first major work and we only have two more works to date, which shows that the author is not in a hurry and prefers to meticulously craft each word, each sentence, while supervising the translations that have been done of her work: into English, in the case of *Empire of Dreams*, into Spanish in the case of *United States of Banana*. Neither translation is her own, even though she is bilingual. Self-translation is an exercise carried out by her compatriots, as in the case of her late friend Rosario Ferré, yet it is a task Braschi has never sought to tackle. The shift from the first work in Spanish, *Empire of Dreams* (1988), to a second that alternates between Spanish and English in a dialectical game that some critics have called Spanglish and others code-switching, *Yo-Yo Boing!* (1998), and to a third written entirely in English, *United States of Banana* (2011), represents "the journey of the immigrant"—namely, the journey taken by those who arrive without knowing the language of the host country and who, little by little, begin mixing the two until they become integrated.[2] Braschi is not a foreigner to the English language, although Spanish was the dominant language of her childhood. She is also not an exile, although we could consider her experience comparable to those of other writers who had to leave their countries of origin in order to write about them, as was the case with T. S. Eliot, Ezra Pound, James Joyce, and Samuel Beckett. It is also true that, despite having lived on the mainland for several decades, Braschi continues to write about the island and its relationship with the United States.

Julio Ortega dedicated an issue of the journal *Ínsula* to the Hispanic literatures of the United States, which included an article dealing specifically with Ferré and Braschi: "Bilingües, biculturales y posmodernas: Rosario Ferré y Giannina Braschi" (Garrigós "Bilingües").[3] These writers are presented as an example of experimental literature from both an aesthetic and a linguistic vantage point, the result of the dynamic exchanges between two cultures, the Anglo-Saxon and the Hispanic. As Braschi put it in an interview: "Yes, I am a hybrid. There are Spanish poets that I know by heart: I have Quevedo, I have Juan Ramón, I have García Lorca, Machado, Bécquer. I arrived in New York grounded in the poetry of García Lorca and Juan Ramón Jiménez. I also had the poetry of Eliot, Joyce, and Beckett" (Garrigós, "Chicken" 150). In addition, we find that many other canonical writers—including Shakespeare, Cervantes, Dante, Petrarch, Neruda, Vallejo, Rubén Darío, Heiner Müller, and Gertrude Stein—mold the personality of the Braschian character and alter ego Giannina, and their voices and names resonate throughout the text, thereby establishing a dialogue between them as channeled through Braschi.

Braschi's literary education, Puerto Rican heritage, and life spent navigating between English and Spanish have contributed to her hybrid personality, which in turn resonates in her work and in her alter ego. Bakhtin defined hybridization in *The Dialogic Imagination* as "the mixture of two social languages within the limits of a single utterance . . . an encounter between two different linguistic consciousnesses, separated from one another by epoch, social differentiation or by some other factor" (358). This hybridization, which is unconscious in culture because it is an intrinsic characteristic in the evolution of all languages, can be intentional or artistically orchestrated (361). Dialogism results from the tension between the inevitable desire for change, implicit in every culture, and the resistance to change.

As Christopher Falzon argues, dialogue is an alternative to the essentialist attitude that sees fragmentation as one of the main concerns of postmodernity. The exchange of ideas through language provides a way to reach, if not total and systematic integration or resolution of conflicts, at least a progression toward valid alternatives that can generate change. It is in this sense that we can consider Braschi's work dialogical—a definition that would also extend to her characters and her own personality as an author. If Braschi is an author of many readings, so are her texts.

We can say that her entire work is a choral exercise in which a dialogue is developed between literature and reality, between the author and other authors, between the author and her characters, and between the characters themselves.

For Braschi, dialogue is enriching, whether it be between a couple of people, nations, or languages. As she states: "I am very interested in couples; I find them quite wonderful. Of course, because of the dialogues. Do you know what inspires dialogue, the confrontation with another human being? It spawns so many ideas, it airs out what you have inside. I find this very interesting. I wish I could talk more with people because this brings out so many things from within, and any exchange gives you something. And I'm also interested in the possibility of non-dialogue. . . . A dialogue of opposites, that's what my work is about" (Garrigós, "Chicken" 155). The notion of dialogue is essential for understanding Braschi's artistic and dynamic concepts. However, this exchange does not need to be logical: "I don't have to answer what you ask me. By asking, what you do is incite my thoughts. And what I have to do is let the thoughts fly" (155). Here, Braschi reacts with defiance when confronted with established parameters that attempt to classify thoughts in any set logical order. Faced with this imposition, she creates a shock dynamic that frustrates the teleological expectations of readers. Hence, the title of her novel *Yo-Yo Boing!* "My title is the sound of the two 'yo's' [self, ego, I] in shock. It is a book of exclamations and interjections" (160).

Braschi has remarked that she prefers not to belong to any land or language. In effect, she lives in an interzone, far removed from Puerto Rico but not entirely assimilated into the United States. She lives in New York, a place of encounters and conflict, of rejection and integration, a culturally contaminated cosmopolitan city, as dramatized in her work by public processions such as the invasion of shepherds and the pageants for "The Queen of Beauty, Charm, and Coquetry" and "The Queen of Solitude," as discussed by a myriad of scholars, including Jerónimo Arellano, Emilie Bergmann, María M. Carrión, Arnaldo Cruz-Malavé, Carmen Haydée Rivera, Laura Loustou, and Diane E. Marting, among others. Thus, the will not to belong, the desire to live in dialogic crossroads between truth and lies, that become palpable in *Empire of Dreams*: "How many lies are told in the name of literature! I was born in San Juan, Puerto Rico. I grew up near the waves of the sea. They showed me that lies are true. And that I should come and go as I please. I'm constantly moving from place to place, like ships, or waves" (*ED* 182). This rootlessness—this constant shifting from place to place—causes the author to unfold into multiple personalities, like the ventriloquist's puppets she collects and which spring to life in her hands, yet which she acknowledges reside in some realm between dependence and independence, clearly as her own creations. There is always some confusion between authorial person and character, between fiction and reality, in Braschi's universe: "I'm sorry to be simultaneously what I write. The narrator is also a product of my imagination. What I write seems unreal, but it's true. I want to lie, but I don't" (*ED* 183).

In the "Postfacio" to *El imperio de los sueños* (1988), Francisco José Ramos identified three distinct lines of poetic autobiography in which the act of poetizing becomes the protagonist of the fiction: the dissolution of the author's self, the reappearance of that integrated self through a new form of anonymity, and the continuous fabrication and transformation of a language that enables a rupture with subjectivist illusion and that maintains the confabulating coherence of the utterance (240). In Braschi's case, this poetics would transform the experience of writing into a protagonist: "Braschi's work is an insistent poetic reflection on the madness of writing, on poetic mania. The 'I' [or 'yo'] that speaks represents the subjectivity of the writer. However, this subjectivity has become completely personified in the utterance of writing: aesthetic possession is an abduction, a theft, a dissipation of subjectivity. To such a degree that the 'I' that appears in the writing is not 'fictional' or 'real,' but credible: it is the result or the perspectivist effect of the confabulating invention" (Ramos, 246–47). Between thought and utterance, a dynamic is formulated in which the author becomes transfigured in her work. She transmutes into various characters, fusing with one or the other through language, as reality and fiction become intertwined in a postmodernist narrative experience that seeks to break the ontological boundaries between these traditionally divided spaces. The intrusion of the author in the text, the appeals to the reader's attention, the irony, and the metafiction are techniques associated with the postmodern. To the label of postmodern writer, Braschi responds:

> Postmodernism is a lizard whose tail has been cut off, yet its tail keeps dancing [laughs]. That is postmodernism for me. Or like a chicken, a chicken whose head has been cut off, yet it still keeps walking without any idea of where it's going. That is the poetry of postmodernism, which doesn't know where it's going, yet it still keeps walking. I know where I'm going. But there's something about not knowing, about ambling decapitated, dismembered. There is something dismembered in postmodernism. . . . If in the Renaissance we had the integration of the human being, the discovery of humanity, the return to our roots, I believe that globalization presupposes the disintegration of the human being, as memory, as history. (Garrigós, "Chicken" 151)

Braschi's work is dismembered and fragmented, but it bears constant connections between one text and another. She is an epic writer, and each of her books is a dramatic act that begins where the last book ends. For example, *Empire of Dreams* closes with a "Requiem for Solitude," in which Braschi proclaims the independence of her work and her right to self-determination: "My handwriting adapts itself to each one of my books. Let them dance. Or let them show the power of their movement. Only then will you notice the flash of their explosion. Soon they'll stop singing. And then they'll die. Like the waves of the sea. And they'll rise again" (*ED* 219–20). Books die when they're closed, and they come back to life each time a reader opens them again.

Braschi's next work is *Yo-Yo Boing!* and dramatic dialogue predominates, as in a play. Sections are included in verse, thereby mixing text genres, styles, and languages: "I want more Spanish. Mixing languages like this is typical of your social class. It's your hang-up, not mine. You discuss philosophical issues in English and leave your feelings in Spanish, reinforcing Hispanic stereotypes—all sex like Almodóvar, all tango—and you leave all the cerebral, intellectual speculations to the Anglo-Saxon tongue. How insulting to Hispanidad!" (*YYB* 181). In *Permissible Narratives,* Christopher González observes, "By seeing the potential of audience to expand Latino/a literary form rather than constrain it, Braschi has set a new standard for how code-switching, bilingualism, and narrative discourse can be used to open up new avenues of expression not only in Latino/a literature but in other literatures of the United States as well (106)". González notes that her "equal prowess with both English and Spanish becomes a crucial aspect of the novel" (106). This to-and-fro between two languages, two cultures, and between reality and fiction are referred to as "Schizo-realism" (*YYB* 182). This term also refers to the split personality of the author, who is projected into the work and who engages in dialogue with herself and with other people, who may be external to the text—such as the publisher "Jonathan" (Brent), the translator "Tess" (O'Dwyer), the Hollywood music editor "Suzana" (Peric) in whose home the party scenes take place, the filmmakers Martin Scorcese and Woody Allen, and so on. The final section of the novel, "Black-Out," employs a film technique of fading out the narrative and presenting Giannina in the foreground in a dialogue with the self: "Lazy, fickle, and rash—eager, tired, and brash—spiteful, truthful, and resentful—or thoughtful like an autumn tree that turns green in the middle of spring—sprouting clichés that sound like words I've mixed with red wine where the vines of my desires grow thick—and the grapes inspire me to think again, and I look in one of the mirrors and see someone else looking back at me" (*YYB* 226). Braschi is reflected in Giannina, who is looking at herself in the mirror, seeking to integrate and reconcile the two and wishing to transcend the limits of language. In the Spanish version, much of the text appears as a run-on sentence, without periods, or interjections, which might hinder the flow of thoughts. The periods and commas that came to life in *Empire of Dreams* disappear, leaving the author alone with her other self. Thus, language is reduced to sound, devoid of relationships. In her dialogic monologue, Giannina seeks to strip her words open and penetrate to the very core of language, to her soul, yet she is aware that this is an impossible task. The words come alive as they relate, like Giannina, to the other characters, and thus to the work and the author herself. Nothing can exist in an absolute vacuum. Only death.

At the end of the novel, Giannina meets up with Zarathustra and Hamlet, who are on their way to bury the twentieth century. The narrator wants to enter the new millennium with a new language and a fresh attitude. As she states earlier: "We have to start tearing down the walls between our two Americas. And we—you and I—we have to be the spokesmen because we're bilingual" (*YYB* 187–88). Ultimately, we cannot bury the past, nor does Braschi really want to. The past will continually resurface, like the living dead, like a soul that has been buried alive.

This reference to being buried alive also appears in *United States of Banana*, specifically in the character of Segismundo. In this novel a conversation is established between politics, literature, and philosophy, which serves to echo the condition of subalternity, invisibility, and silence of Puerto Rico—and of Latinos, in general. Braschi expresses a wish to free Puerto Rico and Latinos through her writing, and this task is given to Giannina, with the help of Hamlet and Zarathustra. This is obviously an ambitious project, one that the author has been developing since the beginning of her career. The objective is not only to seek political freedom, independence, but to achieve an ontological liberation, which can only occur—as the author suggests—by tearing down walls and engaging in constant dialogue.

The end of *United States of Banana* is composed of philosophical dialogues largely inspired by Plato's *Symposium*. Socratic dialogue provides Giannina with a platform for engaging with other literary characters (Hamlet, Gertrude, Zarathustra, Segismundo, Basilio), other writers (Rubén Darío, Pablo Neruda, Antonin Artaud), countries (Puerto Rico, Cuba, Spain, England, China, United States of Banana), philosophers and sages (Socrates, Parmenides, Protagoras, Diotima of Mantineia, Nietzsche), as well as things and creatures (the Statue of Liberty, the Cockroach, Oliver the Exterminator), to reflect on global politics, liberty, the meaning of love, writing, life—in short, all the issues of concern to Braschi. In *Novelization in Decolonization*, Peter Hitchcock notes that

Braschi's characters "debate with humor, irony and anger the tense metrics of seeing freedom. Of course, the text is polemical and…its polyphonies are not simply democratic or equal under the sign of global inequities (189)." In *Precarious Crossings*, Alexandra Perisic theorizes that the chorus of voices represents "a multitude of immigrants, colonized people, and political prisoners. Yet, it is also a literary multitude . . . reflecting on possible dialogues between literary, philosophical, and political multitudes" (166).

One of the main events in *United States of Banana* is the wedding of the century, symbolizing the union between Hamlet and Segismundo in an act of integration that aims to unite the Anglo and Latin cultures, Calderón de la Barca and Shakespeare, and the peoples of North and South America, Spain and the United Kingdom. This metaphoric matrimony takes place in the Statue of Liberty who welcomes everyone under her skirt. Instead of the tower, a phallic symbol in *Life Is a Dream* that represents power of Basil over Segismundo (and of Segismundo himself who, after being triumphant in the rebellion against his father, proceeds to imprison the soldier who freed him), in Braschi's novel the symbol of power and sexuality is situated within the statue that stands for both imprisonment and liberation. It is here that a transference of genders and identities takes place: Hamlet, Zarathustra, and Giannina all act as midwives in the birthing of Segismundo, the statue's son and lover, who has impregnated her by seeking a way out. Calderón's tower, associated with patriarchal empowerment (in Lacanian terms, representing the phallus, negation, and the name of the father: the NON/*nom du père*) is replaced by the uterus of the mother. Sexuality, like literary genres, is fluid in Braschi's novel, melting like the seasons (*USB* 163), fomenting a constant dialogue that joins the brain and the heart. Hamlet is a frustrated poet, trapped by his thoughts, unable to act in his own existential paralysis. Zarathustra, also like Hamlet, lives in his thoughts, yet he speaks. Giannina "writes to feel good" (*USB* 144) and serves as the mediator between thought and speech.

The absence of dialogue between father and son, which structures the works of both Calderón and Shakespeare, is replaced in Braschi's work by a dialogue with the *madre patria* ("motherland," literally "mother/fatherland"). The very concept of "madre patria" is a union of opposites, given that the word *patria* derives from the Latin *pater* (father). *Madre patria* implies a hybrid melding of motherhood and fatherhood, power, and submission. Unlike Spain, which is presented as an oppressive stepmother, the new state, the *United States of Banana*, is a sexually fluid figure: a father figure in the body of a mother. Liberation consists of breaking away from the oppression of the father (United States) and the mother (Spain), in order to find dialogue and a mestizo space that embraces contradictions.

United States of Banana ends with a dialogue between Giannina and Hasib, a taxi driver. Giannina's closing words are in the form of a dialogic monologue with herself, in which she invokes Diotima's help in preventing the doors from being closed to the multiple beings who are knocking, the poets, philosophers, and lovers (*USB* 302). As at the end of Plato's *Symposium*, the doors open to the marginalized masses, in an exercise of unconditional hospitality and absolute acceptance of the other.

If you were to ask me how Braschi's next work might begin, my conjecture would be with someone knocking on Giannina's door. Whether it will open or not and who will be there knocking are questions that the reader will find out if that time comes. There's an old Spanish joke that goes:

> "Knock-knock."
> "Who's there?"
> "Us."

The door opens and there they are. The people knocking may be the many voices that populate Braschi's universe—Giannina and so many more, a thronging crowd, a single individual, but with many heads.

Notes

1. Translated by David Auerbach

2. The quotation is from a conversation with the author in Berlin in the summer of 2014 (notes in my possession).

3. The title of the journal's special edition is "La otra orilla del español; Las literaturas hispánicas de los Estados Unidos" (2002).

Works Cited

Arellano, Jerónimo. *Magical Realism and the History of Emotions in Latin America*. Bucknell UP, 2015.

Bakhtin, Mikhail. *The Dialogical Imagination: Four Essays by M. M. Bakhtin*. 1975, edited by Michael Holquist, translated by Caryl Emerson and Michael Holquist, U of Texas P, 1990.

Barthes, Roland. "La muerte de un autor." 1967. *El susurro del lenguaje. Más allá de la palabra y la escritura*. Paidós, 1987, pp. 65–72.

Bergmann, Emilie L., and Edward H. Friedman. "Imitation and Adaptation: A Meeting of Minds." *Bulletin of Spanish Studies* 93, no. 7–8, 2016, pp. 1445–67.

Borges, Jorge Luis. "Borges y yo." *El hacedor. Obras Completas*, vol. 2. Emecé, 1989.

Braschi, Giannina. *Empire of Dreams*. Translated by Tess O'Dwyer, Yale UP, 1994.

Braschi, Giannina. *El imperio de los sueños*. Anthropos, 1988.

Braschi, Giannina. *United States of Banana*. AmazonCrossing, 2011.

Braschi, Giannina. *Yo-Yo Boing!* Latin American Literary Review, 1998.

Carrión, María M. "Geography, (M)Other Tongues and the Role of Translation in Giannina Braschi's *El imperio de los sueños*." *Studies in Twentieth Century Literature*, vol. 20, 1996, pp. 167–92.

Cruz-Malavé, Arnaldo Manuel. "'Under the Skirt of Liberty': Giannina Braschi Rewrites Empire." *American Quarterly*, vol. 66, no. 3, 2014, pp. 801–18.

Falzon, Christopher. "Dialogue and the Postmodern." *Foucault and Social Dialogue: Beyond Fragmentation*. Routledge, 1998.

Garrigós, Cristina. "Bilingües, biculturales y posmodernas: Rosario Ferré y Giannina Braschi." *Ínsula*, no. 667–68, 2002, pp. 16–18.

Garrigós, Cristina. "Chicken with the Head Off: Una conversación con Giannina Braschi." *Voices of America/Voces de America*, edited by Laura Alonso Gallo, Aduana Vieja, 2004, pp. 147–64.

González, Christopher. *Permissible Narratives: The Promise of Latino/a Literature*. The Ohio State UP, 2017.

Haydée Rivera, Carmen. "Embracing Alternate Discourses on Migration: Giannina Braschi's and Luisita López Torregrosa's Multi-dimensional Literary Schemes." *Revista Umbral*, vol. 8, 2017, pp. 6–20.

Hitchock, Peter. "Novelization in Decolonization, or Postcolonialism Reconsidered." *Other Globes, Past and Peripheral Imaginations of Globalization*. Palgrave Macmillan, 2020.

Loustau, Laura. *Cuerpos errantes: Literatura latina y latinoamericana en Estados Unidos*. Beatriz Viterbo Editora, 2002.

Loustau, Laura R. "Nomadismos lingüísticos y culturales en *Yo-Yo Boing!* de Giannina Braschi." *Revista Iberoamericana*, vol. 71, no. 211, 2005, pp. 437–48.

Marting, Diane E. "New/Nueva York in Giannina Braschi's 'Poetic Egg': Fragile Identity, Postmodernism, and Globalization." *Global South*, vol. 4, no. 1, 2010, pp. 167–82.

Perisic, Alexandra. *Precarious Crossings: Immigration, Neoliberalism, and the Atlantic*. The Ohio State UP, 2019.

Ramos, Francisco José. "Postfacio." *El imperio de los sueños*. Anthropos, 1988, pp. 231–53.

7

The Poetry of Giannina Braschi

Art and Magic in *Assault on Time*

Laura R. Loustau

It is above all by the imagination that we achieve perception and compassion and hope.

—***Ursula K. LeGuin***

Poetry impels us to endure the mystery; it beckons us to follow blindly into inclemency and faith. Faith in the other, without whom I do not exist, yet also with whom I can never be eternally. That is where the poem intercedes.

— ***Diana Bellessi***

"I want people to feel transformed after they have read me. I want them *to memorize* me because that is how I write. To be memorized. To be learned by ear. To be learned by heart," said Giannina Braschi in an interview on the transformative power of poetry (Rivera). *Asalto al tiempo* (*Assault on Time*), Braschi's first work of poetry, was originally published in 1981 and later became part 1 of the trilogy *El imperio de los sueños* (1988) translated into English by Tess O'Dwyer as *Empire of Dreams* (1994).[1] I am interested in identifying instances that unravel a transformational Braschian poetics that speaks to the author's desire for the reader (and the poet) to become transformed through the acts of reading and writing.

In "Breve tratado de la poeta artista" (Brief treatise of the poet-artist), a text that articulates the author's own vital and transformative philosophy, Braschi proposes the concept or figure of the poet-artist. The poet-artist has three beings within: the poet-child who feels, the poet-philosopher who thinks, and the poet-actor who transforms. In the framework of poet-artist, the repetition of the child coexists with the transgression of the philosopher and the metamorphoses of the actor (469). For Braschi, "the child poet is the one who discovers the magic and, above all, the surprise . . . s/he is the one who opens the Pandora's box" (472). In the first poem of *Assault on Time*, the poet-child opens a door to surprise and invites the reader to imagine an animated play space: "Behind the word is silence. Behind what sounds is the door. . . . But if I ring the bell, water jumps, and a river falls out of the water again. . . . And suddenly everything acquires movement. Two travelers meet and their shoes dance. And breeze and morning clash. And the seagull runs and the rabbit flies. And runs and runs, and the current ran. Behind what runs is life. Behind that silence is the door" (3). Like the world in María Elena Walsh's songs, this scene lures us in to a game of wonder and imagination.[2]

According to Puerto Rican philosopher Francisco José Ramos, Braschi's poetry "offers us a delicious opportunity to rethink words and embark upon a journey through the images seen with the eyes of a child."[3] This statement about the importance of seeing can be paralleled with the ideas of Gaston Bachelard, who argued that the real can be explained by the imaginary. For Bachelard this relationship consists not only of forming images but of transforming them with great agility: "imagination, more than reason, is a unifying force in the human soul" (190).

Braschi's treatise qualifies Lorca and Vallejo as the best examples of the poet-child in twentieth-century literature. Their fame, notes Braschi, "was not established through covert intrigues or literary contacts—what enabled them to triumph was authenticity . . . feeling . . . poetic nature . . . [and] the passions of the soul" ("Breve tratado" 474). Braschi sees in them that "poet-child" who condenses the ancient, what belongs to human nature, and reconfigures it to act as transformative agent (474). The influence of César Vallejo's poetry—particularly *The Black Heralds* and *Trilce*—on Braschi's work is palpable. As she stated in an interview: "Vallejo is a jack-in-the-box who performs the movement of my spirit. No matter how much you push him down into the box, the poet always bounces back to affirm his love for life."[4] It is interesting to consider how these canonical texts can be revisited and reappraised after reading Braschi's poetry and her brief treatise (Morris).[5]

In *Assault on Time*, the birth of the word occurs after the origin of the letter, which for Braschi seems to have a greater presence than the word itself. Braschi alludes to the origin of the letter: "A letter comes and visits me. Puts its legs up in the living room. Wanders about speechless. Suddenly it explodes and another shape appears. Welcome! It flees swiftly, and I see two, three, four, five, seven, five hundred letters. Suddenly I hear the word *river* and water runs in another river's space. I repeat *river* two, three, four, five, seven, five hundred times, and cold imprisons twilight. Then this letter's twin slope trembles. There is no return without reaching bottom. The letter is born of life. That's where its limit began. I discover the world underneath" (*ED* 3). This linguistic game becomes poeticized through the personification of the letter, with a rhetorical figure inserting itself into the very "body" of the letter. As we see, the letter "comes," it "flees swiftly," and it is "born of life." The poet attempts to pursue and retrieve the letter, which in turn escapes and becomes transformed. The poet's experience with the movement of the letter can be refracted through the theory developed by Merleau-Ponty in *Phenomenology of Perception*, according to which the origin of human knowledge begins not so much from scientific deduction but from experience and experimentation through all the senses. In Braschi's poem, the speaker sees, listens, repeats, and discovers when faced with the materiality of the letter. The letters become words, which in turn become verse, which eventually create the book of poetry. Thus, words, rather than replacing reality, re-create a certain imaginative version of it. The poet-artist creates a syntax that reveals how it is possible to think, to suffer, and to live. Referring to an ontology of the image, Bachelard finds in the poetic image and the imagination the acts that uncover and release the soul with all that is contained therein, which leads us to an emotional and personal transformation.

A rational understanding of the poems in *Assault on Time* would be a difficult enterprise to achieve if, as Bachelard indicates, "Imagination, more than reason, is a unifying force in the human soul" (190), and the function of the imagination is not only to form images but to transform them with great agility. The reader of Braschi's poetry is invited, and at times challenged, to form images and swiftly move from one to the other. As Francisco José Ramos observes: "Braschi's writing, relying on the voice (phonography) and the (cinematographic) movement or recording of images accords little importance to the description. What is narrated are moments that, instead of being described, are enunciated and, above all, repeated. These are successive moments the spontaneity of which almost leads them to run over each other" (242). Ramos leads us to consider the notion of consciousness and the nomadic subject, as well as the rhizomatic nature of Braschi's poetry. Both concepts allow us to analyze *Assault on Time* from a standpoint of displacement and mobility.[6]

In her introduction to *El cuerpo de la voz (poesía, ética y cultura)*, Francine Masiello observes that "literature traverses our bodies, impacts our bones and resonates within us, that is, it comes into contact with our nerves, with our centers of pain and pleasure." Masiello notes that, by taking us to such a vital space, poetry "leads us to give a name to the voice" (12). This hypothesis proposes that the reader, when approaching the voice of the poem, hears their own voice. This assertion may lead us to ask ourselves: In what way is it possible to hear our own voices in the poems of *Assault on Time*? How can we attempt to hear a multiplicity of voices, voices that are restless, jumping, spirited, voices that also seek to escape from the grasp of our imagination and our feelings? When confronted by so much strangeness, how can we participate in this vital transformation? Julia Kristeva argues (in a context that is quite different from Braschi's poetry) that the antidote to xenophobia, racism, and other forms of discrimination is to recognize that the foreigner is within us. What we fear about others is precisely what we do not wish to face in ourselves (191–92).

Braschi has described *Empire of Dreams*, *Yo-Yo Boing!*, and *United States of Banana*, her three main works, as "stages in my life, like Goya's Black Paintings or Picasso's blue period," while also noting that she "depicts (and inserts) herself, much in the way that Rembrandt did in his works" (Díaz). These allusions to art have tempted us to find pictorial references in Braschi's poetry, as well as poetic references in the work of the Spanish Mexican artist Remedios Varo, whose paintings are infused with dream and travel imagery.[7] Varo's paintings include gothic buildings, androgynous beings, insects, stars, nocturnal forests, spinning objects, hermetic and dreamlike worlds, as well as levitating beings. Similarly, *Assault on Time* is composed of dreamworlds where a series of real and illusory routes and desired and imposed escapes are constructed and deconstructed.

The appearances, disappearances, and the loss of gravity are as germane to Varo's paintings as they are here in Braschi's poem: "The wind and I would have to take off and fly. Behind the closets and under the furniture no one says my name. Yes, I know I'm in a world of invisible sounds. I know its origin. I go toward it and hide. The wind and I would have to take off and fly. My hand says it no longer feels the air" (*ED* 12). The speaker yearns to rise and take flight with the wind. This desire to fly is repeated in the first and fifth lines, underscoring the urgency and yearning of the poetic self. The speaker aches to fly, understand the world she inhabits, recognize her origins, and heed what her hand has to say. However, the poem contrasts the images of presence ("I know") with those of absence ("no one says," "I hide," "no longer feels"). It is a game of hide-and-seek fueled by inspiration (the alluring promise of soaring skyward). Yet the images slip away, the poetic voice escapes, and the body feels, in its disembodied flesh, an absence, though temporary, of the inspiring muse.

For Bachelard, allusions to air in poetry are fundamental because "Through [the air], life and movement are possible" (64). Air acts as "a material element . . . is the principle of a *good conductor* that gives continuity to an imagining psyche" (17). He explains that what is comforting about these air images is that, by feeling connected to them, we become aware of a sense of release, of great joy, of weightlessness (20). In Braschi's poem, however, the reader may not so easily find such an ecstatic sensation of release. Instead, we become ensnared in a nomadic enterprise with departures and retreats that impel us to travel along with the poet through an infinite series of spaces and times:

> And among countless roads and old shoes, among countless objects and questions, the hand acts as an interpreter and the air keeps blowing and the door keeps unlocking and the wind goes back to its place as the door closes. Yes, everything has its place and everything counts when objects empty at the door. But I feel there is something weightless that runs. It's something that rises and never reveals itself and has to hide in some other corner. And that something now raises the same questions. And the wind finds itself back at a point—right where silences fly and objects jump back into the painting. But by then you can't tell one object from another—it's as if they weren't the same objects: watch, mirror, image, wind. But my hand knows the fall, and there's no other question than the same objects striking the frame and the chair. And the air stays still and everything is in its place. (12)

Here the poet becomes a painter, who traces with her pen images and ideas that travel and move. Likewise, the poetic voice depicts herself as a poet-artist, one who ambles incessantly and who becomes this very process of searching.

In another poem, the poet arrives at a house "transformed into art," in which memories are neither romanticized nor defined (*ED* 16). Here, the poet-artist plays with the "frame" of a painting, like the frame of a house, and with the "lintel," that horizontal piece above doors and windows that supports weight loads:

> I arrive at your house transformed into art, framed by my memories. The lintel's color is the guardian of my dream, you the painting. The frame of your house crosses the bottom of the painting. I cross the horizon and sit down to look at it. I arrive home transformed into art, framed behind your memories. (16)

The speaker tells us about memories and wooden structures that frame objects and dreams. If we reflect upon the progression, we realize that, at the beginning of the poem, the poet arrives at the house "framed by *my* memories," yet by the end she is "framed behind *your* memories" (my emphasis). By contemplating this perplexing and potentially infinite space, the magical and itinerant nature of both the poet and the poem becomes magnified. The frame is the poem itself from which one can "feel" one's own memories and the memories of others. Masiello reminds us that "it is the voice of the poem that speaks to us, not in complete transmissions governed by conventional logic, but by a series of whispers and oftentimes latent rhythms . . . and that the strongest form [of poetry] arises from the poet's work with the sensory plane" (173). This observation may bring us to reflect on Braschi's poem and on how the poet (and the reader) can only make the chronotopes of the poem come to life through the senses.

The image of the poet entering and leaving a painting reminds us of the poem "Remedios Varo's Appearances and Disappearances," in which Octavio Paz alludes specifically to the artist's sensibility: "With the invisible violence of wind scattering clouds, but with greater delicacy, as if she painted with her eyes rather than with her hands, Remedios sweeps the canvas clean and heaps up clarities on its transparent surface" (*Alternating Current*, 45). Paz describes the magical worlds of the artist, worlds where beings and objects levitate and become weightless, as "laughter [that] echoes in another world" (46). According to Paz, Remedios does not paint time but the moments when time is resting. One of the most powerful lines of the poem is when Paz states that Remedios "surprises us because she paints surprised" (*Corriente alterna*, 51).[8] In each poem of *Assault on Time*, as in each of Varo's paintings, seemingly senseless logic becomes a language of its own, whose essence is ephemeral. Both artists deploy a playful charm that engages and entrances, and yet, despite their levity, there is a nagging feeling of solitude.

Alicia Ostriker pointed out that solitude forms a subtext in *Assault on Time*. Connections are lost and allusions to distance can have different meanings, such as the distance between word and reality and the distance between lovers and the inability to love (xi). The poet maintains a loving relationship with writing, a game interspersed with pleasure, pain, and loneliness. On the one hand, we find the sheer enjoyment of creation, yet this is contrasted with the anguish of loss. In the last poems of the collection, we are nearly bombarded with references to solitude: "Happiness is solitary" (*ED* 24); "If I have penetrated something, it's only to be alone with all I see" (27); "Streets are crowding solitude" (27); "Nonetheless, solitude doesn't span our hands or move like waves" (28); "Solitude has no enigma when it stays alone. But when your heart is a party, solitude becomes crowded with memories" (28). It may be worth asking if the references to the poet-artist's solitude are related to the overall sense of anguish at the end of the book—of arriving at an unwanted outcome.

Solitude detains us in the now, yet it continues to move onward to tomorrow, opening paths that are marked by the desire to never reach the end of the road, which is to say the end of *Assault on Time*. Thus, loneliness wanders: "I was coming back through the outcome when I found the entrance. I didn't want to go back to the same street, so I went another way" (31). The speaker knows that she must cut short this creative path, but no definitive way seems to satisfy: "You still don't know the way? I can only send you to another one. But I don't know, I really don't know" (31). The poet-artist does not know which paths might lead to the end of her writing. For the poet, this is reality: "Here is reality. The hand touches distance. Touches it, nothing more. That's all. And enough" (31). In these final lines of *Assault on Time*, the poet-artist suggests that the hand (writing) can only "touch the distance" (the reader, in this poetic project). The poet can only draw the reader's attention to the countless ways of the poem. The hand signals us to heed the voices that lead us to encounters with our environment and ourselves. Is it possible that, by listening to the solitary voices of this poetry, we can hear our own voices and yearnings? And if we learn these poems by ear and by heart as Braschi intended, would the poet and the reader realize a certain mental or sensory transformation?

A quote from Shakespeare's *King Lear* serves as the epigraph to *Assault on Time*: "And take upon's the mystery of things / As if we were God's spies." This prompts us to examine with utter resolve the unfamiliar, the unknown, so that we can discover, perceive, and feel. In this way we may be able to explore our own human and spiritual condition. Similarly, when we are reading Braschi's poetry, it is possible that the transformation of the poet-reader and the poet-artist takes place in us by assuming the responsibility and the desire to embrace the strange and mysterious, which may free us from the ties that bind, be they mental, physical, or linguistic. There, in that space of consummate freedom, lies the transformative power of Braschi's poetry.

Notes

1. In this essay, all references are made to the version of *Asalto al tiempo* that appears in the collection *El imperio de los sueños* (1988). The English versions and page references are from the Kindle version of *Empire of Dreams*, translated by Tess O'Dwyer (1994).

2. María Elena Walsh (1930–2011), a renowned Argentine poet and singer, is also considered one of the country's most important figures in children's literature and folklore. In one of her most popular songs, "En el reino del revés" (In the realm of the reversed), the poetic voice asks about this world where everything seems outlandish and unexpected: "Me dijeron que en el reino del revés nadie / baila con los pies que un ladrón es vigilante /

y otro es juez y que dos y dos son tres" (15) [I was told that in the realm of the reversed no one / dances with their feet, a thief is on the lookout / and another is a judge / and two and two are three].

3. Francisco José Ramos, from the back cover, Spanish version of *El imperio de los sueños*.

4. Kristina Puga, "8 Poets Disclose Their Favorite Lines of Poetry," *NBC Latino*, 27 Apr. 2013, https://nbclatino.com/2013/04/27/8-poets-disclose-their-favorite-lines-of-poetry/.

5. Morris understands that, in Braschi's poetry, we should not question the direct influences of other artists, musicians, or writers but, instead, how Braschi's poetry might affect the reception of canonical texts (49). Morris considers the influences and intertexts in Braschi's poetry as a system of contiguity: "With contiguity as the mode of correlation, canonized artists are conceived as metonymic figures rather than metaphorical ones, warps in a fabric of free associations that shape a multiform universe. Diachronic categories of ordering and influence are abandoned in favor of the synchronicity of performances. Braschi's *Imperio* reflects our present perception of texts and contexts as polymorphous configurations molded by casual contiguities" (49).

6. For a detailed study on the nomadic and rhizomatic in Braschi poetry, see Loustau, *Cuerpos errantes*.

7. Varo's oneiric and magical worlds inhabit more than 360 works of art, all heavily indebted to the influence of surrealism (see Kaplan; Arcq, Bogzaran, and Moreno Villareal).

8. This line is translated by David Auerbach. It was omitted in Lane's translation of "Remedios Varo's Appearances and Disappearances."

Works Cited

Arcq, Tere, Fariba Bogzaran, and Jaime Moreno Villareal, eds. *Cinco llaves del mundo secreto de Remedios Varo*. Artes de México, 2008.

Bachelard, Gaston. *El aire y los sueños. Ensayo sobre la imaginación del movimiento*. Editorial Fondo de Cultura Económica, 1993.

Braschi, Giannina. "Breve tratado del poeta artista." *Cuadernos hispanoamericanos*, no. 433–36, September–October 1986, pp. 469–78.

Braschi, Giannina. *Empire of Dreams*. Translated by Tess O'Dwyer, Yale UP, 1994.

Braschi, Giannina. *El imperio de los sueños*. Editorial Anthropos, 1988.

Braschi, Giannina. *United States of Banana*. AmazonCrossing, 2011.

Braschi, Giannina. *Yo-Yo Boing!* Latin American Literary Review Press, 1998.

Díaz, Carmen Graciela. "Avión, sol, y libertad." *El Nuevo Día*, November 17, 2011, www.elnuevodia.com/entretenimiento/cultura/nota/avionsolylibertad-1122361/.

Echandi G., Marcela. "El aire como elemento fundamental de la imaginación." *El aire y los sueños de Gastón Bachelard*. Universidad de Costa Rica, San José, *Revista de Estudios*, no. 18–19, pp. 95–103.

Kaplan, Janet. *Unexpected Journeys: The Art of Remedios Varo*. Cross River, 1988.

Kristeva, Julia. *Strangers to Ourselves*. Columbia UP, 1991.

Loustau, Laura R. *Cuerpos errantes. Literatura latina y latinoamericana en Estados Unidos*. Beatriz Viterbo Editora, 2002.

Marting, Diane E. "New/Nueva York in Giannina Braschi's 'Poetic Egg': Fragile Identity, Postmodernism, and Globalization." *Global South*, vol. 4, no. 1, Spring 2010, pp. 167–82.

Masiello, Francine. *El cuerpo de la voz (poesía, ética y cultura)*. Beatriz Viterbo Editora, 2013.

Merleau-Ponty, Maurice. *Fenomenología de la percepción*. Fondo de Cultura Económica, 1957.

Morris, Barbara. "Paradoxes of Postmodernism in Giannina's Braschi's *El imperio de los sueños*." *Conflictos culturales en la literatura contemporánea. 17 ensayos y una discusión*, edited by R. Orlandini, M. Graniela, and L. Santos, Universidad de Puerto Rico, 1993, pp. 44–53.

Ostriker, Alicia. "Introduction." *Empire of Dreams*, by Giannina Braschi, translated by Tess O'Dwyer, Yale UP, 1994, pp. vii–xxi.

Paz, Octavio. *Alternating Current*, translated by Helen R. Lane. Viking, 1973.

Paz, Octavio. *Corriente alterna*. Siglo XXI Editores, 2006.

Ramos, Francisco José. "Postfacio." *El imperio de los sueños*. Anthropos, 1988, pp. 233–53.

Rivera, Carmen Haydée. "El poder de la palabra y la experiencia transnacional. Una entrevista con Giannina Braschi." *Op. Cit.: Revista del Centro de Investigaciones Históricas*, no. 20, 2011–2012, pp. 181–201.

Walsh, María Elena. *El reino del revés*. Alfaguara, 2015.

8

The Human Barnyard

Rhetoric, Identification, and Symbolic Representation in *United States of Banana*

Elizabeth Lowry

> The Rhetoric must lead us through the Scramble, the Wrangle of the Market Place, the flurries and flare-ups of the Human Barnyard, the Give and Take, the wavering line of pressure and counterpressure, the Logomachy, the onus of ownership, the War of Nerves, the War.
>
> —***Kenneth Burke***

Although there is no evidence that Giannina Braschi is familiar with Kenneth Burke's work, her *United States of Banana* presents a complex tableau of political and social life that takes on new meaning when read through the lens of Burke's "Rhetoric." Burke defines rhetoric according to what he believes it is supposed to do in the world—that is, to bridge social divides and to cultivate a sense of unity among those who might otherwise be at odds. When Burke speaks of the "Rhetoric" leading us "through the Scramble, the Wrangle . . . the flurries and flare-ups of the Human Barnyard," he means that in order to cope with a potentially difficult situation—particularly a political one—it is necessary to temporarily "identify" with another party and then attempt to understand the situation from that "other" perspective. More specifically, in the *Rhetoric of Motives*, he outlines his theory of identification and consubstantiality: "In being identified with B, A is 'substantially one' with a person other than himself. Yet, at the same time he remains unique, an individual locus of motives. Thus he is joined and separate, at once a distinct substance and consubstantial with another" (21). Therefore, consubstantiality can be understood as a way to maintain one's own identity while also acknowledging and accounting for the subject position of another person. Simply put, according to Burke's "Rhetoric," if we want to address social problems, we need to take on different—and often contradictory—identifications rather than repudiating what we are ourselves or distancing ourselves from the "other."

Braschi's *United States of Banana* presents a grim—yet colorful—portrait of American imperialism, false consciousness, and alienation. In this book Braschi offers her own version of the Human Barnyard, making frequent references to animals, including cockroaches, eagles, pigeons, rats, moles, dogs, lambs, rabbits, turtles, cows, bulls, chickens, pigs, peacocks, and buffaloes. *United States of Banana* begins in Lower Manhattan on September 11, 2001, and its opening scenes vary from stark realism to the darkly surreal. Although marketed as a novel, it is in fact a mixed genre work: part memoir, part epic poem, part speculative fiction, part polemic, and at times a stage play. Braschi, the narrator, is sometimes the protagonist of the story, sometimes not. With this in mind, I argue that reading *United States of Banana* through the lens of Burke reveals Braschi's personal attempts to navigate, negotiate, and transcend the cultural chaos of 9/11.

In her novel Braschi maps out the problematic nature of neoliberalism and the policies that she believes precipitated the events of 9/11. Writing from a Latin American perspective, she considers the relationship between the United States and Latin America in the pre- and post-9/11 eras. She speaks of the Latin American experience as being subsumed by Yanqui neoliberal ideology, a view also espoused by historian John Beverly, who states: "Before 9/11, and especially during the Clinton presidency in the 1990s, geopolitically the United States and the neoliberal assumptions of the so-called Washington Consensus were hegemonic in every sphere of Latin American life" (251). But Beverly also argues that, after 9/11, "that hegemony begins to fade," asserting that 9/11 marked a political turn to the right for the United States, which sparked a reactionary turn to the left for Latin America. Beverly asks: "what would be the form of a new Latinamericanism, capable of confronting U.S. hegemony and expressing an alternative future for the peoples of the Americas?" (18).

Entertaining similar questions, Braschi suggests that the events of 9/11 contributed toward a shift in Latin American consciousness, also interpreting 9/11 as being emblematic of a "battle of matter and spirit—the battle of the oppressed that are dispossessed—and want to possess—because they feel possessed. And they are possessed of spirit. It is the call of the oppressed to be possessed by something higher than material dispossession" (*USB* 33). However, much of *United States of Banana* suggests that, despite this "call of the oppressed" to reimagine their lives, many continue to adhere doggedly to the value systems of the pre-9/11 era. Yanquis in particular are seen to be resistant to reconsidering the central tenets of neoliberalism. Although Hispanics in Latin America may be responding to 9/11 by critiquing capitalism, Braschi's work suggests that Hispanics in the United States, particularly those in New York City, remain trapped in outmoded belief systems. Postcolonial subjects are invisible components of the US economy, and faulty postcolonial logics constitute the problematic relationships that the country has forged on a national level.

Braschi is trying to do more than criticize and accuse, however. She attempts to identify with various different subject positions across the political spectrum, emphasizes the need for unity and understanding, and recognizes her own complicity in reifying the social structures that she condemns. For example, following a critique of US imperialism and the harmful psychosocial influence of tourism on her native Puerto Rico, Braschi admits to her audience that she was once one of the very people that she critiques. In Puerto Rico she lived a privileged life, benefiting from the spoils of imperialism: she too spent time at country clubs and fancy hotels. She ate American food, played tennis, and rubbed shoulders with expatriates and wealthy tourists (*USB* 248). This privileged identity is as difficult for Braschi to accept and negotiate as that of the quintessential impoverished "Hispanic immigrant."

How can Braschi account for such conflicting identifications? As a Hispanic immigrant, an ordinary minimum wage worker, she constructs herself as a "piggybank." In Braschi's reckoning, being a piggy bank means a low income, living hand to mouth, and being treated in a manner that suggests an assumption of charity: "You think my brain is a piggybank. The only thing you do is throw some coins inside the piggybank of my brain. I hear the coins drop, drop, drop—but there is no water—they drown the stage in tears seven times salt. Even for an eggshell. My brain is a piggybank. Drop your coins and feel happy because you're contributing to my economy. Fundraiser, you are raising the funds to kill my soul every day a little more" (*USB* 20). When she likens the immigrant brain—or even simply the alienated labor of the immigrant—to a piggy bank, she suggests that, as a receptacle for coins (which aren't "real" money), the piggy bank must be broken once it is full. The worker labors until she is "broken," only to weep at the discovery that the coins she has accumulated are hardly worth anything at all. Here Braschi tentatively occupies subject positions that are simultaneously "me" and "not me" in telling stories from the perspective of an unnamed Hispanic immigrant. She does this by symbolically inhabiting the subject position of the low-income worker (the "piggybank") as well as the subject position of a person profiting from the capitalist system and attaining social status within it (the "cash machine"). The point at which a person is considered to be of worth within the American economy is when she makes the move from being a "piggybank" to a "cash machine"—that is, the point at which she is interpreted as contributing to the economy—not with her labor but by virtue of her ability to hire and pay others.

In her effort to identify with the complementary yet also contradictory subject positions of piggy bank and cash machine, I argue that Braschi engages in what Krista Ratcliffe refers to as "rhetorical listening," by which she means a commitment to self-awareness and to understanding how and why we make certain identifications. When considering the Burkean concept of identification, Ratcliffe asserts that "rhetorical listening may precede conscious identifications" (19). Ratcliffe defines rhetorical listening as being a form of interpretation, a form of invention, and "a stance of openness that a person may choose to assume in relation to any person, text, or culture" (1). This definition relates to the rhetorical work of *United States of Banana* in that Braschi is constantly trying to negotiate where she belongs. Braschi finds herself identifying with a mainstream capitalist mentality that she also repudiates. In addition, she identifies with the Hispanic immigrant who does not readily fit into the paradigm of a mainstream white American capitalist work ethic. Braschi's identifications are always troubled, and they often seem to complicate the notion of the "Human Barnyard" more than they come to terms with it—yet Braschi is trying hard to "listen." Ratcliffe emphasizes that rhetorical listening is a conscious choice, a process of invention that can cultivate a link between the personal and the political without conflating the two. Although we may share political views, what those views mean to us personally within varying individual contexts may be as complex and as contested as they often seem to be for Braschi.

With respect to the personal and political, Ann Keniston and Jeanne Follansbee Quinn ask: "Is it possible to speak in a voice that exceeds the personal, to use a public voice, to launch a political critique in literature? What form can such a literature take, negotiating as it must between the event itself and the dictates of genre, tradition, and the impulse to find an audience?" (308). I contend that reading *United States of Banana* in terms of identification and consubstantiation reveals how Braschi projects a voice that "exceeds the personal." Although much of her writing clearly refers to her own experience, Braschi's work also transcends the personal by addressing a universal problematic of identification. Often this occurs when she moves into second person, addressing the reader directly, assuming that any audience—regardless of heritage or socioeconomic status—will be able to identify with her chicken analogy:

> You walk in the door like a chicken with the head cut off. You don't know what you're doing. You might know what you're doing. Of course you know what you're doing. You're walking. What you don't know is where you're going. But at least you're walking. As the head of the chicken with the head cut off I can't walk. I am lying on the floor—half-dead watching you walk like a chicken with its head cut off. I want to lend you my eyes—so you know where you're going—but now we are two separate entities. (*USB* 26)

Here, the decapitated chicken becomes a placeholder for all forms of false consciousness, for all those who are caught up in the "Scramble" of late monopoly capitalism. These chickens are going "to breed more headless chickens" and to indoctrinate others into their ideology, one in which the individual subject appears to have agency but is actually powerless. The decapitated chicken, with a body violently separated from its head, is also an allegory for colonialism: "The colonizer organizes the invasion but doesn't prepare for the counter-invasion. The colonized moves from the land of the invaded to the land of his invader . . . to infiltrate that new culture and to conquer it with his own culture. Now he is two" (*USB* 45). In this manner the subaltern internalizes his oppressor, experiencing not only false consciousness but also double consciousness and an inevitable crisis of identity. Braschi mentions that, upon moving to the "land of his invader," the experience of the colonized becomes "bilingual," his identity is tied to his language, and he exists in two languages. But the two languages—these two identities—are often in conflict. There is a sense of the self being split, a forced disidentification. The image of the headless chicken walking without knowing where it is going suggests that we are all caught up in a system of compulsive rather than reflective action.

Braschi's frequent references to chickens may allude to the controversial Ward Churchill article that appeared in the *New York Times* on September 12, 2001. In this article, entitled "Some People Push Back: On the Justice of Roosting Chickens," Churchill asserts that the attack on the World Trade Center should be recognized as a backlash to corrupt US and European foreign policy in the Middle East. Churchill suggests that, if we want to understand why September 11 happened and to prevent further similar tragedies, we would do well to engage in some self-reflection. For her part, Braschi appears to be engaging in that reflection from a Latin American perspective, considering the casualties of globalization and a free market economy. However, sharing her perspectives ten years after 9/11 is a judicious move on Braschi's part. In the years closely following the attack on the World Trade Center, a critique of US imperialism would likely not have been well received, for it was a time when the United States was widely perceived as having been victimized. For Braschi to suggest rethinking American political engagement when much of the population was thirsty for revenge hardly seemed prudent. However, as she is well aware, once the emotional turmoil subsides, national and indeed global narratives slowly become ossified in the collective consciousness. It is during this time—a time at which the 9/11 narrative has not yet been wholly "fixed"—that it becomes necessary to question the assumptions underlying patriotic storytelling.

In her own process of storytelling, Braschi is able to retrospectively trace the various nuances of a political climate that helped to spur the post-9/11 Latin American turn toward socialism that Beverly describes. The terrorists, Braschi implies, were successful in that "spectators around the world . . . witnessed the fall of the American Empire on TV. It changed the world's view of the self-proclaimed superpower. It made the superpower appear powerless. When success and impact come together, that event marks an era. There is a before and an after" (*USB* 35). For Latin Americans, "post-9/11" could mean a decreased adherence to the central tenets of capitalism and an increased need to consider one's position as a global citizen, an immigrant, and an expatriate. There is a need to reconsider the meaning of social responsibility and also to consider one's own life on one's own terms. Significantly, chickens are subjects of the "crown"—that is, imperialism of one kind or another—who have hitherto been unable to conceive of themselves as having the capacity for self-actualization: "But chickens with their heads cut off are always rushing around stressed and distressed—from responsibilities and duties—schedules—from sunrise to sunset—always counting hours, minutes, and nanoseconds—they have no time to dwell in themselves—or to feel—as a matter of fact—the fact that they have a life—their life is surpassed by their responsibilities to the crown" (*USB* 305). But to whom or what must the chickens be responsible once they recognize that they "have a life"? Chickens are driven by fear and confusion. They are told what to do and how to think. Instead of prompting us to reflect upon ourselves as a people, a nation, and a culture, the events of 9/11 seem only to have forced us further into a state of brainless compulsion. Instead of thinking about who we are and what we are doing, we have become more chicken-like than ever.

The trope of decapitation recurs at multiple points in the *United States of Banana* narrative. Braschi's first reference to a headless body comes in the novel's opening sequence where she describes the torso of a businessman killed at the World Trade Center:

> I saw a torso falling—no legs—no head—just a torso. I am redundant because I can't believe what I saw. I saw a torso falling—no legs—no head—just a torso—tumbling in the air—dressed in a bright white shirt—the shirt of the businessman—tucked in neatly—under the belt—snuggly fastened—holding up his pants that had no legs . . . and he was dead—dead for a ducat, dead—on the floor of Krispy Kreme—with powdered donuts for a head—fresh out of the oven—crispy and round—hot and tasty. (*USB* 3)

This surreal image draws us into Braschi's 9/11 narrative and inducts us into a world in which the head of the businessman—the symbol of reason, capital, and control—has been replaced by Krispy Kreme donuts. The donuts indicate what is missing, a loss of organization and meaning. Later, Braschi depicts herself eating these very donuts, ripping off little pieces one by one as if to suggest that it is perfectly natural to feed (albeit metaphorically) on the body parts of other human beings. In this sense the Krispy Kreme donuts can be likened to a communion wafer. By eating donuts that replace a man's decapitated head, Braschi attempts to absorb his symbolic power in the same way that a Christian might absorb a wafer. Thus, Braschi addresses the idea of consubstantiation—that is, the idea of "being with." Within the context of a church communion, wafers are eaten as an act of spiritual consubstantiation, a way of connecting with the Christ principle. Similarly, in *United States of Banana*, consuming the host in the form of a donut signifies Braschi's desire for identification and ultimately consubstantiation.

But the donut is a vexed symbol, although it can be likened to a communion wafer and is therefore symbolic of an effort to attain consubstantiality. Braschi also portrays herself as being disconnected from others, consuming donuts while those around her die. Returning to the image of the businessman's torso, Braschi writes: "When the policeman saw the man, he vomited on the stumps of the man's legs—and I felt the horror—but I ate my donut anyway, thinking:—I'm glad I'm not there, I'm here dunking my donut while others are blown to bits and pieces. Good luck. Keep hope alive" (*USB* 8). Despite efforts to identify with the man, Braschi cannot. Although she knows she should feel sick, she continues to eat her donut, apparently frustrated at her inability to identify with others—a frustration that masquerades as casual indifference, highlighting the tension between a desire for consubstantiality and its apparent impossibility. Thus, the donut motif in the text symbolizes both satiety and a profound lack. The enforced satiety of capitalism indicates a recognition that we are divided and alienated even from ourselves. We can confront a terrorist attack without really internalizing it because we are empty inside. The donut represents a fantasy of consubstantiality.

Burke's consubstantiality signifies "a place of bridged differences and common ground, a place from which to act for common cause . . . such consubstantiality may be visualized as the shared space of two distinct but interlocking circles" (Ratcliffe 55). Ratcliffe envisions Burkean notions of consubstantiality as "interlocking circles," but Braschi's consubstantiality—adopting the metaphor of the donut—consists of concentric circles. These circles remain distinct, yet one is subsumed by the other; that is, in Braschi's reckoning, in the relationship between Puerto Rico and the United States the desire for consubstantiality is marked by appropriation—one entity encompassing another—rather than by bridging or interlocking via dialogue and a sense of shared humanity.

Toward the end of the novel, for example, Braschi details a scene where tourists are staying at a fictional luxury hotel in Puerto Rico. The hotel resembles a glazed donut, with an icy-cold pool in its center. When the people in the swimming pool find that they are drowning, they begin to panic: "But once a tourist opened a door to the earth—they all poured out of that door like pennies and penuries out of a piggybank—and they landed in the sand—felt the warmth of the sea, the sun, the suntan and the clouds" (*USB* 252). This is the last time a donut image appears in the novel. And this time, the center of the donut is a swimming pool, a place that appears to present an opportunity for unity. However, this pool is uncomfortably cold and is highly exclusive—only people of a certain economic status can afford to stay in the hotel and the cold water of the pool overwhelms them. The swimmers begin to drown and look for an escape. Upon finding it, they enter an idyllic space—a place of comfort and pleasure and warmth. They pour into this space "like pennies and penuries," indicating that they may have seemed wealthy, but in reality, they were not. In the end their worth amounted to nothing more than that of those who served them. For Braschi, the donut indicates a warped model of identification and consubstantiality—one that must be avoided. Capitalism is immoral because it values the lives of some humans (cash machines) over others (piggy banks). Instead of bridging ideologies between the left and the right, it is possible that 9/11, an opportunity for reflection and change, led only to a widening rift between political ideologies. Ultimately, a belief in American exceptionalism isolated the United States from the rest of the world and contributed to social unrest across the globe. More specifically, this belief in exceptionalism increased the rift between Latin America and the United States, the global North and the global South.

The historical moment at which the proverbial chickens come home to roost marks a time when we must recognize the importance of what Ratcliffe calls rhetorical listening. As a practice, rhetorical listening "turns intent back on the listener, focusing on listening with intent to hear troubled identifications instead of listening for intent of an author" (46). Although we cannot know the "intent of an author," we can recognize "troubled identifications" and attempt to relate to them.

This is particularly significant to discussions of Braschi, much of whose writing is intended to be read aloud to a live audience. In her public reading of the first section of *United States of Banana*, she invites her audience to listen rhetorically—that is, by describing a business man's decapitation on 9/11 she "turns intent back on the listener." In physically facing Braschi, listeners are forced to face their own memories of 9/11 and to attend to her troubled identifications as well as her efforts to negotiate the complexities of cultural violence, race, and social class within a post-9/11 New York City. When readers or listeners of *United States of Banana* are able to experience that complexity along with Braschi, the "meaning of the text" turns into "something much larger than itself, certainly larger than the intent of the speaker/writer, in that rhetorical listening locates a text as part of larger cultural logics" (Ratcliffe 46). The larger "cultural logics" that Braschi addresses become a web of polarizing post-9/11 political ideologies. Despite the fact that we want to be consubstantial, to identify with others, we cannot do so to the extent we would like because of the doctrine that might equals right. When our sense of exceptionalism separates us from one another, language becomes inadequate for us to bridge our differences. Therefore, if language is a condition of identification and identification is a condition of language, then we literally need a new language with which to consider the events of 9/11 if we are to identify with those from whom we have separated ourselves.

Like many other 9/11 authors, Braschi brings her own personal representations of 9/11 to bear on the historical record, deliberately blurring the line between the literal and the figurative—for instance, whether she actually saw the torso of a businessman land among a constellation of Krispy Kreme donuts is irrelevant. What matters is her symbolic memory and how she wishes to comment on the problematics of capitalism and identification as well as her own positionality as a Puerto Rican at "Ground Zero"—a site representative of North American imperialism. In writing *United States of Banana*, Braschi must negotiate between the events of September 11 itself—as she experienced it literally and symbolically—as well as "the dictates of genre, tradition, and the impulse to find an 'audience'" (Keniston and Quinn 308). This awareness of the tension between the individual and the collective as well as the personal and the political spurs Braschi to resist the "dictates of genre" and to challenge fixed meaning, in an effort to communicate that September 11 was at its foundation "incommensurable, inaccessible, and incomprehensible" (308).

After all, "no one wants 9/11 to be misrepresented, politicized, co-opted, or distorted. Yet it seems difficult not to do just this" (Keniston and Quinn 206). I would argue that it is not only difficult but actually impossible "not to do just this," because of the context-driven nature of how we make meaning. Keniston and Quinn address problems of potential misrepresentation and politicization by claiming that the meanings of 9/11 are not—and should never be—fixed. It is essential for many different representations to come to light, for a multiplicity of stories to be told and to become part of our cultural memory. In a similar vein, Braschi's mixed genre "novel" takes on a series of distinct forms that would not immediately designate it as being part of any one recognizable genre. Braschi communicates the problematics of singular representation by resisting formal genre conventions, thus refusing to fix the very shape of her text. Further, she also makes use of extensive wordplay and puns, suggesting not only that contested meanings of individual words (or what Burke refers to as "logomachy") are at the locus of a cultural confusion that results in disidentification but also that a lack of fixed meaning or dominant narrative is (ironically) what makes it possible for us to come together.

Both Braschi and Burke write about times of great social unrest and the pressures to conform to a single worldview or narrative, but all the while they promote not the absorption of one culture into another but, rather, the willingness of one culture to attempt to deploy the tactics of "rhetorical listening," to understand other perspectives, and to negotiate among them. The idea of resisting absorption and negotiating among disparate cultures has been taken up by Marta Caminero-Santangelo, who discusses Latinx writers such as Braschi who "imagine identities as not just bicultural (as is common in 'ethnic' American literature) but insistently transnational, marked by behaviors such as return visits home, remittances, lingering political allegiances, and involvement with home country politics and even return migrations. In the process these texts also often pose significant challenges to the dominant cultural US narrative of the 'American Dream' in which immigrants who arrive in the United States can work hard, climb a ladder of social mobility, and achieve success to a degree unimaginable at home" (Caminero-Santangelo 231).

Braschi recognizes the dominant cultural narrative of the American Dream for what it is—a narrative of absorption and domination rather than one of negotiation and preservation of difference. Meanwhile, scholars have continued to emphasize and present evidence for what Jon

Nieto-Phillips calls a "multitude of narratives that comprise Latinx literatures and arts narratives as wide-ranging as they are numerous" (1). No culture is monolithic, and we do not need to create monoliths to survive. Rather, we find ways to identify with others by listening, by trying to understand what people, places, and politics are trying to tell us about who we are. We identify with others, yet we retain difference by recognizing that we are unwittingly part of the same Scramble. We identify with others by recognizing how the pressure under which we live, the "push and pull" inevitably leads to war and division, not only with others but within ourselves.

Works Cited

Beverley, John. *Latinamericanism after 9/11.* Duke UP, 2011. Kindle.

Braschi, Giannina. *United States of Banana.* AmazonCrossing, 2011. Kindle.

Burke, Kenneth. *A Grammar of Motives: A Rhetoric of Motives.* U of California P, 1969.

Caminero-Santangelo, Marta. "*Historias Transfronterizas*: Contemporary Latina/o Literature of Migration." *The Cambridge Companion to Latina/o American Literature,* edited by John Morán González, Cambridge UP, 2016, pp. 230–32.

Ground Zero: Part I of the United States of Banana. Directed by Michael Somoroff, performed by Giannina Braschi, www.youtube.com/watch?v=p5UdS8DI-ks.

Keniston, Ann, and Jeanne Follansbee Quinn. *Literature after 9/11.* Routledge, 2008. Kindle.

Nieto-Phillips, John. "The Growing Multitude of Latinx Voices." *Chiricú Journal: Latina/o Literatures, Arts, and Cultures,* vol. 2, no. 2, Spring 2018, pp. 1–2.

Ratcliffe, Krista. *Rhetorical Listening: Identification, Gender, Whiteness.* Southern Illinois UP, 2005.

9

Gamifying World Literature

Giannina Braschi's *United States of Banana*

Daniela Daniele

In *United States of Banana*, Giannina Braschi speaks for the Caribbean part of the Americas, and more specifically for the island of Puerto Rico, willing to become an independent state and merge the Northern and the Southern hemispheres of a continent where most people "immigrated with another speech" and whose pronunciation nobody bothers to "correct" (*USB* 22). Indeed, after the rise of the Obamas to power, many a US citizen of Anglo-Saxon origins apparently limited their boasting about their puritan legacy and their presumed (and often, imaginary) descent from the crew of the legendary *Mayflower*. The country, as the poet says, is "becoming a gathering of tribes—a United Nations—without nations" (118), increasingly enriched with the new idioms, traditions, and literary myths carried by the old and current immigration flows. Well aware that "although I am writing in English—they hear and read the foreign accent" (88), Braschi reconfigures her adopted New York identity in constant dialogue with her native Puerto Rico, never assimilating to a level of integration that would prevent her from speaking for the greenhorns and the dispossessed. Braschi writes: "I look like an Arab and walk like an Egyptian" (6).

When she declares, "I am writing in my foreign language, not in my native language" (38), she refers to the mixed idiom of the Nuyorican poets (above all, of Pedro Pietri), grafting onto a Northern American soil a writing form filled with the grotesqueries and the magical realism of a Latinx literary tradition. As it surfaces and flourishes from lower to mid-Manhattan (where Braschi moved after September 11), Giannina's voice grows bolder, never aiming to be fully naturalized but, rather, creatively engaged in the vernacular English of her own migration. She dwells in the linguistic alchemy of multilingual America, lingering in the interlinguistic position of the Puerto Rican expats who mix English with Spanish.[1] It is in that Spanglish intersection that she conceives the funambulist vicissitudes and adventures of a sort of Hispanized New York picaro who declares bankruptcy in the United States while keeping her possessions offshore in her homeland.

This premise on Braschi's multilingual choice is well articulated in Doris Sommer's introduction to *Yo-Yo Boing!* (1998), which illuminates the marginal but not minor vantage point of the hybrid poetics embraced by the writer. It is through her Southern eyes that she peruses and exposes all the flaws of what she irreverently renames the "United States of Banana." Such a provocative denomination designs the globalized world around her, haunted by mobsters and headhunters, struggling to impose the profit-making inclination of its protestant ethos, and the hegemony of a marketplace whose ruthless clocks "keep clicking" (*USB* 21) to spread the "déjà vu" logos (22) of franchising and "copycat commerce" (21). This defamiliarized urban landscape, in which the Xeroxes, Kinkos, Staples, and Starbucks proliferate, fully partakes of a commodified, unsettling scenario that Giannina reconsiders along with the values of democracy represented by her Western intellectual legacy. Starting from the Spanish Golden Age, in her depiction of contemporary New York, she disseminates quotes and characters selected from her most cherished classics (Calderón de la Barca and Cervantes, above all), whom she anachronistically engages in a compelling discussion on the contingent status of the Americas.

Braschi does not flirt with the commodified American landscape the ways in which Wallace Stevens and the New York Poets used to do; she finds little chance of renewal in the depleted landscape of trivia and merchandise. She remains, instead, the alien poet who carries the weight of a bookish tradition while walking with a light foot in the ruins of Ground Zero, until her energetic Latino view of the United States overlaps with her corrupted notion of Caribbean "Banana Republic" of her origins.

Such an imaginary tropical country is not far from the one featured by Steve Goodman and Jim Rothermel in their 1976 homonymous song. Their "Banana Republics" was the effective depiction of the US dissidents and expatriates who spent "those renegade pesos on a bottle of rum and a lime." Such was the southern initiation journey of the many innovative writers of puritan descent who, from Thomas Pynchon in his Mexican days to Rick Moody's *Diviners* (as the song also goes), went "down to the tropical sun . . . [t]ryin' to find what is ailing." Their progress to the southern borders geographically inverted but basically reproduce the political terms of Giannina's invective on the linguistic and cultural creolization of America, as they "learn the naive customs / soon a word of Spanish or two / you know that you cannot trust them / 'cause they know they can't trust you." In such a radical ambivalence, Braschi detects the democratic core of her existential estrangement and social critique, which she locates right at the end of the modernist American century and at the threshold of the era of globalization tragically inaugurated with September 11, 2001.

A Literary Gamification

As she meditates at street level on the ruins of the Twin Towers, Braschi (who was living in the Wall Street area in those horrific days) watches all the papers, bricks, bodies, and "torsos falling" (3) from the sky. Her vision is not the one of the terrified witness ready to provide another emotionally charged report from that universally covered disaster. She focuses, on the contrary, on the estranged and broken landscape, the way in which a surrealist would do. She playfully surfs the ordinary horrors of broadcast communication, manipulating the scene of the attack with the parodic tools of a modernist who never fully trusts reality, and even less the reality broadcast by globalized news. Grinning and hinting at a possible new picaresque way of reading the disarray of the American empire at the turn of the millennium, she discards the self-empowering, official rhetoric of the transatlantic military force to expose the mutilation of a "torso falling" (3) as the ferocious allegory of an empire under attack. As she sees people running for their lives through debris, like a "chicken with the head cut off" (45), she gruesomely lists their physical maiming: "I lost my arms in Vietnam . . . my head in Kuwait . . . my torso in the World Trade Center" (19). Like a satirical comedian she reprocesses America through the meat-grinder of her alien critical lens, showing concern for the state of ruins, while keeping "the eyes of the world on my extravaganza" (25).

With the peculiar cruelty of Artaud's theater, the poet envisions bodies dissected and fragmented as newly surrealist forms.[2] And, as she observes the New York crowd "running and screaming" (3) in the burning towers, she appears strangely immune from the general panic and meditatively lingers on the torso still "dressed in a bright white shirt," grimly representative of a new era of falling businessmen (3). In this disrupted spectacle and the Grand Guignol, which discloses "the white of fear in America's eyes" (35), Braschi prophetically warns that "Oil is coming to an end—and now we have no legs to walk" (18).

The September 11 attacks, which inaugurate this era of "feardom, Not freedom" (21), also start, from Braschi's critical perspective, a long period of agony, whose fear of freedom carried "fire and smoke" (17) in a congested New York, which, no less than Don DeLillo's *Cosmopolis* (2003), appears like a battlefield "full of barricades, tunnels and caves" (*USB* 4). As the narrator treads her uneven path with a quixotic sensibility, the damaged cityscape seems to turn into the hectic scenario of a videogame, into a "first-person shooter" endlessly enacted in a hard time when, as the writer warns us, the "bureaucracy terrorism" of abusive governments imposes its assignments to poorer countries, since "it is your responsibility to comply with the deadline—otherwise—we'll cut your head off or bomb the hell out of your country (28).

As a matter of fact, Braschi critically lingers in the wide gap between North and South, that is, in the contending ground of her virulent geopolitical invectives only mitigated by a maze of literary allusions that serve as the narrator's defensive shield against Western decay and destruction. As she treats the post-traumatic disorder of the United States with the weapons of irreverence and laughter, Braschi parodically surrounds herself with two cartoonish versions of Hamlet and Segismundo, as fellow travelers in an iconoclastic adventure. Such a picaresque trip mimics comics and videogames by mockingly reducing the most celebrated heroes of World Literature to mere caricatures. The diminishing effect of this literary parody is strictly functional to the author's postcolonial critique. Her references to her literary masters are neither reverential nor philologically equipped (like T. S. Eliot's) to recover the redeeming power of the Western literary heritage. On the contrary, Braschi's literary heroes are as disoriented as the New Yorkers in the aftermath of the attacks: they ghostly move with no clear direction in the surrealist disaster scene produced by the fall of the Twin Towers and by the consequent war on terror. Therefore, these literary icons are not resurrected in the inferno of Ground Zero as rescuers but as anonymous passersby plodding in the rubble, no less stunned than the autobiographical narrator in the ruins of corporate capitalism. In the second section of *United States of Banana*, Braschi reclaims them as dignified interlocutors in a compelling apocalyptic dialogue that reveals their inability to vindicate their literary aura and allure into the material devastation of that scene. Segismundo, Zarathustra, and Hamlet become patient and perplexed bosom friends, willing to be questioned in the city ruins on the many issues raised by that attack. In other words, in this anachronic, Socratic dialogue on September 11, Braschi not only invokes her literary masters but walks with them to test their authority in a distressed America, until the world classics and the violated

Americans become absurdly abused and confused, making the author wonder: "*Where is the boss*" (29), now?

It can be argued that the literary heroes revived by Braschi get the same stylized and caricatural treatment reserved for Shakespeare, William the Conqueror, Geoffrey Chaucer, and Anne Boleyn by the African American writer Adrienne Kennedy lost in her wax museum of bleached white icons (Kennedy 30). A similar parodic process seems to inspire Braschi's fictional manipulation of literary classics from her own marginal vantage point, where the ultimate goal is also "burying sameness" (74) and reading "them in exile—in exile from the language of their native land" (46). Her iconoclastic intention to "colonize the colonizers" (46) becomes even more tangible in the pièce that gives the title to the whole book, in which the poet entertains an animated discussion concerning the state of the world with Antonin Artaud and the Statue of Liberty. In a long tirade on the limits of freedom imposed by a new restrictive policy of surveillance after September 11, all the resurrected emblems of Western humanism, which the reader still perceives as landmarks of democratic values, mechanically enter the debate in which she engages them, until they emerge both diminished and distressed from it, despite the author's sturdy resistance to the new "time of tyranny" (Hejinian).

All the cartoonish emblems selected by the poet from the great books of the Western tradition play an outspoken and polemic role in the discussion. They are not meant to outclass the author herself, who immodestly confronts them as a peer with her interrogatives and cutting remarks. This protagonism of the writer who mixes with the literary masters and arrogantly confesses that did not exempt herself from dyeing her "hair blond because I was writing Hamlet and Hamlet is blond" (*USB* 6) is a distinctive exuberant and hyperbolic feature of Braschi's metafiction, in which the author enters her narrative and speaks in the first person, making no distinction between her own person and her persona. Furthermore, she boldly smiles at her reader with her cheeky face from the cover of *Yo-Yo Boing!*, establishing herself as the main character of the stories she tells and somehow dominates.

In this self-centered presentation as both a character and a writing subject, Giannina inhabits her own literary works, both as an author and as an autobiographical narrator with the exuberant energy of another metafictional and parodic writer, the early Kathy Acker of the quixotic series inaugurated with *Kathy Goes to Haiti* (1978). As a Hispanic late version of Acker's piratical writing practice, in *United States of Banana*, Braschi submits the most celebrated protagonist of World Literature to a farcical caricaturization, and assimilates herself to the stylized satirical character of a *Charlie Hebdo* political strip. The cartoonish effect of her travesties is emphasized by the iconoclastic forms that her book takes in the illustrated edition by the Swedish cartoonist Joakim Lindengren, translated into Swedish by the poet Helena Eriksson (2017).

These spectacular inscriptions of Braschi's defiant countenance perfectly reflect her fictional enterprise which, like Acker's, endlessly renews a close complicity with her reader that certainly serves the marketing purposes of her self-promotion. In whatever she creates, her persona partakes of a mock-ironic self-advertising aesthetic, in a self-deconstructing critique of corporate capitalism. Her performative use of fiction as a daring art that transcends the fictional domain and makes her cross-dressed image circulate as a laughing trickster and as a humorous troublemaker in male attire, very similar to the incorrigible tomboyish adolescents Gian Burrasca and Pippi Longstocking who never submitted to the adult code of obedience (Vamba; Lindgren).[3] In all her contending and untamed exuberance, when Braschi cruises with her simplified versions of Segismundo, Hamlet, Gertrude, and other icons roughly selected from the "posthumous" literary firmament, she does not mix with them to increase her own iconic aura. On the contrary, like Kathy Acker who wanders in the "cultural storehouse of Western Literature" (Conte 14), Giannina naughtily draws her literary heroes back down to the disrupted ground commodified America as if to test their ability to apply their wisdom to the environmental crisis and other current dilemmas (*USB* 76). As she squeezes an unattainable material essence out of their symbolic powers, this born-heretic postcolonial writer pushes Hamlet, Segismundo, and the Statue of Liberty far from the sacred temple of arts and letters.

Her greatest skill is to break into the higher field of literary canon while keeping in touch with the prose of life, until her mixture of trivia, literary classics, and global politics achieves a cartoonish and anarchic dimension. Braschi's dramatized dialogues with the cartoon silhouette images of world literature make of them nothing more than stock figures, inevitably blended and vilified by the poet's random use of Spanglish, which adds an unexpected Hispanic variation to her unauthorized appropriation of the Western canon. In this discursive violation, the hybrid vernacular created by the Hispanic community in North America is elevated to a lyrical idiom that oddly switches, at moments, to clarify Braschi's irreducible alien perspective. Like the other vernacular geniuses in postmodern America (from Suzan-Lori Parks to Eminem, from Gary Shteyngart to Eugene Ostashevsky, from Mary Caponegro to Jennifer Scappettone), Braschi searched a rejuvenated validation of her literary myths by juxtaposing famous quotes randomly stolen from the ancient literary lineage with the irregular sentences uttered by her immigrant community in New York. In this way, she reenacts them in an iconoclastic and performative mode that recklessly shifts from prose to poetry, from verse to howl, reshuffling the pages and papers on her shelves in a ravishing, not bookish way, more prone to devour than to dabble in the numberless evoked materials.

So, in *United States of Banana*, which, starting from its very title, announces a subversion of the New World Order, here are Hamlet and Segismundo casually reduced to fellow travelers and confidants. There we find lofty quotes from classics reframed in a setback, informal conversation; there, again, the *Mayflower*'s progress simplistically reconfigured in a cartoonish version in the middle of the current institutional crisis. All of these incongruous revisitings and rewindings of a millennial literary and historical archive converge and implode in this Millennium narrative tour de force. Braschi's pastiche digresses and speculates, centrifuges and meshes the Western imagination in the open sea of random signs, until her alien compost gets caught in a grinding recycling process in which literary echoes and icons can float freely, never to be assimilated nor fully appropriated.

Braschi's proliferation of literary references (which, in many ways, recalls Acker's intensive metafictional game) produces sudden lapses of the sublime into the trivial in sentences: "Artaud storms into my brainstorm, interrupting Joyce who is hard to stop—but Beckett is happy—because they had a stormy marriage." Such a bathos is further intensified by the author's contaminated and contaminating use of Spanglish, as part of her linguistic resistance to cultural assimilation in the foreign land where she lives. The incorporation, in her English dialogues, of Latino expressions such as "Soy boricua" (*USB* 47) adds a Latinized, Catholic layer to the normative Anglo-Saxon alphabet and syntax that, as an inquisitive "intriguer of the imagination" (26), she playfully manipulates. Braschi reshapes and modifies the dominant literary myths of her Hispanic heritage, producing their simultaneous simplification for the sake of her allegorical and satirical purposes: "I love that Segismundo wants to throw his father off the balcony for locking him up in the dungeon" (47). Likewise, her caricatural and simplified reformulation of the Western canon reflects a power in decline, which manifests itself in the generally parodic and mock-heroic tone of a narrative in which the narrator invites the literary icons for coffee at the Starbucks around the corner—and metapoetically comments that incongruous scene, as she learns, along with her readers, how to "see her future condense in her past [in] the moment when the past and the future unite in the present" (15).

In Braschi's critical gamification of great books, quotations and wordplay, masters and disciples, authors and characters, all meet in person and speculate at length as peers and frenemies. With their sincere shared plan to get America back on her feet to honor her old status of promised land, her ill-matched literary emblems "wishfully/washfully" (105) reunite to reenact the salvific trip of the *Mayflower* in the current immigration crisis worsened by the "shock economy" (Klein) as if to advocate for a more inclusive admission policy even in the current age of terror. As Lindengren illustrates this collective resolution in his graphic version of *United States of Banana*, Braschi's apocalyptic imagination brings the Statue of Liberty to her knees, ready to jump into the waters and join the refugees whom she is supposed to welcome and rescue (*USB* 100). As she leaves her much honored pedestal, her crown becomes the emergency raft where Giannina, with her distinctive bodily features, floats along with her distinguished fellow travelers Hamlet, Zarathustra, Antonin Artaud, and Segismundo (101), the latter having finally been released from his Polonized Spain to head back to "the Isle of the Blessed [where he] was born to liberate his people from confinement and isolation, from embargos and diffuminations . . . —from myself—I liberate myself from the United States of Banana" (*USB* 210).

Notes

1. Sollors presents the vivid scenario of multilingual America in the collective volume *Multilingual America* (1998).

2. The mutilations of the female body as a distinctive feature of surrealist art are aptly discussed in Caws 1986.

3. The undeclared American source of the story of naughty Giannino Stoppani is apparently Walter T. Gray [pseud. Metta Victoria Fuller Victor], *A Bad Boy's Diary* (J. S. Ogilvie, 1880); Italian translation, *La vera storia di Gian Burrasca*, ed. S. Proietti (Cooper, 2007).

Works Cited

Acker, Kathy. *Kathy Goes to Haiti*. Rumour, 1978.

Acker, Kathy. *Don Quixote. Which Was a Dream*. Grove, 1986.

Braschi, Giannina. *United States of Banana*. AmazonCrossing, 2011.

Braschi, Giannina, and Joakim Lindengren. *United States of Banana*. Swedish translation by Helena Eriksson. Cobolt, 2017.

Caws, Mary Ann. "Ladies Shot and Painted." *The Female Body in Western Culture: Contemporary Perspectives*, edited by Susan Suleiman, Harvard UP, 1986, pp. 269–87.

Conte, Joseph. "Discipline and Anarchy: Disrupted Codes in Kathy Acker's *Empire of the Senseless*," *Revista Canaria des Etudios Ingleses* no. 39, 1999: 13–31.

Gray, Walter T. [pseud. Metta Victoria Fuller Victor]. *A Bad Boy's Diary*. J. S. Ogilvie, 1880. In Italian, *La vera storia di Gian Burrasca*, ed. S. Proietti. Cooper, 2007.

Hejinian, Lyn. "Time of Tyranny." *Tribunal.* Omnidawn, 2019, pp. 33–59.

Kennedy, Adrienne. "The Owl Answers." *The Adrienne Kennedy Reader.* Minnesota UP, 2001, p. 30.

Klein, Naomi. *The Shock Doctrine: The Rise of Disaster Capitalism.* Knopf, 2007.

Lindgren, Astrid. *Pippi Långstrump.* Rabén and Sjögren, 1945–1948. English translation, *Pippi Longstocking.*

Sollors, Werner. *Multilingual America: Transnationalism, Ethnicity and the Languages of American Literature.* New York UP, 1998.

Sommer, Doris, and Alexandra Vega-Marino. "Either/And." Introduction to *Yo-Yo Boing!* by Giannina Braschi, Latin American Literary Review Press, 1998, pp. 11–18.

Vamba [alias Luigi Bertelli]. *Il giornalino di Gian Burrasca. Il giornalino della Domenica* (1907–1908). Bemporad, 1912.

III

Intermedial Poetics and Radical Thinking

10

Leaping Off the Page

Giannina Braschi's Intermedialities

Dorian Lugo Bertrán

Hybridity is a dominant feature in contemporary culture. Time and again, works are foregrounded because they contain elements of pastiche, bricolage, or heterogeneity. In a seminal article, Fredric Jameson suggests that pastiche is not merely internal to subversive or innovative cultural practices and that there are more political pastiches than others: the Westin Bonaventure Hotel and Suites in Los Angeles by architect John C. Portman Jr. (1974–1976) and Frank Gehry's residences (1974–1975, 1995) are examples of pastiche, with their own respective gradients of the political, from less to more obvious (Jameson).[1] The same article indicates that, for the purposes of cultural production, it is not so much a matter of pure or strident categories as intensities, ones that are marked or potentially markable. The cultural production of Giannina Braschi is no exception.[2] Her genre hybridity is conspicuous in its creative unfolding. The question is whether her work is differentiated by another type of hybridity, one composed of media/mediums.[3]

Braschi's approach to genre hybridity seems tactical. Novel, short story, sketch, essay, diary, theater, poetry (particularly prose poems), all appear effortlessly woven into the same narrative, which has been almost exclusively characterized as literary—not so much as visual or performative. Of her major works, it is often said that *Yo-Yo Boing!* and *United States of Banana* are novels and that *Empire of Dreams* is a collection of prose poems.[4] Certainly, assigning the characterizations of prose poems or novel does not end up being as categorically fitting as it would seem at first glance. Prose poems are in themselves a hybrid, since even one of their own conceptual creators, and not necessarily a first practitioner, Charles Baudelaire, theorized in the nineteenth century that it was a genre halfway between the lyrical and the pictorial-narrative: "l'idée m'est venue de tenter quelque chose d'analogue . . . d'appliquer à la description de la vie moderne . . . le procédé qu'il avait appliqué à la peinture de la vie ancienne, si étrangement pittoresque" ("The idea came to me to try something similar, to apply to the description of modern life . . . the method he used to depict ancient life, so strangely picturesque").[5] A distinction should be made between conceptual creator as opposed to practitioner, given that although the term "poème en prose"(prose poem) is associated with Baudelaire as its founding figure, in practice there are instances of prose poems that historically coincide with or precede those of the French poet. Oft-cited examples of works that feature elements of prose poems include *The Legends* of Gustavo Adolfo Bécquer and *The Traditions* of Ricardo Palma.

If poetry can be seen as diverse in general, with its variants of epic, lyrical, dramatic poetry in addition to the prose poem, the novel is certainly no less so. This aspect extends beyond the diversity of subgenres: byzantine, sentimental, chivalric, *novela morisca*, picaresque, Celestinesque, modern, or polyhedral, and so on. The ascription also extends beyond the morphological diversity of the novel: versified, prosified, or mixed, etc. In his seminal work on the poetics of the novel, Mikhail Bakhtin affirms that the novel is by definition hybrid and, therefore, is less a genre than a polygeneric force, the intrinsic quality of which is none other than to collect genres or dialogize them, in contrast with a genre such as the epic, which is by definition more monologic ("Epic"). The novel is distinguished by its counterpoint of plotlines or discourses, forms and genres, while the epic, for the sake of extolling one ethos or people over another, privileges or centralizes discursive instances through mechanisms of homophony.[6]

As is frequently conjectured in contemporary art theory, genre is not the same thing as medium, nor is medium the same as technique, or technique equivalent to a tool or instrument, nor are tools or instruments the same as a support for a work. In Braschi's "writing," there appears to be an awareness not only of genre/intergenre but also of medium/intermedia and support.[7] Her work evidences a consciousness of the physical or digital "page," which functions as a support to be used for recording or unrecording. The resulting struggles, we suggest, are a part of her signifying and political economies.

The term "intermedial" is complex in English. It might connote, on the one hand, something that occupies a place among other things (intermediary) as well as, on the other hand, the crossing of media that is characteristic of digitality in general and contemporary art in particular. We can compare, for example, the intermediality involved in the mediatic convergence of cell phones, connected by a signal with other electronic devices of a given user, or that of the audiovisual medium, which coincides with what is written on a web platform. The deployment also extends into contemporary art media, which often integrate a range of mediums/media/supports such as the environment, installation, video art, or performance. In Spanish, however, "intermedial" is not so much a noun as a modifier, connoting in-betweenness or intermediariness. In order to convey the second definition above, the noun "intermediality" should be used. In general, I propose the adoption of the anglicized semantics of the term, since it benefits from the necessary amplitude of this semanteme.

Braschi's work has always been intermedial, and its inexhaustible adaptations in other media by other cultural creators emerge in part from the intermediality of the Puerto Rican author herself. While this Braschian intermediality is nourished by intertextual references, it has also spawned a rewriting or material continuation into other works. Braschi's work has been subjected to various adaptations, which include: (1) a photography book, *Two Crowns of the Egg*, by Michael Somoroff, with love poems from *Empire of Dreams* (2011); (2) a limited-edition artist's book of *Libro de payasos y bufones* by printmaker Giorgio Upiglio with aquatint images by Rita Gallé (1987); (3) a theater play titled *United States of Banana*, directed by Juan Pablo Félix (2015); (4) a sculptural object measuring two square feet, *Diario íntimo de Giannina* by Montserrat Pecanins, which opens like a pop-up book and features an illuminated scene from *Empire of Dreams* fashioned in wood, leather, glass, papier mâché, and plastic (1989); (5) a graphic novel in Swedish, *United States of Banana*, by Joakim Lindengren, translated by Helena Eriksson (2017); (6) a series of black-and-white paintings with text from *Yo-Yo Boing!* by Michael Zansky (2011); and (7) a drawing by Tabo Toral, inspired by *Assault on Time* (1985). Projects underway include a critical edition of Lindengren's graphic novel, prepared by Amy Sheeran (Otterbein University) and Amanda Smith (University of California, Santa Cruz), and a wooden triptych with blowtorch and acrylic paint applications by Michael Zansky (measuring twelve by sixteen feet) with texts from *United States of Banana*.[8] And, most recently in 2020, Gabriel Bouche Caro, a young, emerging composer from Puerto Rico, has begun to compose a chamber music piece inspired by political concepts articulated in *United States of Banana* (i.e., Wishy, Wishy-Washy, and Washy).

In discussing these adaptations to other media, it is worthwhile to note that the geographic range of these artists spans Barcelona, Bogotá,

Gothenberg, Mexico City, Milan, Panama City, and New York City. It should also be added that, in the context of linguistic adaptation, Braschi's texts have appeared in Spanish, English, Italian, French, Slovenian, Chinese, and Swedish translations.

Finally, for the sake of balance, applying a broader conception of "intertextuality" (and, therefore, of the textuality of performativity), it seems useful to dialogue with other intermedial adaptations of Braschi's intertextuality or performativity. For Bakhtin, the dialogic—or, as later elaborated by the psychoanalytical theorist Julia Kristeva, the intertextual—is a complex notion and is not limited to dialogues between literal or physical texts. The dialogic may also integrate the image that the reader conjures or creates of the author (whether accurate or otherwise) as well as the instances that correspond to the level of action or performance of things, similar to what nowadays would be called "performativity" (Bakhtin, *Hacia* 96–100). By "performativity," we mean, in this instance, both discursive and counter-discursive practices, occurring within the symbolic, the imaginary (as well as counter-symbolic and counter-imaginary), and the real, which in turn are themselves reinscribed and which urge symbolic production through a non-totalization in the symbolic itself.[9]

Braschi's performativity, or any other dimension of her intertextuality, has also extended into and across a broad spectrum of the intermedial. Braschi has been the subject of numerous portraits—by Puerto Rican artists Francisco Rodón, Jorge Zeno, Víctor Vázquez, John Betancourt, and Eduardo Firpi; New York photographers Michael Somoroff, John Clifford, Beowolf Sheehan, John Stuart, and Michael Zansky; Catalan photographer Gabriel Suau, Italian painter Vita Giorgi, and Swedish photographer Cato Lein.[10] Among the rarest of portraits is one in progress by New York furniture designer Ian Stell, who in 2020 began to build a kinetic sculptural form that is a hybrid in functionality and exists between typologies: a chair that transforms into a lamp. Stell designed the device to exist between typologies and named it after "Giannina" (Braschi), who is a collector of kinetic chairs and illumination devices.[11]

It is not surprising that Braschi's life and work should be equally alluring. For the author, life and work overlap and are interwoven, a fact that she herself readily recognizes. This is a feature that Braschi shares with performers throughout the world. When she reads in her contralto voice—dressed as a nineteenth-century dandy—it is, in a word, mesmerizing.

References to the intermedial appear frequently in her work, especially in the sense of intermediacy. The axiology that links the intermedial to intermediacy (in-betweenness) is mixed. At times, the intermedial as intermediate can have a negative connotation, especially when referring directly or indirectly to the current political status of Puerto Rico. Thus, in *United States of Banana*, the citizens of Liberty Island are availed of the political status options of "wishy," "wishy washy," or "washy." They have thus far opted for "wishy washy," all of which reflects the current political dilemma of Puerto Rico. The country's current status is Commonwealth of the United States (similar to "wishy washy"), which is presented in the novel as a thinly veiled form of colonialism with negative connotations, while the other options are independence (similar to "wishy") and annexation/statehood (similar to "washy"). Of the last two options, "wishy" independence carries a positive charge, while "washy" annexation/statehood is clearly negative and implies culturicide. Similarly, the protagonist Giannina in *Yo-Yo Boing!* asserts that she is against the "in-betweenies" or those who waver between wet rag and ecumenical on certain issues (*YYB* 132).

On other occasions, however, the intermedial in her work takes on liberating and, by extension, relatively positive meanings.[12] In *Empire of Dreams*, her defense of the "poetic egg" simultaneously connotes creative genesis and necessary error, perhaps inspired by the colloquial expression "I laid an egg" (*ED* 196).[13] In *Yo-Yo Boing!* we find her apologetic reference to "Zelig [the] chameleon" (*YYB* 164), the protagonist of the eponymous film by Woody Allen, as well as in her poetic elaboration on the instability of the "yo" (I/ego/self), of the "I" that is you, and of the you that is "I," as the author puts it (120). This results in a bouncing back and forth between "yo" and "yo" (I and I/self and self), as in the rhythmic looping of the children's toy the yo-yo, which, together with the anglicized onomatopoeia "boing," seems to signify the ontological ricocheting not of any toy but of the migrant or the contemporary self ("yo"), or simply of the self that cannot find itself because it is not, nor has it ever been, in any stable place. The semanteme of the liberating intermedial occurs, in turn, when Braschi refers to her linguistic situation as a migrant, in a phrase that is repeated as "my foreign native language," thus underscoring and enhancing the oxymoron.

In *United States of Banana*, the liberating intermedial can be found in the author's positive preferences: (1) the "udderlands," as opposed to the "motherlands" or "fatherlands" (*USB* 734); (2) the dysfunctional metaphor, which fails to make the dissimilar similar (747–48); (3) the "doer" over the mere "being" (793–95); (4) the "parts" that don't "add up," or the irreconcilable chasm between the parts and the whole (836); (5) inequality, which dethrones equality (842); (6) inalienable qualities, as opposed to inalienable rights (845–46); (7) the continual references throughout the work to Puerto Rico as a continent or archipelago, or archipelagic continent, instead of an island (276); (8) other recurring references, this time to America as the parts of an unhinged or scattered continent and to Puerto Rico as a point of irradiation (276); (9) constantly meandering, "lost between languages" (276); (10) for loving multiples, multitudes, or "plentitudes" (a not entirely accepted neologism in Spanish), as opposed to (being part of) the "one" (or of the two that merge in her work) (286–87); (11) love as a "non-god" (in contrast to how the philosopher Diotima sees love in Plato's *Symposium*), as a "desire," always incomplete or "needy," an "intermediary" state existing between heaven and hell; and (12) "gratitude," contrasted against envy, which in many ways links her to the psychoanalytical theories of Melanie Klein (302–3).

However, the intermedial has another application, beyond the notion of in-betweenness. There is also the intermedial representing an amalgamation or hybridization of media. In this sense we can observe how closely Braschi's work can be construed as a house of letters, and literature as a house or closed space, an oppressive construct of its own, from which its author craves unconditional release in some Kierkegaardian leap of faith or Bohrian quantum leap, which would be nothing less than a "leap off the page." Once we examine these allusions throughout her work, we find that the references to high and low culture are relentless, from the myth of Dionysus as trickster or divine rogue to the allusions to a guided travelogue, à la Dante's *Divine Comedy*, with nods to Mahler's post-Romantic and pre-atonal music, Puerto Rican TV commercial jingles, including ads by Oliver Exterminating, a pest-control enterprise based in Puerto Rico, and the career of Puerto Rican comedian Yoyo Boing (Luis Antonio Rivera).

If we focus in on the typeface of the text, we notice a very obvious shifting in font use throughout the work. As an example, the oscillating intercalation of italics and Roman type in *Yo-Yo Boing!* doesn't necessarily serve to indicate narrative voice changes or framing contextualizations, as might occur elsewhere. Instead, these fluctuations sometimes appear as "asides" to the main evolution of the narrative—voices floating in a void—giving Braschi's page the appearance of a canvas, comparable to the abstract-expressionist techniques in the paintings of Clyfford Still or Barnett Newman, with subtle dividing lines echoing the frame, thunderous in the former example, clean and contained in the latter. No less striking is the use of bold typeface, which is employed to indicate interjections or onomatopoeia. These appear almost like comic-book dialogue balloons or the dissonances in post-Romantic, Malherian, or Straussian music. In other instances, calligrams are inserted, with the image of descending steps reproduced into the very flesh of the novel, like the insertion of a Concrete poem (see *YYB* 67, 79, 111, for examples).

More frequent, however, is the use of several fonts or graphic effects in sequence: italics along with bold letters, for example. In *United States of Banana*, these typographic techniques do not appear any less; they are used to mark shifts in narrative voice, framing, or contextualizations, or also for the above-referenced "asides" (*USB* 28–29, 71).

This can also be found in *Empire of Dreams*, which at first glance could seem like a mere layout effect, one that was more in the hands of the publisher or designer than in those of the author herself. Specifically, we find the justified centering of the prose poems running from page to page, in the manner of Donald Judd's minimalist open-fronted drawer-like sculptural forms. In the case of Braschi's book, however, these drawer structures are not empty but, rather, partially occupied by "articles" or, to be more precise, indistinct letters. The effect is also similar to the *Accumulations in a Box* series by French Nouveau-Réaliste artist Arman. All of this leads us to conclude that the result, whether achieved individually or collectively, consciously or unconsciously, was certainly motivated and not arbitrary. These contiguous letter boxes suggest spaces of intimacy, loneliness, and fragility, all on the verge of melting away with childlike innocence, and without resentment, as Nietzsche (one of the philosophers who most influenced Braschi herself) might have envisioned it or as the title of the third section of this lyrical novel, "Intimate Diary of Solitude," indicates. These prose poems also resonate with the dollhouse-like boxes created by the artist Joseph Cornell.

Visual and sound effects in literature carry their own long traditions.[14] Visual aspects extend back to premodern or non-Western conceptions of literature, which were not always intended to be contrasted against or divorced from the visual. We need only consider the illuminated texts of the medieval period or the rich calligraphic tradition of ancient China, where calligraphy was considered an art form, not simply a craft as it was in the West. In the modern literature of the West, precursors to the calligram, among other visual literary effects, can be found from the very beginnings, although these were often associated with humor or were mere illustrations of the more "pure" literary content, or even part of a minor or lesser literary genre. The Romantic movement resuscitated this element, making the visual in literature an autonomous or coexisting system to that the written word, not merely an ancillary component or illustration. Take the "illustrated" texts of William Blake, which combine poetry and art in an inextricable whole. With Symbolist poetry, most notably in the works of Mallarmé and Apollinaire, visual effects in general and the use of calligraphy more specifically gain tremendous importance. The visual there is not understood as paratextual but textual or cotextual. The following decades would add a list of poetry movements and styles, including the Haptic, Visual, Concrete, Léttriste, Neo-Concrete, and Ultra-Léttriste, as well as other avant-garde and post-avant-garde movements that gained prominence as subgenres in Europe, the United States, and Latin America.

The same applies to the use of sound in writing. Again, premodern and non-Western conceptions reflected a performative approach to literature reaching beyond theater. It was common for epic and lyric poetry, for example, to be performed with theatrical gesticulation or musical accompaniment. In modern literature the presence of sound poetry is seen in the avant-garde "Diepalismo" of the Puerto Ricans José de Diego Padró and Luis Palés Matos, in Charles Olson's "Projective Verse," in the performance poetry of Emmett Williams, and in Spoken Word Poetry, Slam Poetry, Poetry Out Loud, but also in the movement that can be more directly linked to Braschi—the performances of the Nuyorican Poets. What is particularly interesting here is that, despite the long-standing tradition of such visual and sound techniques, they have a specific application in Braschi's writing, which suggests the intermediality of image and word or the visual/performative treatment of the written word.

Finally, the adapters of Braschi's work have understood the task well. The baton has been passed to take an intermedial work to another medium/support, not as someone who is following the originator but as someone following a follower. Like love, according to Braschi, her work is and always has been desirous and incomplete. Fortunate are her reader adapters because they have responded to the call of someone who in turn was also called. Like the author's beloved Dionysus, "the god who returns," Braschi's entire opus is a life/work that always returns. It is a work about returning, because it has never completely arrived and never completed departed, in an inextricable *Yo—boing—Yo.*

In its own way, Braschi's work is therefore an inter-work and her poems inter-poems, her novels are inter-novels, her life, inter-life. In images yet to be exhibited (and those already referenced), the artist Zansky meticulously rereads various signs in the works of this Puerto Rican author. His blowtorched drawings—from the technique to the instrument itself—not only capture Braschi's profane tragicomedy, but more importantly they embrace her elemental ferocity. Zansky's adaptations are letters, incisions, inscribed in fire. And his objectives, his characters and subjects, seem more like rhizomes than humans—plantlike forms presaging what is always to come. The path taken by Braschi, or inter-Braschi, is no small thing. It is the same path retaken by her adapters. It is a strange and extraordinary path. It is gratitude.

Notes

1. The term "political" has broad semantic applications in contemporary cultural theory. In current contexts, it can connote "dissident" as well as "pertinent" cultural production.

2. Literary critics have certainly taken note of the hybridity, or its avatars, in Braschi's works. Sarah de Mojica analyzes discourses of hybridity applied as a strategy for reading Braschi's works. Mojica employs various theoretical tools, including the transculturation of Ángel Rama and the heterogeneity of Antonio Cornejo Polar, to illuminate other aspects of the works of Luis Rafael Sánchez and Giannina Braschi.

3. In this chapter (an edited version of a longer article in Spanish, to be published separately), I will first analyze this hybridity of genres and then discuss the expository angle of our reading—the hybridity of media/ mediums/support—in Braschi's work.

4. For the purpose of language congruency we will use the title in English, but the edition consulted was the one in Spanish, as indicated in the Works Cited.

5. *Le Spleen de Paris* (1986), p. 15–16; translation Mackenzie, p. 3.

6. Bakhtin's distinctions between the novel and the epic are well known. He attributes dialogic, polyphonic, and discursive or signifying openness to the former and monologic, homophonic, and discursive or signifying closedness to the latter.

7. Critics have highlighted the dialogic/discursive aspect of Braschi's work from a range of different theoretical standpoints. An example of this can be found in Balboa Echevarría.

8. I am grateful to Tess O'Dwyer for the excellent references to intermedial adaptations of Braschi's work.

9. Here I refer to the terms from the Lacanian psychoanalytic tradition. For Lacan, there are three registers of reality: the symbolic, which is none other than the linguistic-cultural; the imaginary, which is the iconic-prelinguistic; and the real, which is the non-iconic and the non-symbolic aspect of reality, an element that because of its own non-categoricity encourages symbolic production.

10. References provided by Tess O'Dwyer.

11. References provided by Tess O'Dwyer.

12. In this analysis of the discourse in Braschi's work, references will be made to the digital editions. The numbering of these works in the citations or paraphrases reflects the possible textual expansion in digital editions that I used to facilitate reading. In paper editions, the page numbering is uniform.

13. For a detailed analysis of the "poetic egg" in Braschi's work, see Marting.

14. For genres with mix or performative qualities, see Goldberg.

Works Cited

Bakhtin, Mikhail M. "Epic and the Novel: Towards a Methodology for the Study of the Novel." *The Dialogic Imagination.* Translated by C. Emerson and M. Holquist, U of Texas P, 1981, pp. 3–7.

Bakhtin, Mikhail M. *Hacia una filosofía del acto ético: De los borradores y otros escritos.* Translated by Tatiana Bubnova, Editorial de la Universidad de Puerto Rico y Anthropos Editorial, 1997.

Balboa Echevarría, Miriam. "Mirada y marejada en el *Imperio de los sueños* de Giannina Braschi." *Confluencia*, vol. 17, no. 2, Spring 2002, pp. 98–103.

Baudelaire, Charles. *Petits poèmes en prose et choix de textes esthétiques.* Bordas, 1986.

Braschi, Giannina. *Empire of Dreams.* Translated by Tess O'Dwyer, AmazonCrossing, 2011. Kindle.

Braschi, Giannina. *United States of Banana.* AmazonCrossing, 2011. Kindle.

Braschi, Giannina. *Yo-Yo Boing!* AmazonCrossing, 2011. Kindle.

Goldberg, RoseLee. *Performance Art.* Harry N. Abrams, 1979.

Jameson, Fredric. "Lógica cultural del capitalismo tardío." *Teoría de la postmodernidad.* Editorial Trotta, 1998, pp. 37–39.

Mackenzie, Raymond N. *Charles Baudelaire: Paris Spleen and La Fanfarlo.* Hackett, 2008.

Marting, Diane E. "New/Nueva York in Giannina Braschi's 'Poetic Egg': Fragile Identity, Postmodernism, and Globalization." *Global South*, vol. 4, no. 1, special issue "Latin America in a Global Age," Spring 2010, pp. 167–82.

Mojica, Sarah de. "Sujetos híbridos en la literatura puertorriqueña: 'Daniel Dantos y *Yo-Yo Boing!*' Literaturas heterogéneas y creoles." *Revista de Crítica Literaria Latinoamericana*, vol. 28, no. 56, 2002, pp. 187–203.

11

Free-dom

United States of Banana and the Limits of Sovereignty

Ronald Mendoza-de Jesús

Wie weit aber Schelling auch auf neuem Wege in das Wesen der menschlichen Freiheit vordringen mag, die Kantische Grundstellung zur Frage nach der Freiheit wird nicht erschüttert, sondern nur bestätigt. Kant sagt: Die Tatsache der Freiheit ist unbegreiflich; was wir allein begreifen, ist ihre Unbegreiflichkeit. Und die Unbegreiflichkeit der Freiheit besteht darin, daß sie, sofern sie ist, dem Be-greifen sich widersetzt, indem das Freisein uns in den Vollzug des Seyns versetzt, nicht in das bloße Vor-stellen desselben. Der Vollzug aber ist kein blindes Abrollen eines Vorgangs, sondern ist wissendes Innestehen im Seienden im Ganzen, das es auszustehen gilt. Dieses Wissen der Freiheit wird seiner höchsten Notwendigkeit gewiß, weil es allein jene Aufnahmestellung ermöglicht, in der stehend der Mensch imstande ist, als ein Geschichtlicher einem Schicksal zu begegnen, es auf sich zu nehmen und über sich hinweg zu tragen.

—Martin Heidegger

La récurrence du sujet n'est ainsi ni la liberté de la possession de soi par soi dans la réflexion, ni la liberté du jeu ou je me prends pour ceci ou pour cela traversant des avatars sous les masques du carnaval de l'histoire. Il s'agit d'une exigence venant de l'autre, par-delà l'*actif* de mes pouvoirs, pour ouvrir un "déficit" sans limites, ou se dépense sans compter—librement—le Soi. Toute la souffrance et la cruauté de l'essence pèsent sur un point qui la supporte et l'expie.

—Emmanuel Levinas

Free from Freedom. Free.

—Giannina Braschi

It may seem obvious that, when it comes to Puerto Rico, any emancipatory politics worthy of the name must begin by insisting on the need for a full-fledged process of decolonization, which would replace the current political status of the island as an unincorporated territory of the United States with the formation of a truly autonomous, sovereign, free state. Only then would the island come into its own as a properly constituted body politic capable of bestowing upon its citizens the privileges and duties that are proper to political existence—privileges and duties that are themselves based on the freedom that constitutes the very essence of our humanity and our most fundamental human right. And yet, I want to submit to your consideration an alternative scenario. What if, precisely for the sake of emancipatory politics within the island and beyond its shores, another concept of freedom was required—a freedom no longer grounded in the co-implication of sovereignty and selfhood?

It is this possibility that I wish to explore through a reading of *United States of Banana*, the most recent "novel" of Puerto Rican author Giannina Braschi, and some moments in the vast corpus of the French Algerian philosopher Jacques Derrida. Braschi and Derrida have similar backgrounds and interests: both were marked by the experience of exile and the unfinished legacies of colonization, and their work engages with the necessities and impossibilities of translation, undercutting the privilege that is usually granted to first languages or mother tongues as the very linguistic element that unifies a nation, a people, or a community. However, most germane to my concerns today is their common investment in interrogating the limits of political selfhood. Each in their own way, Braschi and Derrida invite us to abandon our expectations of what counts as emancipation by asking us to rethink the very concept of unconditionality—defined broadly as the absence of any internal or external constraints—that we often invoke implicitly as a synonym of freedom, if not as its very essence. Their invitation to rethink unconditionality, and therefore freedom as such, is also an instigation to dismantle the hegemonic political and juridical configurations that transform the force of unconditionality into the power of sovereignty, beginning with that political machine known as the sovereign self, who understands itself as a political entity by making its existence coincide with its ability to *possess itself*.

A Brief Philosophical Excursus on Freedom and Ipseity

But what would this other freedom look like? Consider the first of my epigraphs, which is taken from the end of a lecture course given by the German philosopher Martin Heidegger in 1936 at the University of

Freiburg. This course was devoted to Schelling's famous treatise on the essence of human freedom, *Philosophische Untersuchungen über das Wesen der menschlichen Freiheit*, which was first published in 1809, and which remains to this day one of the crucial texts in the canon of continental philosophy that deals with the question of freedom. For Schelling, as for an entire tradition of philosophical and theological reflection that extends back at least to Augustine, the essence of human freedom is linked to the problem that the existence of evil poses within a theistic worldview in which it is assumed that the universe was created by a God who is omniscient, omnipotent, and absolutely benevolent (Schelling 59). It is telling, however, that Heidegger brings his semester-long engagement with Schelling to a close by identifying Schelling's contributions to our understanding of human freedom with Kant's views on this subject, which are most forcefully exposed in his second *Critique* (Kant, *Kritik der praktischen*). More than anybody else, it was Kant who set the terms for philosophy's renewed interest in the question of freedom by insisting on the "ungraspability" or the *Unbegreiflichkeit* of freedom.

Here, we must take Heidegger at his word, for at least two reasons. The first is because the term *Unbegreiflichkeit* is itself a citation of Kant, who uses this word at least five times in the first *Critique* as part of his attempt to diagnose the pathologies of reason that obtain when pure reason oversteps the realm of possible experience—for instance, when it embraces the idea of a supreme being as a constitutive, and not merely regulative, principle of all possible experience (Kant, *Kritik der reinen* A689/B717). More significantly for the purposes of this essay, the word *Unbegreiflichkeit* appears in the preface of the second *Critique* to characterize freedom as ungraspable for pure speculative reason (Kant, *Kritik der praktischen* 9).

The second is because the common English translation of this word as "ungraspability" is somewhat misleading. Although it rightly accentuates the fact that the German word *Unbegreiflichkeit* has at its core the verb *greifen*, which means indeed "to grasp," this translation does not place enough emphasis on the philosophico-semantic valence of the verb *begreifen*, which means "to conceive" or "to conceptualize," and from which we obtain the German word for "concept," *Begriff*. Freedom is therefore not just ungraspable; it is literally *inconceivable*, in the technical sense that it cannot be represented by means of a concept. And the reason there is no concept of freedom that I could use to represent discursively freedom as an object lies in the simple fact that, for Kant, freedom is not an object I could possibly experience. Nowhere will I encounter a thing called "freedom" that could affect my senses, giving rise to a moment of perception or intuition. Freedom is not of the order of the concept because it does not belong to my phenomenal reality, which I am capable of knowing to the extent that the forms that make the phenomenal world knowable to me are produced by my own consciousness. The fact that freedom resists being captured within a concept only elevates its status to the sublime heights of what Kant calls an idea, which can only be felt—Kant's classic example is the affect of respect or *Achtung*—but can never be fully grasped by means of a concept (Kant, *Kritik der praktischen* 100).

This said, Kant's claim that freedom cannot be objectified has to be qualified, since the whole point of Kant's practical philosophy is to show that freedom is in fact an actual force that has an impact in our world. For Kant, freedom acts in our world through its incarnation in what he calls the "moral law." Kant: "die Freiheit allerdings die *ratio essendi* des moralischen Gesetzes, das moralische Gesetz aber die *ratio cognoscendi* der Freiheit sei. Denn wäre nicht das moralische Gesetz in unserer Vernunft eher deutlich gedacht, so würden wir uns niemals berechtigt halten, so etwas, als Freiheit ist (ob diese gleich sich nicht widerspricht), anzunehmen. Wäre aber keine Freiheit, so würde das moralische Gesetz in uns gar nicht anzutreffen sein" ("freedom is indeed the *ratio essendi* of the moral law, the moral law is the *ratio cognoscendi* of freedom. For, had not the moral law already been distinctly thought in our reason, we should never consider ourselves justified in assuming such a thing as freedom [even though it is not self-contradictory]. But were there no freedom, the moral law would not be encountered at all in ourselves" [Kant, *Kritik der praktischen* 4; Kant, *Practical Philosophy* 140]). Although freedom is the ontological ground, the very being that subtends the existence of the moral law, we would have no knowledge of freedom if we couldn't conceive of the possibility of moral law. Conversely, the moral law would neither be lawful nor, above all, moral if it were not adopted as a law through an act of my own free will. As such, the moral law concretizes freedom by transforming the latter into the autonomy of a subject that freely subjects itself to the universality of a law that demands to be obeyed in an unconditional and pure manner—a law that is followed simply because it is the law, and as law it allows me to experience the fullness of my essence as a being who not only knows the natural world and its laws but also is capable of acting freely, in ways that may even contravene or supersede the causal mechanisms that characterize natural laws.

Returning to the passage from Heidegger that is cited as our first epigraph, we can see that he follows Kant when he insists that our human freedom "contradicts con-ceptualization, as being-free transfers us into the fulfillment of beyng, and not into its mere re-presentation" (Heidegger 281, my translation). But, for Heidegger, who at this point was still committed to his own brand of *spiritual* National-Socialism, the fulfillment of *beyng* is not realized through the morl law but, rather, is to be found in humanity's encounter with its historical *Schicksal* or "destiny" (Heidegger 281), through which a people (and for Heidegger this word almost always means the "German" people) appropriates its own essence, becoming an authentic self.[1]

A similarly humanist thinking of freedom informs Levinas's remarks in the passage I quoted as my second epigraph. But from Heidegger to Levinas a major displacement has nonetheless taken place. Heidegger substitutes the Kantian figure of the moral law for the fulfillment of being, out of which a people or a community receives its historical destiny.[2] Levinas radicalizes Kant's thinking of the moral law in the direction of a thinking of radical alterity that enables us to distinguish between two kinds of freedom: on the one hand, there is the active substantive liberty that is the very ground of the existence of those selves who possess themselves; on the other hand, we would have adverbial freedom of a passive movement in which the self freely ceases to possess itself and instead wastes itself away, spends itself in a moment of generosity for the sake of responding freely to the demand of the other.[3] And yet, in spite of their differences, both Levinas and Heidegger think freedom within the humanist purview of a notion of selfhood according to which the self can only be free either by taking up the historical destiny that has been sent to it, or by submitting itself to the law of the other. Is there perhaps another freedom that may be beyond appropriation or submission?

It is in order to approach this question that I want to take up the phrase from Braschi's *United States of Banana* that I quoted as my third epigraph: "Free from freedom. Free" (Braschi 186). What kind of life would be that which exists so freely that it has freed itself of the idea of freedom, perhaps a freedom freer than freedom? If thinkers as opposed to the tradition of liberalism as Heidegger and Levinas continue to think of freedom within the horizon either of an appropriation of the other or of a voluntary submission to the alterity of the other, Braschi's mantra perhaps formulates the demand for a free-dom *other* than freedom *itself*, inviting us to think an emancipation without horizon that cannot be *dom*-esticated by any concept nor assimilated to any idea. A freedom that is not the freedom of a sovereign self—the freedom of ipseity—but, rather, that is free from ipseity.

Puerto Rico's Sovereign Crises

Before we turn to this question, consider the case of Puerto Rican sovereignty, a place that Justice Trías Monge—one of the architects of the territory's current constitution—referred to as the oldest colony in the world (Trías Monge). Although it has been submitted to external rule since the establishment of a Spanish colony on the island in 1508 under the leadership of Juan Ponce de León, at no other point in Puerto Rico's history have the seams of colonial rule been so visible as during the summer of 2016. If, since 1952, Puerto Rico has enjoyed a degree of self-government that, in the words of the Supreme Court of the United States, is comparable to that of any other state of the union, and if Puerto Rico was officially removed from the list of colonies by the UN Committee on Decolonization in 1953, this summer all branches of the federal government decided to put an end to the fictive sovereignty under which some members of the political class of Puerto Rico—mostly gathered in the Partido Popular Democrático—have sought to perpetuate colonial rule on the island under the misleading banner of the Estado Libre Asociado (ELA).

The first blow to the Commonwealth (as the ELA is known in English) came on June 9, 2016, when the US Supreme Court decided that Puerto Rico does not possess enough sovereignty to deprive two criminals, Luis Sánchez Valle and Jaime Gómez Vazquez, of their right not to be tried twice for the same crime, a right enshrined in the Fifth Amendment of the American Constitution and known as the Double Jeopardy Clause. As you may know, one of the major exceptions to the Double Jeopardy Clause is known as the separate sovereigns doctrine, which allows putting someone on trial twice for the same crime if two different sovereign jurisdictions—for instance, the federal government and a state government—can prove to have been wronged by the crime committed. According to the Supreme Court:

> [The creation of the Commonwealth in 1952] made Puerto Rico "sovereign" in one commonly understood sense of that term. At that point, Congress granted Puerto Rico a degree of autonomy comparable to that possessed by the States. If the dual-sovereignty doctrine hinged on measuring an entity's self-governance, the emergence of the Commonwealth would have resulted as well in the capacity to bring the kind of successive prosecutions attempted here. . . . But the dual-sovereignty test focuses not on the fact of self-rule, but on where it first came from. And in identifying a prosecuting entity's wellspring of authority, the Court has insisted on going all the way back—beyond the immediate, or even an intermediate, locus of power to what is termed the "ultimate source." On this settled approach, Puerto Rico cannot benefit from the dual-sovereignty doctrine. True enough, that the Commonwealth's power to enact and enforce criminal law now proceeds, just as petitioner says, from the Puerto Rico Constitution as "ordain[ed] and establish[ed]" by "the people." P. R. Const., Preamble. But back of the Puerto

> Rican people and their Constitution, the "ultimate" source of prosecutorial power remains the U. S. Congress. Congress, in Public Law 600, authorized Puerto Rico's constitution-making process in the first instance, and Congress, in later legislation, both amended the draft charter and gave it the indispensable stamp of approval. Put simply, Congress conferred the authority to create the Puerto Rico Constitution, which in turn confers the authority to bring criminal charges. (*Commonwealth of Puerto Rico v. Sanchez Valle et al.*, 579 U.S. 3, 2016)

In adjudicating this seemingly technical issue, the US Supreme Court settled the issue as to whether Puerto Rico's autonomy constituted what legal scholar Thomas Aleinikoff refers to as a "semblance of sovereignty" (Aleinikoff). Puerto Rico may have attained a degree of self-rule comparable to that of the states of the union, but the source and the ground of such self-governance remains an act of US sovereignty and not a moment of self-determination of the Puerto Rican people. In other words, whatever functional sovereignty Puerto Rico may exercise occurs on the basis of an act of Congress—and what Congress gives, Congress could take away.

And indeed it has. On the last day of that same month, President Obama signed into law project S. 2328, also known as the Puerto Rico Oversight, Management, and Economic Stability or PROMESA. The law reestablishes undemocratic colonial rule in the island by creating the Fiscal Oversight Board—known in the island as the "Junta de Control Fiscal," or, simply, "La Junta." Composed of seven men and women appointed by the Speaker of the House of Representatives and the President of the United States, "La Junta" has ultimate control over the commonwealth's budget, with a mandate to maneuver the liquidity crisis that the island's government faces, oppressed by a shrinking economy and a whopping debt of 72 billion dollars (almost 100 percent of the GDP). The board also has the power to ensure "the prompt enforcement of any applicable laws of the covered territory prohibiting public sector employees from participating in a strike or lockout" (PROMESA, 559). Moreover, the law not only grants the "La Junta" the power to fast-track approval of infrastructure projects and public-private partnerships in key sectors of the Puerto Rican economy, such as energy and higher education (which are currently largely in the hands of the commonwealth's government). The law also gives total immunity to the board members in the fact of any possible future lawsuits, stipulating that "The Oversight Board, its members, and its employees shall not be liable for any obligation of or claim against the Oversight Board or its members or employees or the territorial government resulting from actions taken to carry out this

Act" (PROMESA, 561). Finally, Section 108 of the law, aptly titled "Autonomy of Oversight Board," clarifies the extent to which colonial rule in the classical sense of the term has returned to the island, stipulating that "(a) IN GENERAL.—Neither the Governor nor the Legislature may—(1) exercise any control, supervision, oversight, or review over the Oversight Board or its activities; or (2) enact, implement, or enforce any statute, resolution, policy, or rule that would impair or defeat the purposes of this Act, as determined by the Oversight Board" (PROMESA, 563). As you can imagine, the question of Puerto Rico's relationship to the United States is now even more at the center of political debates on the island. Many, myself included, feel that the time has come to finally dispel the fantasy of Puerto Rico's sovereignty under US rule and to take up again the question of the economic and ontological implications of striving to become a sovereign nation.

Braschian Allegories 1: Wishy-Washy

The philosophical and political contexts I have discussed are crucial if we are to grasp the pertinence of Giannina Braschi's political intervention in her 2011 novel, *United States of Banana*. In a truly Nietzschean fashion, her text constitutes an "untimely" if not even prophetic observation of the situation that the island now faces. In this novel she not only revisits the question of Puerto Rico's colonial relation to the United States (a topic that had ceased to be a primary concern of literary authors since, at least, the 1980s), she also dares to imagine a scenario in which the island attains its independence from the United States . . . of Banana, wreaking havoc in the geopolitical order of neoliberal capitalism. Furthermore, I would also argue that Braschi's text runs against the grain of many contemporary ways of theorizing political action well beyond the Puerto Rican context, resisting simplistic notions of identity politics that go in tandem with an understanding of the political as a name for struggles around hegemony, while also insisting, against a certain reception of post-structuralism or postmodernity, on the need to disentangle notions such as freedom and sovereignty from their inscription within liberal and neoliberal political frameworks.

Before continuing with this line of thought, I want to give a brief and partial account of some of the main features of Braschi's recent work. Not unlike its predecessors *El imperio de los sueños* and *Yo-Yo Boing!*, *United States of Banana* defies generic boundaries: it is partly a novel, partly a prose poem, partly a play, though always a performance. The book is set in post-9/11 New York City. It is divided into two parts: the first is titled "Ground-Zero" and is composed of a series of prose poems punctuated by dialogues; the second is titled "United States of Banana" and is decisively more theatrical and plot driven. The second part also seems to be more immediately allegorical than the first part, at least if we subscribe to the notion of allegory that Frederic Jameson articulates in an influential and problematic essay published in 1986. Jameson argues that "[t]hird-world texts, even those which are seemingly private and invested with a properly libidinal dynamic, necessarily project a political dimension in the form of national allegory: *the story of the private individual destiny is always an allegory of the embattled situation of the public third-world culture and society*" (Jameson 69). Indeed, at first sight, the section "United States of Banana" appears to be nothing more than another allegory of Puerto Rican independence, though, this time, the emblem of Puerto Rico's liberation is Segismundo, the main character of Calderón de la Barca's *La vida es sueño*. Like the play it parodies, *United States of Banana* begins with Segismundo imprisoned by his father, Basilio, who is the head of state of the United States of Banana. But this time around, his cell is located in a dungeon on top of the fortress that serves as the base of Lady Liberty on Liberty Island. The plot of *United States of Banana* unfolds in the following way: Shakespeare's Hamlet, Nietzsche's Zarathustra, and a character named Giannina decide to cross the Hudson River to go to Liberty Island, penetrate the Statue of Liberty, and free Segismundo, subsequently freeing Puerto Rico from its colonial captivity. This act of defiance produces a response from Gertrude—Hamlet's mother—who concocts a plan to marry Basilio, free Segismundo, and bring him into the same family as Hamlet as the only possible way to save the ancien régime of the imperial United States of Banana from collapsing. As part of her plan, Gertrude convinces Basilio that Puerto Rico should be granted admission into the United States of Banana, that all illegal immigrants should be granted citizenship, and that the borders of the United States of Banana should be opened. Her efforts to mitigate the revolution by granting concessions to Giannina and the other insurgents fail. Giannina and her comrades declare unilaterally the independence of Puerto Rico after realizing that the changes in the United States of Banana's policies toward Puerto Rico and Latin America were an attempt to perpetuate a sort of imperial Pax Banana under the joint leadership of Basilio and Gertrude. War erupts between Puerto Rico, Cuba (which has claims to Puerto Rico and seeks to create its own Caribbean empire), and the United States of Banana. Giannina and her comrades can only rely on coconuts and philosophical conversation to fight the soldiers of the empire. But the timely intervention of China—the USB creditor—secures the independence of Puerto Rico and brings Braschi's geopolitical comedy to a close.

That the allegorical intention of *United States of Banana* is linked to the issue of imagining Puerto Rico's emancipation from US colonial rule can be seen from the very first section of the first part of Braschi's text, titled "Death of a Businessman." After recounting having seen the dismembered body of a businessman (a torso, to be more precise) falling from the Twin Towers, the narrative voice (who is clearly Braschi herself, or Giannina) gives us an account of her plans to write *United States of Banana*. It is here that one of the most important allegories in the book makes its first appearance. I am referring to the words: "Wishy" "Wishy-Washy" and "Washy." I cite Braschi *in extenso*:

> That same fortress over which Bartholdi erected the Statue of Liberty will be the fortress where Segismundo will be imprisoned. . . . Segismundo thinks that he depends on liberty, but the truth be said—liberty has more need of him than he of the statue. . . . The military is afraid that some terrorist group will plot to rescue him. The people want to liberate him. So, in order to prevent the coming insurrection, a voting system is created to give the people the impression that Segismundo's destiny is in their hands. They are given three options: Wishy / Wishy-Washy / Washy. If they vote for Wishy—Segismundo will be liberated from the dungeon. If they vote for Wishy-Washy, the status quo will prevail. If they vote for Washy, he will be sentenced to death, and nobody will have the honor of hearing his songs rise from the gutters of the dungeon of liberty. Every four years the citizens of Liberty Island vote for Wishy-Washy. They can choose between mashed potato, French fries, or baked potato. But any way you serve it, it's all the same potato. (*USB* 7)

The allegorical valence of Segismundo as the image of Puerto Rico's political dilemma is here doubled by another set of allegories that signify the options of political status that determine the configuration of partisan politics in the island. Wishy stands for independence; Wishy-Washy stands for the commonwealth or the ELA; and Washy stands for statehood. Although the narrator describes Washy in terms that are more immediately negative (that is, a death sentence), it is telling that the following sentence neutralizes any significant difference between these three options by comparing them to three different ways of serving the "same potato." Later on in another section of "Ground Zero" titled "Chicken with the Head Cut Off," Braschi adds more layers of allegorical significance to the set of Wishy-Washy-Wishy-Washy by invoking these figures in order to designate the entanglement of language and politics not only in the broader context of the Puerto Rican experience but also in her own work as writer: "In spite of my family and in spite of my country, I'm writing the process of the Puerto Rican mind—taking it out of context—as a native and a foreigner—expressing it through Spanish,

Spanglish, and English—*Independencia*, *Estado Libre Asociado*, and *Estadidad*—from the position of a nation, a colony, and a state—Wishy, Wishy-Washy, and Washy" (*USB* 47).

Reading these two passages together produces an ironic effect, which is linked to a discrepancy between the politics of language and the language of politics when it comes to Braschi's own work. For something in these sets of triads does not line up. The book of Puerto Rican independence (that is to say, the book of Wishy or *United States of Banana*) ought to have been written in Spanish. And yet that book is written in English, the language of Washy or statehood. The implications of this chiasmus—of the crossing of Spanish into English, of independence into statehood, and of Wishy into Washy—are far-reaching. In fact, this reversal is what truly accounts for the passage I quoted above where the narrator says that ultimately Wishy, Washy, and Wishy-Washy are three versions of the same potato. In other words, they are nothing other than the internal differentiations of sameness, or Wishy-Washy.

It is here, in this point where Wishy and Washy become indistinct, that I want to locate what I take to be Braschi's most compelling contribution to another thinking of politics. The realization that Wishy and Washy are ultimately the same leads the narrator to radically question the framework of representational politics, identity positions, and linguistic fluencies that determines the political configuration of the game of Wishy-Washy, which has kept Puerto Ricans at the mercy of a political process that can only provide a semblance of freedom. It is here also that another allegory is grafted onto the national allegory of the *United States of Banana* and pushes this text beyond the limits of the notions of allegory that Jameson puts forward in his essay—closer to the work on allegory of Erin Graff Zivin, who has recently argued for the political valence of allegorical structures that foreground the impossibility of any aesthetic and political regime of representation to produce and ensure its own semantic closure (Graff Zivin).

Braschian Allegories 2: "Free-dom"

This other thinking of politics is articulated allegorically around the character of the Statue of Liberty. At a textual level, this allegory is at work in the repetition of a phrase that functions like a motif or a refrain throughout the text, repeated by several characters, though primarily by Segismundo and Giannina. The phrase is what stands as my paper's title: "Free from freedom. Free." Within the plot of Braschi's novel the liberation of Segismundo was not only meant to liberate Puerto Rico; it was also meant to free freedom from freedom. The closest we ever get to that moment occurs in the section of "United States of Banana" titled "Wedding of the Century." After Segismundo challenges his father to a duel, the Statue of Liberty utters the following words through a loudspeaker:

> I am speechless. He is fulfilling his promise to his people. I am speechless—soon—my genie—soon. I will leave—when he leaves—somebody—or myself—I might have to do it myself—self-reliance. . . . I have been waiting—and waiting—all these years as a frigid statue—soon—my genie—not soon enough—this dawn—when the cock crows—*cuando vengan los rosarios de la aurora*—when the cocks fight and kick their spurs—my genie—uncorked—free from freedom. Free. My genie uncorked. And I will ride away on the back of his horse—wherever his spurs lead me. Free from freedom. Free. (*USB* 186)

"Free from freedom. Free." The syntactic concatenation of four words and two sentences results in a paradoxical juxtaposition that produces both tautology and its opposite—namely, an extreme form of dissociation of what is commonly held to be the same or to belong together. Moreover, even if we bracket the concrete modifications that these two sentences undergo throughout *United States of Banana* so as to treat them as an isolated set of statements, their mere juxtaposition generates an allegory of emancipation whose interpretation would demand more time than I have at my disposal. I will thus limit myself to bring to your attention two aspects of this allegorical set with the goal of sketching out the contours of what I would be tempted to call *freedom's double bind*. On the one hand, we should note that these two statements not only *deal* exclusively *with* the concept of freedom but also seem to *belong to* freedom. Freedom would be both the subject and the object of this set of statements, which would be not so much *about* freedom as *of* freedom itself. Ironically, it is only if we consider what Roman Jakobson calls the "poetic function" of language that the genitive, possessive relation that the concept of freedom has with regard to this set of statements becomes more salient (Jakobson 356). First, we must observe that the three units that make up this set are almost exhaustively unified through the interplay of alliteration and assonance—*fr*ee, *fr*om, *fr*eedom and fr*ee*, fr*eedom*, fr*om*. Second, and most important, the noun "freedom" is the only member of the set that contains in itself all the possible combinations that make up this set in its totality. If, according to its referential function, the first sentence of the set amounts to a declaration of independence *of* freedom *from* freedom, its poetic dimension would seem to undermine the possibility of such a liberation. For the very *tongue* in which the freedom *from* freedom is stated, demanded, or petitioned continues to speak the language *of* freedom and is, in fact, contained *within* that freedom, which ought to have been excluded for *another* freedom to finally ring. Taken to its most extreme and perverse limit, this set seems to give way to an absolute tautological schema, which reassures freedom in its power to control its boundaries by turning any declaration of free-dom *from* freedom into a declaration *of* freedom. As if the very attempt to free freedom from freedom were a ruse of liberty, which would feign to expose itself to *its own* undoing while continuing to rule over the conditions of its demise, all the while saving for itself the right to preside over its exclusion unconditionally, autonomously, and thus in a certain way, freely. Excluding itself from itself in order to better rule over its inner-most interiority—such would be the claim of *freedom proper.*

Is it possible to draw a limit—at once from without and within—to freedom's tautology? In "Tympan," the preface to *Marges de la philosophie*, Derrida poses precisely this question, although his target is not strictly speaking the concept of freedom but, rather, any and all philosophemes—that is, the philosopheme in general—including the very concept of the concept:

> Subsequently, what are the conditions from which one could *mark* a *limit* to a philosopheme in general, mark a margin that it may not be able to reappropriate for itself infinitely, *conceive* as its own, engendering and internalizing in advance the process of its expropriation (Hegel still, always), going from itself to its inversion? . . . For *being* hears itself in this way: its *proper.* It assures without rest the sublating movement of reappropriation. Subsequently, can one *pass* this singular limit which is not one, which no longer separates the inside from the outside nor assures a permeable and transparent continuity? What may be the form of this play of limit/passage, of this logos that poses and denies itself in letting its own voice to emerge? Is this a well-formed question? (Derrida, *Marges* viii–ix; my translation)

Derrida's question also haunts Braschi's *United States of Banana.* The novel's mantra-like repetition of the words "Free from freedom. Free." betrays a desire to finally interrupt the circle of appropriation that turns any moment of emancipation into another instantiation of the most traditional concept of liberation. Moreover, I would argue that the incessant repetition of these words not only conveys a desire to break this circle but also effectively transgresses this limit, provided that this set of statements is read *otherwise.* For if on the one hand these utterances can be read as another affirmation of freedom's tautology, on the other hand they also can be read as an allegory of the interruption of said tautology.

This interruption becomes legible as soon as we pay attention, first of all, to the grammatical form of these statements. Both sentences are closed off by periods: "Free from freedom. Free." But these produce different semantic effects in each case. Whereas the first period ends the process through which freedom sets in motion *its proper* liberation and reaffirms itself precisely by placing itself outside of itself, the second period takes place abruptly, near the very beginning of the sentence. Although the second sentence begins by repeating the first one, the period cuts the sentence short of reasserting freedom's *own* freedom, leaving the word "Free"—which could be read as an adjective or as a verb—alone, independent, absolved, delivered, free from everything else including the prepositional phrase "from freedom," which enables the unfolding of the circular movement of the concept of freedom as the uncanny conclusion of the first sentence. As if within the space that separates the first and the second sentence, in the interval between the first and the second period, a difference at the heart of the concept of freedom had emerged—a difference that is intended by the first sentence but that is only produced by the second sentence, which not only brings to a halt the repetition of freedom's self-liberation but also renders questionable whether these two appearances of the word "free" mean, name, refer, indicate, or figure the same thing. The difference between these two "freedoms" would be indicated by the fact that Braschi places the second appearance of the word "free" by itself, that is, out of the reach of both the noun-concept "freedom" and the preposition "from," which mediates the relation between "free" and "freedom" in the first sentence. As if the second sentence affirmed that what the first sentence intended—a freeing from freedom—had already taken place—namely, that "the free" and "freeing" have been dissociated from the name of "freedom." Moreover, it is not any coincidence that this other thinking of freedom requires not only the transposition of the noun "freedom" into the adjective "free" but also the effacement of the suffix "-dom." As the *Oxford English Dictionary* (*OED*) tells us:

> [The prefix "-dom" is an] abstract suffix of state, which has grown out of an independent n., orig. putting, setting, position, statute, Old High German *tuom*, position, condition, dignity, in Old English *dóm*, statute, judgment, jurisdiction. . . . Frequent already in Old English as a suffix to ns. and adjs., as *biscopdóm*, the dignity of a bishop, *cyningdóm*, *cynedóm*, royal or kingly dominion, kingdom, *ealdordóm*, the position or jurisdiction of an elder or lord; *þeowdóm*, the condition of a þeow or slave; *fréodóm*, *háligdóm*, *wisdóm*, the condition or fact of being free, holy, or wise. The number of these derivatives has increased in later times, and *-dom* is now a living suffix, freely employed to form nonce-derivatives, not only with the sense of "condition, state, dignity," but also with that of "domain, realm." (*OED* s.v. "-dom")

We do not need to posit some dubious etymological connections—for instance, we do not have to trace the English suffix "-dom" back to the

Proto-Indo-European themes of **dem* or **dēmh2*, from which the Latin noun for house, *domus*, and the verb for taming, *domō*, are respectively derived—to grasp the significance of what is at stake in Braschi's gesture of severing the word "free" from its suffix "-dom."[4] For this suffix domesticates the unconditionality of "freedom" in at least two different ways: first, by translating the enigmatic experience of freeing into a condition or a state of a subject who may go in and out of this condition; second, by erecting freedom as the sovereign concept that has jurisdiction over anything that may claim to be free or demand to be freed. The sentences "Free from freedom. Free." can be read now also as a call for *another* free-dom, a free-dom whose unconditionality ought to remain heterogeneous to any "statute, judgment, jurisdiction," insofar as it resists being put in its *proper* place, positioned in the *right* manner, erected as a *legal* statute or as the very statue that represents the law (*OED*, "s.v. -dom"). Unconditionally free, perhaps an *improper* freedom.

Derrida's Unconditionality—Free from Freedom

For the time that I have left, I want to turn to several moments in Derrida's corpus where he engages explicitly with the question of freedom, in order to flesh out the ways in which the concept of unconditionality is no longer the same after Derrida. More specifically, I would like to highlight two of the very concrete ways in which Derrida transformed this traditional philosopheme. On the one hand, for Derrida the very notion of unconditionality is irreducibly linked to the history, the politics, and the metaphysics of the university as the *proper* place of freedom within an Anglo-European culture that continues to expand the reach of its institutional hegemony across the entire globe. Indeed, for Derrida, the problematic relation between the university and its outsides cannot be approached as a special case of the general philosophical problem of freedom and its limits since the university is one of the concrete places in which the deconstruction of freedom may happen and since the freedom that may correspond to the idea of the university may well go against the grain of the metaphysical concept of freedom—what I have called, throughout this talk, *freedom proper*. On the other hand, during the last few years of his life, Derrida's work was primarily engaged in a task outlined explicitly for the first time in *L'Université sans condition* as the dissociation of unconditionality from sovereignty. This task remains unfinished and is most likely interminable in its very structure. Still, Derrida's earlier and later writings on the university provide the best point of departure if we are to grasp the extent to which the task of deconstructing sovereignty requires rehabilitating the name and the concept of freedom beyond its political and ethical determination as the very essence and element of ipseity, defined in the most general sense as the power that secures all possibilities in their possibility.

One of the earliest and most affirmative appearances of the French word *liberté* in Derrida's corpus occurs near the beginning of "Violence et métaphysique" ("Violence and Metaphysics"), first published in 1964 and later collected as one of the essays in *L'écriture et la différence* (*Writing and Difference*). After characterizing the question of the death of philosophy as the sole element that constitutes the community of philosophers as the community of questioners, Derrida makes the following series of striking moves:

> Through . . . this discipline [of the question] . . . , an injunction announces itself: the question must be guarded. As question. The freedom of the question (double genitive) must be said and sheltered. If this commandment has an ethical meaning, it is not because it belongs to the *domain* of the ethical, but because it authorizes—later on—any ethical law in general. . . . There is no commandment that is not addressed to a freedom of speech. There is therefore neither law nor commandment that does not confirm and enclose—that is to say, which does not dissimulate by presupposing the possibility of the question. (Derrida, *L'écriture* 118–19; my translation)

There is a law or a commandment of the question that exceeds the realm of the ethical (and, I would add, that it also exceeds the realm of the political) and whose sole content consists in the injunction to safeguard the freedom of the question. This commandment is neither ethical nor political because it only orders to keep open the possibility of an outside with regards to the modes of ethical and political subjectivation that occur through the agency of the law. This outside would be the very experience of a free question that, at any moment, may turn itself against the totality of political and ethical commands in which we are always already entangled. Rather than constituting a subject, the law of the question renders the questioner destitute, restoring the speaker and the force of its interrogation to the status of a possibility that has become impossible, incapable of being appropriated by anyone or anybody. This explains why Derrida has freedom and possibility exchange places in a movement of metaphorical substitution. The question that is free is the question that remains a question—the question that not only has not found itself by finding its answer but that has not even found itself as a question. For Derrida, only such a question could qualify as the question "as such": the question that questions itself but does so in such a way that it separates its self from itself and thus remains exposed to the chance arrival of further interrogations. In obeying the commandment from which the question as such proceeds, the questioner is obliged only to keep open the space for the possibility of a disobedience of every ethical and political law.

To measure the extent to which Derrida's thinking of the freedom of the question *as such* in "Violence and Metaphysics" remains still, and to a large extent, on this side of philosophy's margins, we could turn to the preface of *Du droit à la philosophie* (*Who's Afraid of Philosophy: Right of Philosophy I*), titled "Privilège: Titre justificatif et remarques introductives" ("Privilege: Justificatory Title and Introductory Remarks"), published for the first time in 1990. In a context that is decisively inflected by the question of the university and the place of philosophy within it, Derrida decides to revisit his engagement with the question in order to better demarcate the limit that separates philosophy's relation to the question as such from that which ought to characterize deconstructive thinking:

> The question (and with it, all forms of negation, research, critique) envelops in it an affirmation, at least the "yes," the affirmation without any content other than the other, precisely, to which a trace is addressed, be it at night. The thought of this "yes" before philosophy, before even the question, . . . traces a strange form of limit between all the determinations of the philosophical and a deconstructive thought that is engaged by philosophy without belonging to it, faithful to an affirmation whose responsibility places it *before* philosophy but also always *ahead* of it, thus below or beyond the question-form of thought. (Derrida, *Du droit* 28–29; my translation)

Notice how the notions of the law and freedom that dominate Derrida's thinking regarding the possibility of the question in "Violence et métaphysique" undergo a drastic transformation here. The place from which the question comes is no longer described as a speaking law, and its addressee is not any more a free speaker. These two places are now "occupied" by the wholly other and the singularity of whoever is responsible for the alterity of the other, which is nothing other than the exigency—the demand, petition, but also prayer—of a response. We may be justified in reading these conceptual shifts as the result of Derrida's own transformed relation to the philosophical tradition. And yet, we would be wrong in assuming that the substitution of freedom for responsibility is indicative of Derrida's resistance to the possibility of deploying the concept of freedom in a more affirmative way. The case is quite the opposite, and Derrida in fact concludes "Privilège" by raising the possibility that "the interest on truth" (one of the fundamental traits of the philosophical) may "*correspond* to a freedom or *answer* to a freer freedom, free otherwise than that which proportions itself to objectivity" (Derrida, *Du droit* 107–8; my translation).

Before beginning to conclude, it would be necessary to confront the obvious question that this passage implicitly poses. Is this *other* freedom conceivable? Is it possible to think of a freedom *otherwise*, a freedom whose difference vis-à-vis the traditional concept of freedom would not be simply quantitative, as a quick reading of Derrida's use of the comparative particle *plus* would make us believe? Wouldn't the establishment of the slightest comparison between these freedoms run the risk of ruining the proportions of this other freedom, by making it proportionate vis-à-vis the proportion of freedom as subjectivity? At this point would reemerge what I called earlier the freedom's double bind, which arranges the scene and the juridical process of freedom's undoing in such a way that the end result confirms the archaic, archic primacy of this concept.

Without being necessarily able to dissolve this double bind, I want to gesture to two aspects of this passage that point to a possible way of sidestepping this paradox. For this passage can be read as doing something other than asserting a quantitative or qualitative distinction between two kinds of freedoms. To begin to do so, we just have to keep in mind that the French particle, *plus*, as you may know, not only means "more" but also "no more." Bending the rules of English grammar for a second, we could say that the freedom that is "more free" than freedom is also freedom "no more," liberated from the rule of the concept "Free from freedom. Free." Then, Derrida italicizes the verbs "cor-respondait" and "répondait" in a way that recalls the earlier passage I quoted above concerning the unconditional character of an absolute affirmation of responsibility for deconstructive thought. As if Derrida were suggesting that this freedom, rather than being a *liberté de parole* as in "Violence et métaphysique," would instead be a *liberté de réponse*, a freedom that would not only hail from the other in me but that would also interrupt both me and freedom from ever becoming each other's master.

Although Derrida himself never pursued explicitly, directly, and in a robust manner this task of thinking freedom otherwise, or an otherwise than freedom, I would like to conclude by turning to a text by Derrida from 1998, written against the backdrop of the Kosovo War, translated as "Unconditionality or Sovereignty: The University at the Frontiers of Europe." Derrida gave this text in a ceremony at Pantion University, which gave Derrida an *honoris causa*. As its title suggests, it is in many ways the sequel to *L'Université sans condition*, where Derrida for the first time explicitly argued for the need to dissociate unconditionality and sovereignty ("Unconditionality" 76). Perhaps the most striking difference between these two texts lies in the way in which Derrida introduces the question of freedom from the very beginning of "Unconditionality or Sovereignty."

> Does the university also aim to be sovereign, with a sovereignty analogous to the one nation-states are presumed to have, a sovereignty that is today going through, everywhere and very close to here, the torment of which you are aware and which surpasses no doubt a simple crisis? Unless the supposed independence of the university, the immunity, the freedom, the absolute exemption that it claims are still more demanding: neither superior nor lesser but of a completely other nature. How should the university decide, then, in complete freedom and whether that freedom is sovereign or not, as to its own "politics," its own "ethics" with respect to all the powers, state powers, powers of the nation-state, powers of the church, ideological powers, economic powers, powers of the media, and so forth, wherever these powers fight over sovereignty or wage war with each other on the subject of sovereignty? (116)

Moreover, if *L'Université sans condition* devotes only its last pages to formulating why the dissociation of unconditionality from sovereignty is almost impossible, "Unconditionality or Sovereignty" presents a bolder case for the chance of this distinction. Consider the following passage:

> Why insist so much, here and now, on an unconditional freedom of the university that should allow one to put in question the principle of any power—first of all in order to think it with full independence and to the point of resistance, disobedience or dissidence? Because no one will have failed to notice that this freedom can resemble and sometimes seem to be linked to what one rightly calls sovereignty, for example, the sovereignty of God, the sovereignty of a monarch, the sovereignty of a nation-state, the sovereignty of the people itself. What, then, allows one to distinguish between, on the one hand, the freedom of thought that is *in principle* unconditional, which seeks its best example and its established right [*droit de cité*] in the university and, on the other hand, sovereignty, notably state-nationalist sovereignty? It is ultimately a theologico-political history of power. I cannot deploy here the argumentation but it would make apparent first of all the theological origins of the concept of sovereignty ("sovereign," "superanus," from "superans," designates first of all the almightiness, predominance and superiority of God, of the Lord-God, then of the absolute monarch by divine right). (127)

To conclude, I want to point out the fact that Derrida himself points to history—more precisely, to a theological history of the concept of power—as what needs to be interrogated and, indeed, deconstructed, if an unconditionality without sovereignty is to be experienced. The deconstruction of this legacy is still ongoing, in spite of the calls from several quarters of the philosophical and critical work to finally bring to a close the project of deconstruction:

> The unconditionality of thought, the thought that ought to find its place or its example in the university, may be identified wherever, in the name of freedom itself, it can put in question the principle of sovereignty, as principle of power. Let us not pretend that this question is anything but formidable and abyssal. For thought thereby, the one that finds its place of freedom there, also finds itself, to be sure, without power. It is an unconditionality without sovereignty, which is to say at bottom a freedom without power. But without power does not mean "without force." And there, discreetly, furtively, another frontier is perhaps passed through, at once inscribing itself and resisting the passage, the barely visible frontier between the unconditionality of thought . . . and the sovereignty of power, of all powers, theologico-political power down to its national or democratic guises, economic-military power, the power of the media, and so forth. The affirmation I am speaking of remains a principle of resistance or of dissidence: without power but without weakness. Without power but not without force, be it a certain force of weakness. This thought of the university must prepare, with all its force, a new strategy and a new politics, new thinking of the political. And of political responsibility. For that, it must ally itself, in the world, in Europe and outside Europe, with all the forces that do not conflate the critique of sovereignty with servitude, not even with voluntary servitude, quite the contrary. (Derrida, "Unconditionality" 129)

In this precise moment in which those of us whose lives are marked by our relationship to this small complicated place known as Puerto Rico feel more than ever the need to fight for the establishment of a Puerto Rican sovereign state, it would be imperative in my opinion to insist on the political and philosophical task that both Braschi and Derrida have outlined for us: to resist both the politics of sovereignty and the ethics of servitude and obedience that deprive us of the possibility of resisting the unbridled destructive effects of sovereign power.

United States of Banana and the Right to Have an Other Right

"Free from freedom. Free." Toward the end of the novel Giannina turns this notion of a freedom that is paradoxically free from itself into the principle of a demand and a claim launched against the minister of the United States of Banana government, Cockroach, the Exterminator: "I can no longer deny that I am not free—and that my country is not free—and that the voting system has cancelled the right to be a right—and has reduced it to a clause—a presupposition—a condition—if. If is not the issue—and liberty is not an issue—nor a ballot box—but a right" (*USB* 271). The sudden reappearance of the language of rights in such a positive manner ought to come as a surprise to any reader of *United States of Banana* since one of the most lucid sections in the first part of the book deals with the fallacy of rights discourse, which is ultimately predicated on the sovereignty of the subject and its claims to moral superiority and certainty: "Righteous are those who grant themselves rights. Not only are they right, but they have the right to do what they want because they grant themselves the right. They don't doubt their righteousness. That would be to doubt their entitlement" (*USB* 60). Giannina's response is precisely to challenge the very desire to be right, insisting on a different notion of right: "What you'll never understand is that I don't want to be the boss because I am not always right and when I am right I start doubting I am right because my power has always been in doubting what is right" (*USB* 61). Paradoxically, the liberation of freedom from freedom is the entrance into a space of doubt without end. It is from this highly unstable place, from the right to doubt, to question, and ultimately to disobey any command for unconditional obedience, that Braschi and Derrida invite us to rethink what we mean by freedom, what we regard as a right, and what we understand by sovereign power. It is in the force of their will to disobey that their writings can offer us resources to live through these destructive times.

Notes

The epigraphs are from Heidegger 281; Levinas 161; and Braschi 186. Here are English translations of the first two epigraphs. Heidegger: "Regardless of how far Schelling might have also advanced along new paths into the essence of human freedom, the Kantian fundamental position was not shaken, rather only confirmed [by Schelling]. Kant says: the fact of freedom is inconceivable, what we grasp is only its inconceivability. And the inconceivability of freedom consists in this: that freedom, insofar as it is, defies conceptualization, as being-free transfers us into the fulfillment of being, not into its mere representation. This fulfillment, however, is not the blind unrolling of a process; rather, it is the knowing standing-within in beings as a whole, which must be withstood. This knowledge of freedom becomes certain of its highest necessity because it only can enable that position taking in which the human, standing, is able to encounter a destiny as a historical being, taking it up to itself and carrying it over and beyond itself" (my translation). Levinas: "The recurrence of the subject is thus neither the freedom of the possession of the self by itself in reflection, nor the freedom of that game in which I take myself as this or that, traversing avatars under the masks of history's carnival. It is a matter of an exigency that comes from the other, on the other side of *the active* of my powers, in order to open a 'deficit' without limits, where the self spends itself—freely—without counting. All the suffering and the cruelty of essence weigh on a point that withstands it and expiates it" (my translation).

1. The formula of a "spiritual National-Socialism" recurs often in the *Schwarze Heften*, Heidegger's notebooks, whose publication since 2013 has reopened the debate about Heidegger's thinking and its relation to Nazism. For an informative analysis of this motif in the Heidegger of the 1930s, see Mitchell.

2. For an affirmative—and, for this precise reason, problematic—reading of these motifs in Heidegger, see Nancy.

3. On the relation between Kant and Levinas, see Basterra.

4. For an analysis of the Indo-European roots of the Latin family of words that cluster around the "-dom" particle, see Benveniste.

Works Cited

Aleinikoff, Thomas. *Semblances of Sovereignty: The Constitution, the State, and American Citizenship.* Harvard UP, 2002.

Basterra, Gabriela. *The Subject of Freedom: Kant, Levinas.* Fordham UP, 2015.

Benveniste, Émile. "Les quatre cercles de l'appartenance sociale." *Vocabulaire des institutions indo-européens.* Minuit, 1969, pp. 293–319.

Braschi, Giannina. *United States of Banana.* AmazonCrossing, 2011.

Commonwealth of Puerto Rico v. Sanchez Valle et al., 579 U.S. 3, 2016.

Derrida, Jacques. *Du droit à la philosophie.* Galilée, 1990.

Derrida, Jacques. *L'écriture et la différence.* Seuil, 1967.

Derrida, Jacques. *Marges de la philosophie.* Minuit, 1972.

Derrida, Jacques. "Unconditionality or Sovereignty: The University at the Frontiers of Europe." Translated by Peggy Kamuf, *Oxford Literary Review,* vol. 31, 2009, pp. 115–31.

Derrida, Jacques. *L'Université sans condition.* Galilée, 2001.

Graff Zivin, Erin. "Beyond Jameson: The Metapolitics of Allegory." *Yearbook of Comparative Literature,* vol. 61, special issue "Allegory and Political Representation," edited by Tara Mendola and Jacques Lezra, 2015, pp. 156–73.

Heidegger, Martin. *Gesamtausgabe* vol. 42, *Schelling: Vom Wesen der menschlichen Freiheit.* Klostermann, 1988.

Jakobson, Roman. "Linguistics and Poetics." *Style in Language,* edited by T. Sebeok, MIT P, 1960, pp. 350–77.

Jameson, Fredric. "Third-World Literature in an Era of Multi-national Capitalism." *Social Text,* vol. 15, no. 15, 1986, p. 69.

Kant, Immanuel. *Kritik der praktischen Vernunft.* Meiner, 2003.

Kant, Immanuel. *Kritik der reinen Vernunft.* Meiner, 1998, A689/B717.

Kant, Immanuel. *Practical Philosophy.* Edited and translated by Mary J. Gregor, Cama bridge UP, 1996.

Levinas, Emmanuel. *Autrement qu'être ou au-delà de l'essence.* Martinus Nijhoff, 1978.

Mitchell, Andrew. "Die Politik des Geistes und die Selbst-Zerstörung des zukünftigen Staates. Heideggers Rektorat in den *Schwarzen Heften*." *Heidegger, die Juden, noch einmal*, edited by Peter Trawny and Andrew Mitchell, Klostermann, 2015, pp. 167–90.

Nancy, Jean-Luc. "L'histoire finie." *La communauté désœuvrée*. Christian Bourgeois, 1999, pp. 235–78.

PROMESA, P. L. 114–87, 130 Stat. 559 (2016).

PROMESA, P. L. 114–87, 130 Stat. 561 (2016).

PROMESA, P. L. 114–87, 130 Stat. 563 (2016).

Schelling, F. W. J. *Philosophische Untersuchungen über das Wesen der menschlichen Freiheit und die damit zusammenhängenden Gegenstände*. Meiner, 2011.

Trías Monge, José. *Puerto Rico: The Trials of the Oldest Colony in the World*. Yale UP, 1999.

12

The Holy Trinity

Money, Power, and Success in *United States of Banana*

Francisco José Ramos

"Life is born from death. From the death of *Assault on Time* came the birth of *Profane Comedy*, and from the death of *Profane Comedy* came the birth of *The Intimate Diary of Solitude*. And what will be born will die later. The dying will reach the limits of the undying. . . . I was born on an island, so every character acting in any show in this building also depends on the movement of the waves of the sea. We imitate the nature of the sea" (*ED* 187). When reading this passage by Giannina Braschi in *Empire of Dreams*, we may wonder what the nature of the sea is. The answer may be found in Paul Valéry's words: it is the essence of the sea to be the sea, always recommencing. "La mer, la mer toujours recommence. . . . The sea, the sea, always recommencing."

There is a *poetic logic*, as the author herself indicates, that traverses the work of Giannina Braschi from start to finish. There is also the operative sense of an *opera aperta* (an open work of art), to use Umberto Eco's expression. A work of theater turns into a philosophical essay, one that reads as a story that turns into a prose poem or, eventually, turns into an operetta, an *opera buffa*, or a farce as in the Ubu plays by Alfred Jarry. In any event, the endless journey of poetry recommences at any given moment, at any given turn.

It is on this journey that the poet denounces, sometimes in sotto voce, the fallacies of modern democracy with which the United States has seduced a large swath of the globe, in its systematic distortion of the reality of capitalism, and its imposition of some supposed national destiny upon the Western Hemisphere. These fallacies extend to the conflation of democracy with capitalism and economic freedom; the distortion consists of making power, money, and success the exclusive criteria for an adequate representation of reality; and the fraudulent plays out by identifying the United States with the name of an entire hemisphere: America.

United States of Banana unfolds as a lucid, scathing, and sardonic confrontation with what we might call the *Holy Trinity of the American Way of Life: Power, Money, and Success.* What happens to be, though increasingly less so, the universal model for a brand of political *recta ratio*, or virtuous reason, is little more than camouflage for an extremely violent society, impotently enthralled with its own culture of death. It is thus that the marketing gimmicks for the manufacturing of docile, submissive individuals are devised, which are simultaneously shredded by an undercurrent of deep dissatisfaction with what, paradoxically, they never cease to exalt.

We could delineate the profound transformations that have occurred on a planetary scale in the last sixty years as a trend that extends from the "one-dimensional man" (Marcuse), the "society of the spectacle" (Debord), and brainwashing by the media, to the ultimate consolidation of the "societies of control" (Deleuze) based on the logic of capital, technocracy, and software engineering exported by the mind-suckers of Silicon Valley. Nothing and no one is to be left unscathed by the cogs of banalization that whir beneath some vast analgesic bubble, calculated to *anesthetize* intelligence and sensitivity, swallow up minds and bodies, and spew out faithful fools. Against this universal campaign of ignorance, which is no longer inventive or daring but merely robust and voluptuous, the "Tongue Machine" in *United States of Banana* wags away with its vigorous and vivacious parade of words.

It should be emphasized that *United States of Banana* is the nominal syntagma that allows us to denounce the sham that prevents us (the redundancy seems fitting) from recognizing the true greatness of the United States, which runs against the grain of its economic/military insolence. That greatness is to be found in its musical ingenuity, its artistic and intellectual bravado, its adventurous and inquiring spirit, and a literature that has "an exceptional power to produce writers who can recount their own memories, but as those of a universal people composed of immigrants from all countries" (Deleuze).

That greatness has been dismantled, neutered, and confined to the ghettos of academia. The entire apparatus of the American capitalist machine is designed to *exempt* the state from its political and social responsibility, safeguarding the strict legal forms of the rule of law while endlessly expanding the profit margins of the market, whose excess it deigns to use for sustaining the arts and the sciences: philanthropy, that "arrogance of the powerful," as Pedro Albizu Campos aptly called it. In this context, the eccentric racket of cities such as New York and writings such as Giannina Braschi's, which are nourished by an anarchic and cosmopolitan "in-sub-ordination," is allowed to be *ex*hibited almost as an exotic modality. *United States of Banana* functions as a kaleidoscopic artifact that subverts, with its diverse and volatile intensities, the abridged imbecility of the contemporary cybernetic apparatus.

It seems particularly apt, in this context, to quote the words of a Mexican writer, commenting on a recent book about the current US president: "More than half the book could be considered an oil landscape of how the United States slowly became a banana republic."[1] This observation also resonates with *United States of Banana*. The cover design for the Amazon edition, with its image of a bright banana-yellow Boeing, speaks eloquently of both this particular tragedy and the forces that have triggered it: the imperial aspirations of the USA and its hypocritical defense of a notion of freedom at the service of lucre.

As a consequence, it seems impossible not to pore over the eschatological beginning titled "Death of the Businessman," with its evocation of the deadly explosion at the Twin Towers on September 11, 2001, when two jets were hijacked midflight and crashed into the structures: "It's the end of the world. I was excited by the whole situation. Well, if everyone is going to die, die hard, shit, but what do I know. Is this the atomic bomb—the end of the world—the end of the millennium? . . . there came a point when that sunny sky turned into a hellhole of a night—with papers, computers, windows, bricks, bodies falling, and people running and screaming" (*USB* 1). This heart-wrenching scene of suffering also becomes a motif that illuminates the background of the American tragedy. Later in the text, in the form of musical counterpoint, we hear one of the various exchanges between the servile Segismundo and the imperial Hamlet:

> Hamlet: I feel for you. I've come to liberate you.
>
> Segismundo: Did I ask for help?
>
> Hamlet: I heard you complaining about your lack of freedom. I said: what an unjust father. What is he doing—with his son in the dungeon of liberty—enclosed in a nutshell. I had to help you. I had to let you know that I care for you. That I thought your father was unjust. . . .
>
> Segismundo: The method of your madness is not my method. You were born on the top—and you fell into the pit of Ground Zero. I was born to raise hell as the voice of the dungeon. Nobody expected anything of me—nothing. And that is when the unexpected unfolds its wisdom against all the expectations that amounted to zero to the

> bone. Stop creating hard labor for my people—labor that doesn't develop their higher standard of expectation—only your method of extermination. (*USB* 160)

The novel poses a profound meditation on artistic experience and the saturation of modernity that ushered in the twenty-first century. Saturation means the point of maximum infiltration as with the condensation of vapor at the exact moment before a downpour, or the utter satiation (to the point of ennui) with those same ideals that were made possible by the French Revolution: liberty, equality, fraternity. It has certainly been acknowledged that these ideals led to experiments in so-called democratic populism and the dictatorships of the proletariat of the past century and that their failure and the ensuing disenchantment have ultimately transformed capitalism into a new branch of secular, universal religion.

The supposed triumph of capitalism and its liberal democracy is mounted on the fragile scaffolding of distrust and disbelief. That is why the same ideals are constantly reiterated and underscored in the most fraudulent ways and in the name of "positive thinking" and "hopeful longing"—to make people believe they still believe. There is a curious linguistic detail contained in the second syllable of the word "believe" that can be construed as the noun "lie" or the verb "to lie," which also brings us to that sense of lying back on a lie, of believing one's own lie.

It can thus be construed that "liberty" is reduced to that liberty to enrich and arm oneself to the teeth in the name of "legitimate self-defense," as if we were still living in the times of the Native American genocide. In the same way, "equality" becomes a false premise, because no one is equal to anyone else, not even to itself. It would be more appropriate to reclaim, rather, the singular and distinctive power that each one of us contains or, more specifically, the singular reality and temporality that the logic of capital annuls with its uniformity of lifestyles. Within this same logic, the term "fraternity" can only point to the special interest groups and trust funds, and to the plutocracy that, de facto, governs society. The term can also point to the increasing prominence of the mafia and drug trafficking in all social strata, as well as the conversion of political parties into fraternities or clienteles as evidenced by the legitimate organization of lobbies and the legal structural corruption of capitalism. In any event, it all ends up being a matter of plundering the public treasury and converting the res publica into a matter of personal interest and private benefit. "Neoliberalism" is another euphemism for looting and plundering.

This is the logic of capital, "the logic of destruction" and "the system of demolition" that have reached the peak of saturation (*USB* 173). This is why poetic logic becomes simply unbearable, no matter how much it is published and even encouraged, when we ignore so deeply what that poetry is about and what it unleashes. Against this logic of capital, the poetics of the exception exhibits itself, out in the open, and in the most transparent way: "Originality is to go back to the origins—and that's why I go back to the exceptional—what is extra—what gives gifts—generosity and light. The writing that goes overboard and over borders—and that is on the edge of breaking—and finds a light—and beams. The writing that is not good but extra—because it has extra points, extra credit—and it goes higher and lower with charm" (*USB* 235–36). This is the poetics that unfolds in "Wedding of the Century," with its fiery condemnation of the passions of entertainment: "by the enemies of greatness and the lovers of entertainment who have spit in the eyes and slapped the cheeks of poetry and philosophy—with the cheapening of the heart—the cheapening of all that is high and noble—the cheapening of all the greatness, the magnificence, the beauty, the good, the noble" (189).

Against the nihilism that triggers Zarathustra's nausea ("Ekel, Ekel, Ekel") in Nietzsche's great philosophical poem we are met with Giannina's hiccup, which also evokes Aristophanes in Plato's *Symposium*. This is how the saintly words are understood when he says "Yes"—the innocence of becoming (*Umschuld des Werdens*). With *United States of Banana*, we enter a script that is inscribed in the classic parody of tragicomedy and in the theatrical parody performed by Lewis Carroll, Alfred Jarry, Ramón del Valle Inclán, Samuel Beckett, Eugène Ionesco, Antonin Artaud, and (why not?) Bertolt Brecht. That parody winds its way from Parmenides to Nietzsche and from Nietzsche to Deleuze, into the noble love of wisdom, the φιλοσοφία, until it becomes realized when words spring to life with an unprecedented appearance of things: "Creation means discovery of a new reality that exists but that has not yet been noticed. The words are alive again. The verbs are in revolt" (*USB* 229–30).

Every great work of literature presents an affirmation or, better yet, a sheltering of some poetic logic. The great Rubén Darío would define it as follows: "I pursue a form that my style does not find."[2] Who does not find what? The syntactic ambiguity brings out the core of the literary experience as it is represented in the infinite odyssey of poetry. Poetry is not simply the composition in verse of a poem. Poetry is what is done or created with word, with thought, with sound, with color, with the body. Poetry is daily life, every moment of life: "For a true poet, every moment of life, every act, should be poetic, since they are all profoundly so" (Borges). From that imperative springs, *sponta sua* (from its own source), the poet's style. *Stylo* in French means "pen," and both the English and French "style" derive from *stilus*, also meaning a writing instrument (*stylus*) in Latin. And so, style is to writing what form is to poetry. Form is not what is finished but, on the contrary, what is unfinished that does not cease to become something else, another/an other; another and an other, ad infinitum. Form is also unformed, because its boundaries open, like flowers, unfathomably, to the boundless, to the void that envelopes life and death, and which extends beyond life and death.

The practice of writing consists of giving form to what is to be done, created, brought to fruition. Writing, in its artistic and poetic sense, is the expression of the unfinished and the immeasurable. Wherever the end point concludes, everything recommences again, as if there were always, without needing to assign it, that indefinite insertion of ellipses. Leibniz has said it well: "I thought I had reached port, but when I set myself to meditate . . . I was, as it were, thrown back out onto the open sea" (Strickland 73). At the end of *United States of Banana*, we are confronted with the following:

> Even death has to be an open dialogue with life—it has to go on—to move along—not to enclose a body—but to open the body to the multiples and multitudes—like at the very end of *The Symposium*—when the crowd of revelers comes marching in—knocking on the door—from the beginning of *The Symposium* to the end—all those people entering the same house of wisdom and wine—all drunk on life—no doors closed—all in different degrees of light and life—in layers of colors and depths of soul—in progression into the limelight—all moving—knocking—and entering—all talking—drinking—sleeping—dancing—and leaving—entering and leaving—the passing of energy from the individual to the multitudes—from the multiples of the single-handed. (*USB* 302–3)

Entering into *United States of Banana* means also becoming an accomplice not only to the practice of writing but also to an exercise in freedom. The transfigurations we run across extend from the theatrical (Hamlet, Segismundo, Basilio, Gertrude), conceptual (Zarathustra, Socrates, Protágoras, Diotima), poetic (Antonin Artaud, Rubén Darío), geopolitical (Puerto Rico, Cuba, Argentina, England, Denmark, Spain, China, United States of Banana), nominal (Statue of Liberty, Cockroach, Oliver, How, Hu, Hau, Reptile, Soldier, Cato Lein, Wishy, Washy, Wishy-Washy), and autobiographical (Giannina), making the novel quite unique in the history of American literature. Braschi's profound sense of humor has nothing to do with entertaining or amusing but, rather, with pouring out everything in abundance and gratitude, with the multiple ways of creating, and not just make-believe, or made-believed.

As we have observed, the practice of writing represents a detachment from oneself. It might also be said that it represents the obliteration of the "I," of the ego, the euthanasia of the first person singular (Ramos, "Postfacio"). To the extent that whenever one says "I," that "I" always becomes the other. To paraphrase Rimbaud: not the "other I" but the always other, the most other of others says "I." Nietzsche touches on this theme in the *Birth of the Tragedy*: "The 'I' of the lyric thus echoes out of the abyss of being [*Abgrunde des Seins*]. What recent aestheticians mean by its 'subjectivity' is mere fantasy" (Nietzsche 63). The character Giannina exposes the artistic expression of truth, which allows her to defrock the precarious principle of reality with which the logic of capital and its most vulgar and hypnotic modes prevail. And it is the persona Giannina, the actress who writes, who echoes the words of Descartes, "like actors who, to play their parts, put on masks to hide their blushing faces."[3]

In the manner of a specular game—Alice leaping through the looking glass—we can witness the movement of the writing and the characters who inhabit that writing. The act of depersonalization gives rise to the character Giannina and her persona gives rise to the author's identity. It can also be confirmed that "the face is most revealed by its mask of words."[4] The background to these words is not "individuality," the "I/ego" or "subjectivity." It is not even what could be called "reality." It is about the unfathomable dimension of the real from which poetry springs forth and, therefore, the creative force of language that invents "a new reality that exists but that has not yet been noticed" (*USB* 230).

It is only from the vantage point of artistic experience that the artist can politically censure the democratic fallacy, and it is from this fallacy that the artist must liberate herself. As Segismundo says "Everything in me will be free from freedom free"—the freedom imposed in the name of liberty is really a prison (doom) for the foolhearted and unwary who flock to the skirts of liberty transformed into a statue (*USB* 206). It is this statue that abandons its obdurate condition to grovel before a trusted lie that is played out in its name, thereby expressing the overarching ennui with the systematic falsification of the real thing, of the Big Fake Global Enterprise (which nowadays could publish its own "fake news").

Giannina asks the Statue, "What is your job?" (*USB* 99). To which she responds: "To inform the government of the U. S. of B. about suspicious activities taking place in my domain. I supervise the undergrounds—the gutters, the subways, the channels, the tunnels. I was a monument to immigration. Now I'm a border patrol cop. . . . You know, I'm laissez faire. But I never applied for this government job. I am not a spy. Nor a policeman. I'm a slave of liberty. My sympathies go out to all of the prisoners. I am a prisoner too" (*USB* 99). To which Giannina adds: "You are a war criminal. You should be judged by an international tribunal. How many dead bodies are in your cellar? You were supposed to protect us—give me your tired, your poor, your hungry—and then you put us to work" (*USB* 100).

The poetic drama of *United States of Banana* is also a political satire, a trenchant dramatization of Puerto Rico's pathological dependence on the nation that invaded the island in 1898 and imposed US citizenship in 1917, which was consecrated in 1952 as a colonial experiment that has since served as a launching pad for America's imperial proclivities. This political reading has been brilliantly illustrated in the Swedish-language graphic novel by Joakim Lindengren (translated by Helena Eriksson). This version also highlights the "mechanics of the spirit," (*USB* 215) in Giannina's words, which confront the "churning, floating, hypnotic value that is capital" (Marx 158). What is the spirit? The vital breath (*spiritus*) of thought, of poetry. Thus, the "Declaration of Independence" in the second part of *United States of Banana* offers a visionary vanishing point of what Puerto Ricans have not done or carried out. As Giannina states just prior to this chapter:

> Segismundo will slip away with Hamlet, you and me. The crown will be floating on the water—after the statue has hurled her crown into the river. All the people who were at gala on the balconies of the crown will drown or swim away to the Jersey shore except you—the poet philosopher, me—the poet child—Hamlet, the poet actor—and Segismundo—the poet statesman who will sail—on the four peaks of the crown—north, south, east and west—Zarathustra, Giannina, Hamlet, and Segismundo—the poet statesman who will be crowned Prince of the Isle of the Blessed, directing its energies and sailing against the wind and the sea toward the Isle of the Blessed where Segismundo was born to liberate his people from confinement and isolation, from embargos and diffuminations, from the bread and butter of daily routines—from isolation and confinement—from myself—I liberate myself from the United States of Banana. (*USB* 209–10)

Political drama cannot be separated from the mettle and integrity of poetry, from its emancipating power. Independence here relates to the revolution created by thought and the corporeal power to invent the future of a people and the enterprise of health that can become literature, against any prognosis. "Health as literature, as writing, consists in inventing a people who are missing. It is the task of the fabulating function to invent a people. We do not write with memories, unless it is to make them the origin and collective destiny of a people to come still ensconced in its betrayals and repudiations" (Deleuze, 11).

The appropriation that Braschi makes of the language of the invader is a strategy employed to invent those people who are missing in the very belly of the beast, as José Martí might say. What transpires along the way is, simply, a literary feat, which cannot be so readily pigeonholed into any category, be it "Spanglish" or the cultural marketing label of "postmodern literature." The literary experience, taken to the limit of its possibilities, overflows the boundaries of such delimitations conceived for the flat "demagogic satisfaction of popular taste" (Bordieu 27). It is a writing practice that is fully installed out in the open air, and its flight rises skyward, like the birds, those prodigious and free messengers of the void.

Notes

1. *El País*, Madrid, January 7, 2018.

2. "Yo persigo una forma que no encuentro mi estilo." (Rubén Darío, "Yo persigo una forma..." *Prosas profanas y otros poemas*, Biblioteca virtual Miguel de Cervantes, http://www.cervantesvirtual.com/obra-visor/prosas-profanas-y-otros-poemas--0/html/fedc2602-82b1-11df-acc7-002185ce6064_2.html).

3. Line from René Descartes, 1619 notebooks, as quoted in Richard Watson, *Cogito, Ergo Sum: The Life of René Descartes*, rev. ed., Boston: David R. Godine, 2007, p. 155. See also Descartes, *Preámbulos*, Buenos Aires: Sudamericana, 1967.

4. "No hay más cara que la máscara de las palabras" (Ramos, *Estética*).

Further Reading

Bordieu, Pierre. *Sobre la televisión*. Barcelona: Anagrama, 1997.

Borges, Jorge Luis. *El oro de los tigres*. Buenos Aires: Emecé, 1972.

Braschi, Giannina. *Asalto al tiempo*. Barcelona: Ámbito literario, 1981.

Braschi, Giannina. *La comedia profana*. Barcelona: Anthropos, 1985.

Braschi, Giannina. *Empire of Dreams*. AmazonCrossing, 2011.

Braschi, Giannina. *Estados Unidos de Banana*. AmazonCrossing, 2016.

Braschi, Giannina. *El imperio de los sueños*. Barcelona: Anthropos, 1988.

Braschi, Giannina. *United States of Banana*. AmazonCrossing, 2011.

Braschi, Giannina. *Yo-Yo Boing!* Pittsburgh: Latin America Review Press, 1998.

Braschi, Giannina. *Yo-Yo Boing!* AmazonCrossing, 2011.

Deleuze, Gilles. *Crítica y clínica*. Barcelona: Anagrama, 1996.

Descartes, René. *Obras escogidas*. Buenos Aires: Sudamericana, 1967.

Lindengren, Joakim, and Giannina Braschi. *United States of Banana*. Swedish translation by Helena Eriksson. Cobolt, 2017.

Marx, Karl. *Le Capital*. Paris: Éditions Sociales, 1975.

Nietzsche, Friedrich. *El nacimiento de la tragedia*. Madrid: Alianza, 1981.

Ramos, F. J. "Postfacio." Giannina Brasch, *El imperio de los sueños*. Barcelona, Anthropos, 1998.

Ramos, Francisco José. *Estética del pensamiento (I): El drama de la escritura filosófica*. Madrid: Fundamentos, 1998.

Roberts, Edward A., and Bárbara Pastor. *Diccionario etimológico indoeuropeo de la lengua española*. Madrid: Alianza, 2013.

Strickland, Lloyd, ed. *The Shorter Leibniz Texts: A Collection of New Translations*. London: Continuum, 2006.

Valéry, Paul. *Algunos poemas*. Translation into Spanish by Jorge Guillén. Barcelona: Ocnos. 1972.

13

My Dinner with Giannina

Rolando Pérez Interviews Giannina Braschi

Sometime in 2018, after more than two decades of not seeing each other, Giannina Braschi and I met again happily by happenstance at a cultural event that took place at the King Juan Carlos Center at New York University. From this point on we continued to meet in social settings, often dinner parties at her home, which gave us the wonderful opportunity to connect and reconnect in many ways. Heraclitus said that one cannot step into the same river twice, meaning that the river's currents are ever changing, and that's what had happened with Giannina and me. We weren't the same river. The world(s) that we had known in the 1990s had changed drastically. We had changed. In the meantime Giannina had written *United States of Banana*, a work that pretty much painted a picture of where we are now (unfortunately), economically, culturally, and politically in the gilded age of Trump.

In 2019, I met Giannina at her art-filled loft overlooking the High Line in Chelsea, and over a bottle of wine and dinner we began to talk. And we talked and talked and talked. I had come with some ideas of things that I wanted to ask her about her work, but at the end, the river's currents made the conversation flow in a sundry of unexpected directions. The initial conversation was in Spanish, with occasional code-switching moments, and afterward I translated it into English. Since then we have had other far-ranging dialogues, spanning the question of love—a topic that is so important in Latin American and Spanish thought—to the cruel inanities of the Trump era and the raging pandemic. We have conversed about the lives and writings of Santa Teresa and Sor Juana—and about the timely and untimely mediations of Giorgio Agamben, Alain Badiou, Franco "Bifo" Berardi, Anne Carson, Byung-Chul Han, and Paul Virilio, among others.

The following interview is the first of a series that will become a book project. And this, I believe, is significant for both of us, because as admirers of ancient Greek culture, we feel that the dialogue is an indispensable way to understand ourselves and the world. Not to mention, that as Latinos we just simply love to talk. It's what Gustavo Pérez Firmat calls our "logo-eroticism." I hope you enjoy reading this dialogue, as I much as I enjoyed my dinner with Giannina.

RP: You conceived of the title *Yo-Yo Boing!* as two "I"s—two subjects—that confront each other. The clash is not between an "I" and a "not-I," nor between "I" and the "other," but rather between two equal subjects. I think of that first encounter between Columbus and the indigenous world, where Columbus sees the "Indian" as an "other" that has nothing to do with him.

GB: Do you think that was an encounter between an "I" and a "not-I"?

RP: I think so. I think that for Columbus the "other" was radically different and inferior to him; and perhaps that's what we generally do when we want to negate the humanity of someone who is different from us, but what you do is to bring together two "I"s, and that seems to me not only ingenious but also highly important.

GB: An encounter is always the coming together of two beings, "dos seres," which regardless of their differences are at the same level.

RP: Exactly, and that is what I see you do in *Yo-Yo Boing!* and where we should go as a society.

GB: Of course, but on the other hand, the encounter between the two "I"s is *boing*—a clashing of two cultures—and their differences can also lead to war. And that war is still there and exists.

RP: That war to which you allude in *Yo-Yo Boing!* is that a cultural or a linguistic war?

GB: Both. For me there is no difference between language and culture. The linguistic is born out of the cultural; it's not the opposite. And when I sat down to write the work, what I thought about was how do

I enter into this culture? Or perhaps, rather, since I have never had any interest in being part of it—how do I understand the other that is different from me?

RP: How do you think the other sees you?

GB: I would say with certain violence. It's a violence that one doesn't know from where it comes. It emerges unexpectedly. It is a culture of repression. While mine, on the other hand, is a culture of expression. They say that love is out of fashion, but that's not true.

RP: *Totalmente de acuerdo. El amor para mí es una fuerza de unión, o comunión, como decía Octavio Paz.* He says that in order to escape the labyrinth of solitude one has to be willing to open one's self up to the world, *rajarse.*

GB: That entails a certain risk, for perhaps you'll lose it all, but when you lose everything, you also gain everything, as it happened with Oedipus. All of a sudden you don't have anything, and then you have everything. So strange, and so beautiful. The moment Oedipus loses everything is the moment he becomes a sacred man.

RP: If I'm not mistaken, your work calls not only for the decolonization of literary language but also for the decolonization—as Severo Sarduy says in his radio play *Los matadores de hormigas*—of the body. And all your books are very critical of this society; while, of course, also calling for liberation.

GB: Always. Liberty is always very important for me, regardless of how it's achieved.

RP: And how is it realized at the moment of writing?

GB: I let things flow. Unlike other people who begin with a plot, I don't have a plot in mind. I have ideas, feelings—above all, feelings, because my ideas come from my feelings. I walk through the world, and I see life like an adventure, like Don Quijote, and like Don Quijote those adventures transform me because everything that you live transforms you in some way. I also believe in what the Greeks used to say: that "what is is"—that the world presents itself as it is. I'm interested in what is, in the way things are.

RP: You have a Greek aesthetic. You allow things to be as they are.

GB: Exactly, there is a being in things. One has to look for that being.

RP: You said that each object in your collection of contemporary art and kinetic design has a life of its own.

GB: For me each thing has its own corresponding depth.

RP: You write about the life of objects. In a humorous passage of *Empire of Dreams* that bears the title "The Things That Happen to Men in New York!" you say: "Las cosas son hombres y mujeres."

GB: Yes, things are men and women.

RP: Although the question of lexical gender in Spanish can be problematic at times, it also brings a certain richness to Spanish, don't you think?

GB: I agree. We think of *la luna* as a woman and of *el sol* as a man. And there is love between the moon and the sun—whether it's husband and wife or not—there is a love.

RP: Just as there is between *una silla* [a chair] *y una puerta* [a door].

GB: *Sí, sí, sí*, and there is.

RP: It's a beautiful, ontological way of seeing things. You then write: "[Las] Apples look for [las] pears. And [las] pears love [los] peaches. Listen, sir, to the things that happen to [las] pears in New York! Nothing new. We already know that men like [las] pears, and that [los] peaches like [las] oranges. We also know that an orange is an orange. And that an apple is a peach. That, I didn't know—says the apple's mother. I thought my daughter liked [los] peaches, but [las] pears? Gentlemen, ladies—and she puts her hands on her head—I didn't know that happened to women in New York. Ladies, gentlemen, says the peach's father solemnly, I didn't know it would happen to my son."[1] Fantastic! Precious! A way of applying this ontology of things to something that has to do with human *beings*.

GB: Exactly, I love what you have just said. Human beings are objects because they are subjects.

RP: Sometimes people say "don't treat me like an object," and I always think, "why not?" Many people have died protecting an object that was very dear to them: because they shared a life with that object, and it had a sentimental meaning for them.

GB: The liberation of objects.

RP: I am fascinated by all of this in your work because of my own recent interest in object-oriented ontology, a new and very exciting philosophical approach to ontological issues.

GB: Objects have a life of their own, and sometimes, they last more than we do. When my brother died, I used an umbrella that had been his, and I told my mother, "I can't believe that the umbrella lasted more than he did," but when I said this, I said this in recognition of the life the two had had together.

RP: In "The Financial Statement of Mariquita Samper," a chapter in *Empire of Dreams*, you write: "The building had chosen its land, even if I had thought that the building was going to be located elsewhere. The author of *Assault on Time* [Giannina Braschi] used to say that this is what's called the mandate of things, and I believe she's completely right."[2] You speak of this mandate of things as if things asked us or demanded us to act.

GB: Not only things, human beings also demand that we accept them as they are. The objects themselves tell us where they have to be. So I don't have to force them into any order, because they will find it by themselves. The only thing I have to do is observe them until they find their place. Like I was telling you before, one has to let things *be*. People are always looking to find our weaknesses and not our strength—and the economy in no way represents our strength. The problem with capitalism is that it wants to reduce us to an economic thing. And since when is Puerto Rico poor? Christopher Columbus called it "Rich Port" not "Poor Port." Puerto Rico is not poor. Puerto Rico is rich. The economy has made it poor, but Puerto Rico can't be reduced to economy. Puerto Rico is sun, nature, abundance, creativity, ingenuity, humanity. You take away a country's nature and you make it poor, because you are looking for its weakness. That is, one has to begin by looking at the strength of a people, and work with that strength and not with its weakness.

RP: The problem comes when you reduce everything in life to exchange value. If I can't impose some kind of economic value on an object—be it a banana, a beach, or even the sun—it has no value.

GB: Precisely; it's the belief that if I can't use something for my own ends, then it's no good. It's a very selfish way of seeing the world. Not to see the generosity of the world. The economy is not our forte. Our strength resides in love, happiness, the vitality that we have. If you take that away from me and you make me doubt myself, and make me a "business woman," I will never be as good as you, because you were born in a country whose nature is not like mine.

RP: The mountain, for example, is important in and of itself, not necessarily because I may be able to extract some kind of economic profit from it—that's the idea, isn't it? The contrary leads us to the destruction of the planet.

GB: The other day a friend of mine said, "We have to take advantage of solar energy," and I said to her, "Leave the sun alone." The idea of extracting energy from the sun as if . . .

RP: As if the sun doesn't already give us energy that we don't have to, in any way, extract it from it.

GB: Yes, and moreover, turn it into economy.

RP: How interesting. I had never thought of it that way—in terms of the exploitation of the sun.

GB: Imagine that! What can I take from the sun to make it work for me, for us human beings—so insignificant! We want to make a profit from everything in the universe.

RP: We think we are more important than the entire universe, than the entire "not-I."

GB: They call us minorities when we are the majority. That's why they have invented the notion that "less is more," because it's convenient for them that less be more.

RP: That's what happening in politics today in this country.

GB: Yes, and that's why you see the little American flag on the lapels of all the politicians: because the flag no longer means anything. When it meant something, it was not on the lapels of the politicians. It's a false nationalism that comes from the fear that they have ceased to be the majority.

RP: Like the word "community," constantly bandied about in the media, but which in reality does not exist. I've lived in my apartment building for more than twenty years—and there is no community there. It's very strange. You greet people in the morning, and instead of saying "good morning" back to you, they respond with an empty smile. Very strange.

GB: And then you pass them on the street and they don't even look at you.

RP: It's a very curious thing, because in our culture such a relationship with neighbors would be impossible. One of the things that is evident in your writings is the notion of diverse worlds. In *United States of Banana*, the multiple is everywhere: the multiple of literary language, the multiple of English, the multiple of Spanish, the multiple of Spanglish, the multiple of genders and genres. The text is sometimes a novel, at times poetry, at times theater, and that, seems to me, is the way you look at the world.

GB: After 9/11, when the Twin Towers came down, I thought here begins everything.

RP: In what sense?

GB: In the sense that the things that seemed to function, really didn't function. And it was a major crisis: at a personal, national, emotional, physical level. At every level. And we had to question everything. Suddenly the Statue of Liberty became like the flag on the lapels of the politicians—a little symbol of something that no longer exists. I found myself talking to Hamlet and Zarathustra.

RP: At the beginning of *Thus Spoke Zarathustra*, Zarathustra comes down from the mountain. Is that what happened to the intellectual, to the writer, after 9/11?

GB: I have always had three poets in my life: the poet-child, the poet-actor, and the poet-philosopher. And so I think Hamlet is the poet-actor, and Zarathustra is the poet-philosopher. And I'm the poet-child, so I walk with the other two, the actor and the philosopher.

RP: That's so beautiful, and it reminds me of the moment in which Nietzsche describes the metamorphosis of the spirit.

GB: Yes, yes, from the camel to the lion and from the lion to the child.

RP: The camel is big and strong.

GB: And says "I ought" to do that.

RP: It represents heaviness. The lion says . . .

GB: "I am."

RP: And later the innocence of the child . . .

GB: Who acts . . .

RP: Creates something new.

GB: Well, those three poets have always been with me: the philosopher, the actor, and the child. They are always there, at my side.

RP: The poet and the philosopher are very present in your work, but at times I think that the reader doesn't recognize the actor.

GB: Nor the drama. My work is full of drama. I'm a dramatic writer.

RP: That's how I think of your work—as a theatrical performance—something like Artaud's theater of cruelty—someone you mention quite often in your work.

GB: Strictness, diligence, cruelty, Artaud used to say.

RP: You "yourself" appear in all of your works, as a character.

GB: It was only when I began re-reading Plato's dialogues that I noticed the many transformations of Socrates: where you see him as a young person in one dialogue, and then as an older person in another. I realized that was what I was doing. Or when you see Rembrandt, in his self-portraits, you see him from his youth on, from a young boy all the way to an old man. That's what I wanted to do: capture the different stages of life.

RP: So that was the idea, then, of leaving a series of self-portraits?

GB: Of leaving a sort of witness to this life that exists. That person transforms herself, and [she] is not the same in all the works; she has changed. She has been Shepherd Giannina, Mariquita Samper, "Giannina," and "Giannina Braschi."

RP: And Berta Singerman.

GB: All those transformations.

RP: Who is Mariquita Samper?

GB: I went to see fortune teller, a psychic in Newark, whose name was Jeannie Beauchamp. She offered me a plate of mariquitas, which are plantain fritters. And out of that word, like the madeleine of Proust, a whole work emerged. Mariquita Samper was my aunt who was from Colombia. When she first arrived in Puerto Rico they told her, "here we can't call you Mariquita because 'mariquita' here means something else. We'll call you Maria." But my mother continued calling her Mariquita. I like Mariquita—it reminds me of *muñequita*.

RP: At times you identify yourself with her in the text, and at times with Berta Singerman or with Uri Eisensweig.

GB: Uriberto Eisensweig was a professor at Rutgers. He could not believe that I had turned him into a character.

RP: *In Ecce Homo*, Nietzsche says, "at bottom, I am all the names in history." I have the feeling that for you all the names in your work, whether real or fictitious, are ways of connecting with certain lines or drives of intensity. Correct me if I'm wrong.

GB: Well, I would say of connecting with the passions. I walk into a boutique that sells eye glasses, and I say to the woman who works there, "I am a poet," and she says to me "but Giannina, you are not only a poet. Don't tell me that you're only a poet, because you are that and many other things." And she was right, for I also love art, design, fashion, architecture, music, philosophy. Not with only one thing; I connect with all that.

RP: And when you connect, for example, with Zarathustra or with Hamlet, it's *your* Zarathustra and *your* Hamlet—exclusively yours. It's not Nietzsche's Zarathustra, nor Shakespeare's Hamlet.

GB: Exactly, it's nobody else's. But Nietzsche would have screamed.

RP: No, no, I think he would have liked the affective way with which you connect.

GB: Really? I adore Nietzsche. I feel him at the core of my being. I mean, he is very close to my way of being. I would marry him. He would not have been so alone if he had married me. What do you think?

RP: You would have understood him.

GB: I think he may not have died had he found someone in his life, but he became desperate, like Van Gogh. They didn't have the patience to wait for someone who understood them. They weren't able to move to the next stage, and life is made up of stages. It's like if I had died after *Empire of Dreams*. And essentially, I did die after *Empire of Dreams* because what I did afterward was different.

RP: Which is to say, to change is to leave something behind, and that implies a certain death.

GB: When I was living in Madrid, Claudio Rodríguez stopped by my house and said to me, "Giannina, you have no idea what it's like to be a fifty-year old poet," and I, who was then eighteen, asked him, "What do you mean?" And he said to me, "To be a poet when you're eighteen, twenty, that's easy, but to be a poet when you're fifty, that's something else." How can you continue to believe in poetry, after all the blows that life has dealt you? How does one still believe in feelings and innocence?

RP: That's the idea of the metamorphosis of the spirit in *Zarathustra*, isn't it?

GB: Exactly.

RP: You have to cease to be a camel and a lion to become a child and continue to create.

GB: Now I understand what Claudio Rodríguez was saying to me. It's not easy to remain a poet.

RP: How did you feel when you finished *Empire of Dreams*? Did you feel it was an end of a stage in your life?

GB: I felt very happy because it had been so easy, and things should be easy. What was difficult was what came before—getting my PhD. But when the time came to write *Empire of Dreams* it was like a celebration. And when I finished it, I felt great because I felt that I had done it. But then I felt empty because I had said everything—everything that I wanted to say.

RP: What you have just said is incredibly important. I have always envied those poets who can get up in the morning, have breakfast, and sit down to write a poem about their breakfast. Unfortunately, I don't work that way. I work in terms of projects, and I write when I think I have something to say, and if I don't have anything in particular to say, I simply don't write. But there are people who write for its own sake—the very act of writing inspires them. I'm not one of those. I would like to be, but I'm not.

GB: The same thing happens to me.

RP: So your next thought after you were done was "now what?"

GB: Yes, and really everything came out so easily.

RP: You mean, the writing itself came out easily?

GB: Yes. And in *Empire of Dreams*, everything comes from the inside.

RP: It's a very personal book; a beautiful book.

GB: It is. But afterward I felt empty because I had already said what I had to say. And then I had to write from the outside, and to listen to people, and what people had to say, and that's how *Yo-Yo Boing!* came about. In that sense, *Yo-Yo Boing!* is a book about other people, not about me. And after that book I felt empty again, because I was only listening to others. And so I began to write *United States of Banana*, which came from the inside.

RP: How fascinating: it's about the movement from a book that emerges from the inside, to a book that emerges from the outside.

GB: Yes. With *Yo-Yo-Boing!* you feel that I'm empty, that I'm listening to people, that I'm taking from people. I'm being creative as an artist, but I'm not talking about myself. It is not a poet who is speaking, but more like a poet disguised as a novelist. What I have done with poetry is similar to what James Joyce did with the novel. James Joyce took the novel out of the novel and sent it walking into different literary genres.

RP: In that sense, I think the relation between *Yo-Yo-Boing!*, *United States of Banana*, and *Ulysses* is that they're all trans-genre "novels."

GB: Yes, but with James Joyce you never cease to feel that he is a novelist, not a poet. But in my case, what you see is a poet—a poet who has said: Let's take poetry out of poetry, and set her free to walk the world, and see what she learns from the world. Poetry has been cloistered in a convent made of verses and stanzas for too long. Santa Teresa put her in a convent and made her a nun. I said No: we have to take her out of the convent, set her free to walk the world, and let her date and mate with other literary genres. I took her out. I turned poetry into novel, into theater, into musical, manifesto, treatise, essay, diary, advertisement, interview, and yet in the end, it is none and all of those things—it is still poetry.

RP: You have taken poetry out of the verse.

GB: I would never have been happy if I had stayed with verse. That's why I left Spain. I studied with Claudio Rodríguez and Blas de Otero who both wanted me to learn the metrical compositions of Garcilaso's sonnets, which I did. I even wrote an article, "La metamorfosis del ingenio en la Egloga III de Garcilaso." And yet despite knowing Garcilaso and loving him, I wasn't going to write sonnets nor in hendecasyllabic verses. Not interested, you know?

RP: It's a very rigid way of writing . . .

GB: It worked in the Renaissance, but not today, not in the modern world, and not for me. I'm American—in the sense of being a citizen of the Americas, plural.

RP: What I like about your *ars poética* is that it breaks, in an original way, with conventional notions of poetry. You have no idea how many times I meet a writer, who from the outset hands me a business card with the title "POET" printed on, and whenever this happens, I feel like running. What does that mean? Does that mean that he writes sonnets or hendecasyllabic verse, like you say? Now, your work, that's something else. I suppose one could call it "experimental." After all, the majority of narrative writing today pretty much follows the conventions of narration, in Aristotelian fashion, and poetry adheres to the usual practices of free verse.

GB: All great writers have worked outside the limits of their genre, be they philosophers or poets.

RP: You break barriers, but I don't think you do so just to break them.

GB: That's very true. I do so because it's the way I see things, as with the apples [*las manzanas*] and the pears [*las peras*].

RP: Now that you mention your "apples" and your "pears," I think of Cézanne's apples, which are exclusively Cézanne's. When I read your poetry, I think of a writer like Severo Sarduy, who didn't belong to any group, or of Kathy Acker, who unfortunately died so young, and also of Vallejo, whom you often mention, and who didn't belong to any group either.

GB: No, nor did Cervantes. Quevedo and the rest had nothing but awful things to say about him.

RP: But in contrast to the work of someone like Acker—your work is positive. And by that I don't mean that it doesn't have its dark side; it does, but it never ceases to believe in life.

GB: Yes, I go down to the depths but then I always return to the light. Like Vallejo, I'm a jack-in-the-box. No matter how much you push us down into the box, we always bounce back to affirm a love for life.

Hoy me gusta la vida mucho menos,
pero siempre me gusta vivir: ya lo decía.

Today I like life much less,
But I always like living: I've often said.

Notes

1. "Las cosas son hombres y mujeres. Las manzanas buscan a las peras. Y las peras aman a los melocotones. ¡Oiga, señor, las cosas que les pasan a las peras en Nueva York! No es ninguna novedad. Ya sabemos que a los hombres les gustan las peras. Y a que los melocotones les gustan las naranjas. Ya sabemos también que la naranja es naranja. Y que la manzana es un melocotón. Eso no lo sabía—dice la mamá de la manzana. Yo creía que a mi hija le gustaban los melocotones. Pero ¿las peras? Señores, señoras—y se puso su mano sobre la cabeza. Eso no sabía que les pasaba a las mujeres en Nueva York. Señoras, Señores—dice con seriedad el padre del melocotón—esto tampoco lo que le pasaba a mi hijo" (*El imperio de los sueños* 176; translation by Rolando Pérez).

2. "El edificio había escogido su terreno aunque yo hubiera pensado que el edificio iba a estar colocado en otro lugar. Decía la poeta de *Asalto al tiempo* [Giannina Braschi, 1981] que esto se llama el mandato de las cosas y creo que tiene toda la razón" (204–5).

Works Cited

Braschi, Giannina. *Asalto al tiempo*. Anthropos Editorial del Hombre, 1981.

Braschi, Giannina. *Empire of Dreams*. Translation by Tess O'Dwyer. AmazonCrossing, 2011.

Braschi, Giannina. *El imperio de los sueños*. 1988. AmazonCrossing, 2011.

Braschi, Giannina. *United States of Banana*. AmazonCrossing, 2011.

Braschi, Giannina. *Yo-Yo Boing!* 1998. AmazonCrossing, 2011.

Contributors

Frederick Luis Aldama is Distinguished Professor of English at the Ohio State University. He is the author, coauthor, and editor of thirty-six books, including the 2018 *Latinx Superheroes in Mainstream Comics*, which won the International Latino Book Award and the Eisner Award. His areas of research include Latinx cultural phenomena from literature, film, and television to music, sports, video games, and comic books.

Anne F. Ashbaugh is professor and department chair of Philosophy and Religious Studies at Towson University and Professor Emerita at Colgate University. She is the author of *Plato's Theory of Explanation* (State University of New York Press). She holds a PhD from Duquesne University. Her research spans ancient Greek philosophy, Nietzsche, and philosophy of literature.

David Auerbach is a tenured professor of the Graduate Program in Translation at the University of Puerto Rico, Río Piedras Campus, where he specializes in legal, financial, literary, and cultural translation. He has been a professional translator and editor for twenty-five years. A native of New York City, he currently resides in San Juan, Puerto Rico.

Dorian Lugo Bertrán is full professor and chair of the Interdisciplinary Program at the University of Puerto Rico, where he earned his PhD in Hispanic Studies. Former cochair of the Film Studies Section of the Latin American Studies Association, he specializes in gender and queer studies in the areas of early modernist literature and Latin American audiovisual production.

Daniela Daniele teaches Anglo-American literature at the University of Udine in Italy. She has published research on the Victorian American novelist Louisa May Alcott and contemporary American poets and fiction writers including Don DeLillo, Grace Paley, Jerome Rothenberg, and Mary Caponegro. She edited a literary anthology in the aftermath of September 11, *Undici settembre*, featuring Laurie Anderson, Paul Auster, John Barth, Giannina Braschi, Judith Butler, Toni Morrison, and Patti Smith.

Cristina Garrigós is professor of English philology at the Universidad Nacional de Educación a Distancia in Spain. She has a PhD from University of Seville and teaches American postmodernism as well as gender and comparative studies. She collaborated on the book *God Save the Queens: Pioneras del Punk* with Paula Guerra and Nuria Triana. She published critical works on American authors of the twentieth and twenty-first centuries, including Kathy Acker, Gloria Anzaldúa, John Barth, Giannina Braschi, Don DeLillo, and Rosario Ferré.

Madelena Gonzalez is professor of Anglophone literature at Avignon University in France. She has published widely on minority theater, postmodern literature, and contemporary culture and is head of the multidisciplinary research team Cultural Identity, Texts, and Theatricality. She is the author of *Fiction after the Fatwa: Salman Rushdie and the Charm of Catastrophe* and her most recent publications include *Aesthetics and Ideology in Contemporary Literature and Drama* and *Contemporary Publishing and the Culture of Books*.

Laura R. Loustau received her PhD in Hispanic languages and literatures from the University of California, Berkeley. She teaches US Latinx and Latin American literature at Chapman University. She is the author of *Cuerpos errantes: Literatura latina y latinoamericana en Estados Unidos*, which explores notions of borders and de(re)territorialization in the works of Giannina Braschi, Cristina García, and Luisa Valenzuela.

Elizabeth Lowry earned a PhD in rhetoric and composition from Arizona State University where she teaches. Her research interests include religious rhetorics, indigenous rhetorics, Latin American studies, and gender studies. She is the author of *Invisible Hosts: Performing the Nineteenth Century Spirit Medium's Autobiography* (SUNY) and *The Seybert Report: Rhetoric, Rationale, and the Problem of Psi Research* (Palgrave Pivot).

Ronald Mendoza-de Jesús is assistant professor of Spanish and comparative literature at the University of Southern California. He helped to conceptualize this volume with Frederick Luis Aldama and Tess O'Dwyer. His first book project, *Reading Danger: Literary History After History*, develops a non-historicist theory of literary history by exploring the modernist strategies of thinkers and authors such as Walter Benjamin, Jacques Derrida, Giannina Braschi, and Julia de Burgos.

Francisco Moreno-Fernández holds a PhD in Hispanic linguistics and is a professor of Spanish language at the University of Alcalá in Spain. He served as director of the Instituto Cervantes at Harvard University. He is a member of the North American Academy of the Spanish Language. He is executive editor of *Lengua & Migracion*, editor of *Spanish in Context*, and a member of the editorial board of the *International Journal of the Sociology of Language*, the *Journal of Linguistic Geography*, and the *Journal of World Languages*.

Tess O'Dwyer served as coeditor of this volume with Frederick Luis Aldama and as coeditor of *Review: Literature and Arts of the Americas* with Doris Sommer. She has won the Columbia University Center Translation Award, and her books in translation include *Empire of Dreams* (Yale University Press) and *Yo-Yo Boing!* (AmazonCrossing) by Giannina Braschi, and *Martin Rivas* (Oxford University Press) by Alberto Blest Gana. She runs an eponymous arts management firm in New York City and has served on the boards of PEN America, the *Evergreen Review*, and the Academy of American Poets.

Francisco José Ramos is professor of philosophy emeritus at the University of Puerto Rico. He earned a PhD in philosophy at the Universidad Complutense de Madrid. He is a member of the Academia Puertorriqueña de la Lengua Española and a correspondent for Real Academia Española. His books include *Estética del pensamiento, La significación del lenguaje poético*, and *Erothema*.

John "Rio" Riofrio is director of Latin American Studies at the College of William and Mary where he also teaches in the Department of Modern Languages and Literature. His scholarly interests range from popular representations of US Latinxs in film, literature, and media to Latinx counternarratives. With a PhD in English from University of Wisconsin–Madison, he has an abiding interest in hemispheric Latinx identities and their impact on understanding the complexities of Latinx presence in the Americas. He is author of *Continental Shifts: Migration, Representation and the Search for Justice in Latin(o) America.*

Rolando Pérez is professor of Spanish and Latin American literature and philosophy at Hunter College at the City University of New York. His research focuses on the relations among literature, the visual arts, and philosophy. His critical books include *Severo Sarduy and the Neo-Baroque Image of Thought in the Visual Arts* and *Agorapoetics: Poetics after Postmodernism*. His creative titles include a contemporary version of Dante's *Divine Comedy, The Electric Comedy* and a poetry collection *Tea Ceremonies for Winter*. His creative writings can be found in *The Norton Anthology of Latino Literature*.

Maritza Stanchich is a professor of English at the College of Humanities at the University of Puerto Rico, where she teaches literature of the Puerto Rican diaspora, US Latinx, Caribbean, and US American literatures and currently coordinates her department's masters and doctoral programs. She holds a PhD from the University of California–Santa Cruz. She has published scholarly essays and lectured widely on Giannina Braschi, Martín Espada, William Faulkner, and Tato Laviera, among others. Her columns for the *New York Times*, the *Huffington Post*, and the *Guardian* have brought international attention to recent crises in Puerto Rico.

Ilan Stavans is Lewis-Sebring Professor of Humanities, Latin American, and Latino Cultures at Amherst College and the publisher of Restless Books. He is a renowned and prolific cultural critic, linguist, translator, TV host, and author. His recent titles include *Latinos in the United States: What Everyone Needs to Know*, *I Love My Selfie*, *Angelitos: A Graphic Novel*, *The Wall*, and *Don Quixote of la Mancha* (in Spanglish).

Index